Learning Go Programming

An insightful guide to learning the Go programming language

Vladimir Vivien

BIRMINGHAM - MUMBAI

Learning Go Programming

First published: October 2016

Production reference: 1201016

Published by Packt Publishing Ltd.
Livery Place
35 Livery Street
Birmingham
B3 2PB, UK.
ISBN 978-1-78439-543-8

www.packtpub.com

Credits

Authors

Vladimir Vivien

Reviewers

Quintessence Anx
Parth Desai
Abhishek Kumar
Chris Schaefer

Commissioning Editor

Akram Hussain

Acquisition Editor

Manish Nainnani

Content Development Editor

Aishwarya Pandere

Technical Editor

Mohita Vyas

Copy Editor

Safis Editing

Project Coordinator

Nidhi Joshi

Proofreader

Safis Editing

Indexer

Aishwarya Gangawane

Graphics

Disha Haria

Production Coordinator

Nilesh Mohite

About the Author

Vladimir Vivien (@vladimirvivien) is a software engineer living in the United States. He is a previously published author and has written code in languages such as Java, JavaScript, Python, C to name a few. Vladimir has work in diverse industries including technology, publishing, financial, and healthcare. After years of building enterprise systems using Java, Vladimir came to Go for its simplicity and stayed for its concurrency and fast build time. Vladimir continues to use Go as his primary language to build and create open source software (https://github.com/vladimirivivien).

About the Reviewers

Quintessence Anx. is a superhero (also called as Cloud Engineer) at Stark & Wayne LLC by day and an astronomer with a passion for the Internet of Things by night. She is a chapter leader for her local Girl Develop It, where she empowers women programmers of all levels and abilities through classes and hands-on project experiences, as well as co-founder of City of Light 2.0, an organization working to bring more affordable, reliable, and faster internet to Western New York

Parth Desai is a polygot programmer and architect, and has worked on almost all popular languages like Golang, python, C#. He regularly contributes to various open-source golang projects, like a notification engine called "Khabar", a http framework written in golang called "Gottp", and media server called "moire". He implemented url signing protocol using cryptography in python, from scratch.

He has also written custom single sign on solution (SSO) in c#, with proper implementation of oauth and saml protocols. He also developed pluggable architecture to facilitate easier adding and removing of authentication providers for the SSO. Currently, He is working as a lead backend engineer, and designing and implementing scalable systems in golang and python. You can reach out to him on linkedin at `https://in.linkedin.com/in/parthdesa i08`. Or on his email-id `desaiparth08@gmail.com`.

Abhishek Kumar is a technologist in IT Industry since 2010 mainly working in Systems Programming, DevOps Practices and Security. He likes to keep in sync with all domains, paradigms and up-coming technologies to get a wholistic approach for problem solving and planning ahead. He loves to learn new programming languages. Abhishek has been using Golang since 2012. He started a timeseries datastore project in Golang by Sep'2013 and is currently pivoting it. [`@abionic` | `https://abhishekkr.github.io`]

Want to thank my mother ShivPyari to enable me choose my own path

Chris Schaefer software developer with a passion for learning new things. He enjoys writing code and participating in local community software events.

www.PacktPub.com

For support files and downloads related to your book, please visit www.PacktPub.com.

Did you know that Packt offers eBook versions of every book published, with PDF and ePub files available? You can upgrade to the eBook version at www.PacktPub.com and as a print book customer, you are entitled to a discount on the eBook copy. Get in touch with us at service@packtpub.com for more details.

At www.PacktPub.com, you can also read a collection of free technical articles, sign up for a range of free newsletters and receive exclusive discounts and offers on Packt books and eBooks.

https://www.packtpub.com/mapt

Get the most in-demand software skills with Mapt. Mapt gives you full access to all Packt books and video courses, as well as industry-leading tools to help you plan your personal development and advance your career.

Why subscribe?

- Fully searchable across every book published by Packt
- Copy and paste, print, and bookmark content
- On demand and accessible via a web browser

Table of Contents

Preface

Go is an open source programming language that lets programmers easily build reliable and scalable programs. It does this by offering a simple syntax which makes it fun to write correct and predictable code using concurrency idioms and a robust standard library.

Go has a large and active online community and there are several Go conferences that take place around the world yearly. Starting with `https://golang.org/`, you will find numerous places on the web that provide documentations, blogs, videos, and slides that cover a wide range of Go-related topics. On GitHub, the story is no different; some of the best known projects that are driving the future of cloud computing, for instance, are written in Go with an ever growing list.

As you would expect, getting started with Go is simple, fast, and well documented. However, "getting into" Go can be more challenging, especially for newcomers from other languages. My first attempt at Go failed. Even after reading the prescribed documentations and going through the tutorials, there was a gap in understanding driven by my own biases from previous programming experiences. Months later I returned to Go and got into it. This time I read the language specs, I read blogs, watch videos, and searched the web for any discussion that provided design motivations and in-depth explanations of the language.

Learning Go is a book intended to help new, and seasoned programmers alike, to get into the Go programming language. With this book, I have attempted to write the book I would have like to have read when I was starting out with Go. It distills the language specs, the documentations, the blogs, the videos, slides, and my own experiences of writing Go into content that carefully provides the right amount of depth and insights to help you understand the language and its design.

I hope that you enjoy it.

What this book covers

Chapter 1, *A First Step in Go*, the reader is introduced to Go at a high-level and take a tour of the features that have made the language a favorite among its adopters.

Chapter 2, *Go Language Essentials*, this chapter starts with a deeper exploration Go's syntax and other language elements such as source files, variables, and operators.

Chapter 3, *Go Control Flow*, examines Go program control flow elements including if, loop, and switch statements.

Chapter 4, *Data Types*, introduces its readers to Go's type system including detail about built-in types, type declaration, and conversion.

Chapter 5, *Functions in Go*, discusses the characteristics of the Go function type including definition, assignment, variadic parameters, and closures.

Chapter 6, *Go Packages and Program Structures*, introduces readers to the organization of functions as a logical grouping known as packages and programs.

Chapter 7, *Composite Types*, this chapter continues the discussion Go types by introducing the reader to Go's composite types such as arrays, slices, maps, and structs.

Chapter 8, *Methods, Interfaces, and Objects*, introduces the reader to Go idioms and features that can be used to create and compose object structures.

Chapter 9, *Concurrency*, introduces the reader to the topics of writing concurrent programs in Go using language constructs such as goroutines and channels.

Chapter 10, *Data IO in Go*, covers the built-in interfaces and APIs to achieve streaming input, output, and encoding of data.

Chapter 11, *Writing Networked Services*, explores the Go's standard library for creating connected applications using covering topics from low-level TCP protocols to HTTP an RPC.

Chapter 12, *Code Testing*, here readers are introduced to Go's inherent support and tools for code testing and benchmarking.

What you need for this book

To follow the examples in this book, you will need Go version 1.6 or later. Go supports architectures including AMD64, x386, and ARM running the following operating systems:

- Windows XP (or later)
- Mac OSX 10.7 (or later)
- Linux 2.6 (or later)
- FreeBSD 8 (or later)

Who this book is for

If you have prior exposure to programming and are interested learning the Go, this book is designed for you. While it assumes that you are familiar with concepts such as variables, data types, arrays, methods, and functions, the book is designed to allow you to follow chapter by chapter or skip around to the topics you want to learn about.

Conventions

In this book, you will find a number of text styles that distinguish between different kinds of information. Here are some examples of these styles and an explanation of their meaning.

Code words in text, database table names, folder names, filenames, file extensions, pathnames, dummy URLs, user input, and Twitter handles are shown as follows: "Save the source code in a file called `helloworld.go` anywhere inside your GOPATH."

A block of code is set as follows:

```
package main
import "fmt"
func main() {
   fmt.Println("Hello, World!")
}
```

Any command-line input or output is written as follows:

```
$> go version
go version go1.6.1 linux/amd64
```

New terms and **important words** are shown in bold. Words that you see on the screen, for example, in menus or dialog boxes, appear in the text like this: "If all goes well, you should see the message **Hello, World!** output on your screen.."

Warnings or important notes appear in a box like this.

Tips and tricks appear like this.

Reader feedback

Feedback from our readers is always welcome. Let us know what you think about this book-what you liked or disliked. Reader feedback is important for us as it helps us develop titles that you will really get the most out of. To send us general feedback, simply e-mail feedback@packtpub.com, and mention the book's title in the subject of your message. If there is a topic that you have expertise in and you are interested in either writing or contributing to a book, see our author guide at www.packtpub.com/authors.

Customer support

Now that you are the proud owner of a Packt book, we have a number of things to help you to get the most from your purchase.

Downloading the example code

You can download the example code files for this book from your account at http://www.packtpub.com. If you purchased this book elsewhere, you can visit http://www.packtpub.com/support and register to have the files e-mailed directly to you.

You can download the code files by following these steps:

1. Log in or register to our website using your e-mail address and password.
2. Hover the mouse pointer on the **SUPPORT** tab at the top.
3. Click on **Code Downloads & Errata**.
4. Enter the name of the book in the **Search** box.

5. Select the book for which you're looking to download the code files.
6. Choose from the drop-down menu where you purchased this book from.
7. Click on **Code Download**.

Once the file is downloaded, please make sure that you unzip or extract the folder using the latest version of:

- WinRAR / 7-Zip for Windows
- Zipeg / iZip / UnRarX for Mac
- 7-Zip / PeaZip for Linux

The code bundle for the book is also hosted on GitHub at `https://github.com/PacktPubl ishing/Learning-Go-Programming`. We also have other code bundles from our rich catalog of books and videos available at `https://github.com/PacktPublishing/`. Check them out!

Downloading the color images of this book

We also provide you with a PDF file that has color images of the screenshots/diagrams used in this book. The color images will help you better understand the changes in the output. You can download this file from `http://www.packtpub.com/sites/default/files/downl oads/LearningGoPrograming_ColorImages.pdf`.

Errata

Although we have taken every care to ensure the accuracy of our content, mistakes do happen. If you find a mistake in one of our books-maybe a mistake in the text or the code-we would be grateful if you could report this to us. By doing so, you can save other readers from frustration and help us improve subsequent versions of this book. If you find any errata, please report them by visiting `http://www.packtpub.com/submit-errata`, selecting your book, clicking on the **Errata Submission Form** link, and entering the details of your errata. Once your errata are verified, your submission will be accepted and the errata will be uploaded to our website or added to any list of existing errata under the Errata section of that title.

To view the previously submitted errata, go to `https://www.packtpub.com/books/conten t/support` and enter the name of the book in the search field. The required information will appear under the **Errata** section.

Piracy

Piracy of copyrighted material on the Internet is an ongoing problem across all media. At Packt, we take the protection of our copyright and licenses very seriously. If you come across any illegal copies of our works in any form on the Internet, please provide us with the location address or website name immediately so that we can pursue a remedy.

Please contact us at copyright@packtpub.com with a link to the suspected pirated material.

We appreciate your help in protecting our authors and our ability to bring you valuable content.

Questions

If you have a problem with any aspect of this book, you can contact us at questions@packtpub.com, and we will do our best to address the problem.

1
A First Step in Go

In the first chapter of the book, you will be introduced to Go and take a tour of the features that have made the language a favorite among its adopters. The start of the chapter provides the motivation behind the Go programming language. If you are impatient, however, you are welcome to skip to any of the other topics and learn how to write your first Go program. Finally, the *Go in a nutshell* section provides a high-level summary of the characteristics of the language.

The following topics are covered in this chapter:

- The Go programming language
- Playing with Go
- Installing Go
- Your first Go program
- Go in a nutshell

The Go programming language

Since the invention of the C language in the early 1970s by *Dennis Ritchie* at Bell Labs, the computing industry has produced many popular languages that are based directly on (or have borrowed ideas from) its syntax. Commonly known as the C-family of languages, they can be split into two broad evolutionary branches. In one branch, derivatives such as C++, C#, and Java have evolved to adopt a strong type system, object orientation, and the use of compiled binaries. These languages, however, tend to have a slow build-deploy cycle and programmers are forced to adopt a complex object-oriented type system to attain runtime safety and speed of execution:

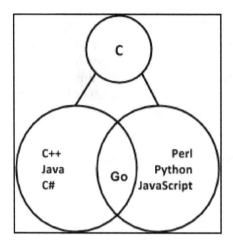

In the other evolutionary linguistic branch are languages such as Perl, Python, and JavaScript that are described as dynamic languages for their lack of type safety formalities, use of lightweight scripting syntax, and code interpretation instead of compilation. Dynamic languages have become the preferred tool for web and cloud scale development where speed and ease of deployment are valued over runtime safety. The interpreted nature of dynamic languages means, however, they generally run slower than their compiled counterparts. In addition, the lack of type safety at runtime means the correctness of the system scales poorly as the application grows.

Go was created as a system language at Google in 2007 by *Robert Griesemer*, *Rob Pike*, and *Ken Thomson* to handle the needs of application development. The designers of Go wanted to mitigate the issues with the aforementioned languages while creating a new language that is simple, safe, consistent, and predictable. As Rob Pike puts it:

> *"Go is an attempt to combine the safety and performance of a statically-typed language with the expressiveness and convenience of a dynamically-typed interpreted language."*

Go borrows ideas from different languages that came before it, including:

- Simplified but concise syntax that is fun and easy to use
- A type of system that feels more like a dynamic language
- Support for object-oriented programming
- Statically typed for compilation and runtime safety
- Compiled to native binaries for fast runtime execution
- Near-zero compilation time that feels more like an interpreted language
- A simple concurrency idiom to leverage multi-core, multi-chip machines
- A garbage collector for safe and automatic memory management

The remainder of this chapter will walk you through an introductory set of steps that will give you a preview of the language and get you started with building and running your first Go program. It is a precursor to the topics that are covered in detail in the remaining chapters of the book. You are welcome to skip to other chapters if you already have a basic understanding of Go.

Playing with Go

Before we jump head-first into installing and running Go tools on your local machine, let us take a look at the **Go Playground**. The creators of the language have made available a simple way to familiarize yourself with the language without installing any tools. Known as the Go Playground, it is a web-based tool, accessible from `https://play.golang.org/`, that uses an editor metaphor to let developers test their Go skills by writing code directly within the web browser window. The Playground gives its users the ability to compile and run their code on Google's remote servers and get immediate results as shown in the following screenshot:

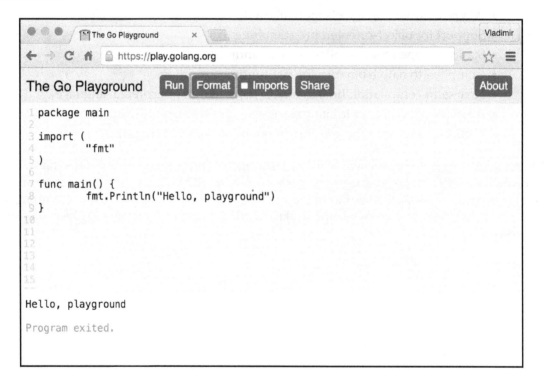

The editor is basic, as it is meant to be used as a learning tool and a way to share code with others. The Playground includes practical features such as line numbers and formatting to ensure your code remains readable as it goes beyond a few lines long. Since this is a free service that consumes real compute resources, Google understandably imposes a few limitations on what can be done with Playground:

- You are restricted on the amount of memory your code will consume
- Long-running programs will be killed

- Access to files is simulated with an in-memory filesystem.
- Network access is simulated against the loopback interface only

No IDE required

Besides the Go Playground, how is one supposed to write Go code anyway? Writing Go does not require a fancy **Integrated Development Environment (IDE)**. As a matter of fact, you can get started writing your simple Go programs with your favorite plain text editor that is bundled with your OS. There are, however, Go plugins for most major text editors (and full-blown IDEs) such as Atom, Vim, Emacs, Microsoft Code, IntelliJ, and many others. There is a complete list of editors and IDE plugins for Go which can be found at `https://g ithub.com/golang/go/wiki/IDEsAndTextEditorPlugins`.

Installing Go

To start programming with Go on your local machine you will need to install the **Go Toolchain** on your computer. At the time of writing, Go comes ready to be installed on the following major OS platforms:

- Linux
- FreeBSD Unix
- Mac OSX
- Windows

The official installation packages are all available for 32-bit and 64-bit Intel-based architectures. There are also official binary releases that are available for ARM architectures as well. As Go grows in popularity, there will certainly be more binary distribution choices made available in the future.

Let us skip the detailed installation instructions as they will certainly change by the time you read this. Instead, you are invited to visit `http://golang.org/doc/install` and follow the directions given for your specific platform. Once completed, be sure to test your installation is working before continuing to use the following command:

```
$> go version
go version go1.6.1 linux/amd64
```

The previous command should print the version number, target OS, and the machine architecture where Go and its tools are installed. If you do not get an output similar to that preceding command, ensure to add the path of the Go binaries to your OS's execution `PATH` environment variable.

Before you start writing your own code, ensure that you have properly set up your `GOPATH`. This is a local directory where your Go source files and compiled artifacts are saved as you use the Go Toolchain. Follow the instructions found in `https://golang.org/doc/install #testing` to set up your GOPATH.

Source code examples

The programming examples presented throughout this book are available on the GitHub source code repository service. There you will find all source files grouped by chapters in the repository at `https://github.com/vladimirvivien/learning-go/`. To save the readers a few keystrokes, the examples use a shortened URL, that starts with `golang.fyi`, that points directly to the respective file in GitHub.

Alternatively, you can follow along by downloading and unzipping (or cloning) the repository locally. Create a directory structure in your `GOPATH` so that the root of the source files is located at `$GOPATH/src/github.com/vladimirvivien/learning-go/`.

Your first Go program

After installing the Go tools successfully on your local machine, you are now ready to write and execute your first Go program. For that, simply open your favorite text editor and type in the simple Hello World program shown in the following code:

```go
package main
import "fmt"
func main() {
   fmt.Println("Hello, World!")
}
```

golang.fyi/ch01/helloworld.go

Save the source code in a file called `helloworld.go` anywhere inside your GOPATH. Then use the following Go command to compile and run the program:

```
$> go run helloworld.go
Hello, World!
```

If all goes well, you should see the message **Hello, World!** output on your screen. Congratulations, you have just written and executed your first Go program. Now, let us explore the attributes and characteristics of the Go language at a high level.

Go in a nutshell

By design, Go has a simple syntax. Its designers wanted to create a language that is clear, concise, and consistent with few syntactic surprises. When reading Go code, keep this mantra in mind: *what you see is what it is*. Go shies away from a clever and terse coding style in favor of code that is clear and readable as exemplified by the following program:

```go
// This program prints molecular information for known metalloids
// including atomic number, mass, and atom count found
// in 100 grams of each element using the mole unit.
// See http://en.wikipedia.org/wiki/Mole_(unit)
package main

import "fmt"

const avogadro float64 = 6.0221413e+23
const grams = 100.0

type amu float64

func (mass amu) float() float64 {
    return float64(mass)
}

type metalloid struct {
    name   string
    number int32
    weight amu
}

var metalloids = []metalloid{
    metalloid{"Boron", 5, 10.81},
    metalloid{"Silicon", 14, 28.085},
    metalloid{"Germanium", 32, 74.63},
    metalloid{"Arsenic", 33, 74.921},
```

```go
        metalloid{"Antimony", 51, 121.760},
        metalloid{"Tellerium", 52, 127.60},
        metalloid{"Polonium", 84, 209.0},
}

// finds # of moles
func moles(mass amu) float64 {
    return float64(mass) / grams
}

// returns # of atoms moles
func atoms(moles float64) float64 {
    return moles * avogadro
}

// return column headers
func headers() string {
    return fmt.Sprintf(
        "%-10s %-10s %-10s Atoms in %.2f Grams\n",
        "Element", "Number", "AMU", grams,
    )
}

func main() {
    fmt.Print(headers())

    for _, m := range metalloids {
        fmt.Printf(
    "%-10s %-10d %-10.3f %e\n",
        m.name, m.number, m.weight.float(), atoms(moles(m.weight)),
        )
    }
}
```

golang.fyi/ch01/metalloids.go

When the code is executed, it will give the following output:

```
$> go run metalloids.go
Element    Number     AMU        Atoms in 100.00 Grams
Boron      5          10.810     6.509935e+22
Silicon    14         28.085     1.691318e+23
Germanium  32         74.630     4.494324e+23
Arsenic    33         74.921     4.511848e+23
Antimony   51         121.760    7.332559e+23
Tellerium  52         127.600    7.684252e+23
Polonium   84         209.000    1.258628e+24
```

If you have never seen Go before, you may not understand some of the details of the syntax and idioms used in the previous program. Nevertheless, when you read the code, there is a good chance you will be able to follow the logic and form a mental model of the program's flow. That is the beauty of Go's simplicity and the reason why so many programmers use it. If you are completely lost, no need to worry, as the subsequent chapters will cover all aspects of the language to get you going.

Functions

Go programs are composed of functions, the smallest callable code unit in the language. In Go, functions are typed entities that can either be named (as shown in the previous example) or be assigned to a variable as a value:

```
// a simple Go function
func moles(mass amu) float64 {
    return float64(mass) / grams
}
```

Another interesting feature about Go functions is their ability to return multiple values as a result of a call. For instance, the previous function could be re-written to return a value of type error in addition to the calculated float64 value:

```
func moles(mass amu) (float64, error) {
    if mass < 0 {
        return 0, error.New("invalid mass")
    }
    return (float64(mass) / grams), nil
}
```

The previous code uses the multi-return capabilities of Go functions to return both the mass and an error value. You will encounter this idiom throughout the book used as a mean to properly signal errors to the caller of a function. There will be further discussion on multi-return value functions covered in Chapter 5, *Functions in Go*.

Packages

Source files containing Go functions can be further organized into directory structures known as a package. Packages are logical modules that are used to share code in Go as libraries. You can create your own local packages or use tools provided by Go to automatically pull and use remote packages from a source code repository. You will learn more about Go packages in Chapter 6, *Go Packages and Programs*.

The workspace

Go follows a simple code layout convention to reliably organize source code packages and to manage their dependencies. Your local Go source code is stored in the workspace, which is a directory convention that contains the source code and runtime artifacts. This makes it easy for Go tools to automatically find, build, and install compiled binaries. Additionally, Go tools rely on the workspace setup to pull source code packages from remote repositories, such as Git, Mercurial, and Subversion, and satisfy their dependencies.

Strongly typed

All values in Go are statically typed. However, the language offers a simple but expressive type system that can have the feel of a dynamic language. For instance, types can be safely inferred as shown in the following code snippet:

```
const grams = 100.0
```

As you would expect, constant grams would be assigned a numeric type, float64, to be precise, by the Go type system. This is true not only for constants, but any variable can use a short-hand form of declaration and assignment as shown in the following example:

```
package main
import "fmt"
func main() {
  var name = "Metalloids"
  var triple = [3]int{5,14,84}
  elements := []string{"Boron","Silicon", "Polonium"}
  isMetal := false
  fmt.Println(name, triple, elements, isMetal)

}
```

Notice that the variables, in the previous code snippet, are not explicitly assigned a type. Instead, the type system assigns each variable a type based on the literal value in the assignment. Chapter 2, *Go Language Essentials* and Chapter 4, *Data Types*, go into more details regarding Go types.

Composite types

Besides the types for simple values, Go also supports composite types such as array, slice, and map. These types are designed to store indexed elements of values of a specified type. For instance, the metalloid example shown previously makes use of a slice, which is a variable-sized array. The variable metalloid is declared as a slice to store a collection of the type metalloid. The code uses the literal syntax to combine the declaration and assignment of a slice of type metalloid:

```
var metalloids = []metalloid{
    metalloid{"Boron", 5, 10.81},
    metalloid{"Silicon", 14, 28.085},
    metalloid{"Germanium", 32, 74.63},
    metalloid{"Arsenic", 33, 74.921},
    metalloid{"Antimony", 51, 121.760},
    metalloid{"Tellerium", 52, 127.60},
    metalloid{"Polonium", 84, 209.0},
}
```

Go also supports a struct type which is a composite that stores named elements called fields as shown in the following code:

```
func main() {
  planet := struct {
      name string
      diameter int
  }{"earth", 12742}
}
```

The previous example uses the literal syntax to declare struct{name string; diameter int} with the value {"earth", 12742}. You can read all about composite types in Chapter 7, *Composite Types*.

The named type

As discussed, Go provides a healthy set of built-in types, both simple and composite. Go programmers can also define new named types based on an existing underlying type as shown in the following snippet extracted from `metalloid` in the earlier example:

```
type amu float64

type metalloid struct {
    name string
    number int32
    weight amu
}
```

The previous snippet shows the definition of two named types, one called `amu`, which uses type `float64` as its underlying type. Type `metalloid`, on the other hand, uses a `struct` composite type as its underlying type, allowing it to store values in an indexed data structure. You can read more about declaring new named types in `Chapter 4`, *Data Types*.

Methods and objects

Go is not an object-oriented language in a classical sense. Go types do not use a class hierarchy to model the world as is the case with other object-oriented languages. However, Go can support the object-based development idiom, allowing data to receive behaviors. This is done by attaching functions, known as methods, to named types.

The following snippet, extracted from the metalloid example, shows the type `amu` receiving a method called `float()` that returns the mass as a `float64` value:

```
type amu float64

func (mass amu) float() float64 {
    return float64(mass)
}
```

The power of this concept is explored in detail in `Chapter 8`, *Methods, Interfaces, and Objects*.

Interfaces

Go supports the notion of a programmatic interface. However, as you will see in Chapter 8, *Methods, Interfaces, and Objects*, the Go interface is itself a type that aggregates a set of methods that can project capabilities onto values of other types. Staying true to its simplistic nature, implementing a Go interface does not require a keyword to explicitly declare an interface. Instead, the type system implicitly resolves implemented interfaces using the methods attached to a type.

For instance, Go includes the built-in interface called Stringer, defined as follows:

```
type Stringer interface {
    String() string
}
```

Any type that has the method String() attached, automatically implements the Stringer interface. So, modifying the definition of the type metalloid, from the previous program, to attach the method String() will automatically implement the Stringer interface:

```
type metalloid struct {
    name string
    number int32
    weight amu
}
func (m metalloid) String() string {
  return fmt.Sprintf(
    "%-10s %-10d %-10.3f %e",
    m.name, m.number, m.weight.float(), atoms(moles(m.weight)),
  )
}
```

golang.fyi/ch01/metalloids2.go

The String() methods return a pre-formatted string that represents the value of a metalloid. The function Print(), from the standard library package fmt, will automatically call the method String(), if its parameter implements stringer. So, we can use this fact to print metalloid values as follow:

```
func main() {
  fmt.Print(headers())
  for _, m := range metalloids {
    fmt.Print(m, "\n")
  }
}
```

Again, refer to Chapter 8, *Methods, Interfaces, and Objects*, for a thorough treatment of the topic of interfaces.

Concurrency and channels

One of the main features that has rocketed Go to its current level of adoption is its inherent support for simple concurrency idioms. The language uses a unit of concurrency known as a goroutine, which lets programmers structure programs with independent and highly concurrent code.

As you will see in the following example, Go also relies on a construct known as a channel used for both communication and coordination among independently running goroutines. This approach avoids the perilous and (sometimes brittle) traditional approach of thread communicating by sharing memory. Instead, Go facilitates the approach of sharing by communicating using channels. This is illustrated in the following example that uses both goroutines and channels as processing and communication primitives:

```go
// Calculates sum of all multiple of 3 and 5 less than MAX value.
// See https://projecteuler.net/problem=1
package main

import (
    "fmt"
)

const MAX = 1000

func main() {
    work := make(chan int, MAX)
    result := make(chan int)

    // 1. Create channel of multiples of 3 and 5
    // concurrently using goroutine
    go func(){
        for i := 1; i < MAX; i++ {
            if (i % 3) == 0 || (i % 5) == 0 {
                work <- i // push for work
            }
        }
        close(work)
    }()

    // 2. Concurrently sum up work and put result
    //    in channel result
    go func(){
```

```
    r := 0
    for i := range work {
       r = r + i
    }
    result <- r
}()

// 3. Wait for result, then print
fmt.Println("Total:", <- result)
}
```

golang.fyi/ch01/euler1.go

The code in the previous example splits the work to be done between two concurrently running goroutines (declared with the go keyword) as annotated in the code comment. Each goroutine runs independently and uses the Go channels, work and result, to communicate and coordinate the calculation of the final result. Again, if this code does not make sense at all, rest assured, concurrency has the whole of Chapter 9, *Concurrency*, dedicated to it.

Memory management and safety

Similar to other compiled and statically-typed languages such as C and C++, Go lets developers have direct influence on memory allocation and layout. When a developer creates a slice (think array) of bytes, for instance, there is a direct representation of those bytes in the underlying physical memory of the machine. Furthermore, Go borrows the notion of pointers to represent the memory addresses of stored values giving Go programs the support of passing function parameters by both value and reference.

Go asserts a highly opinionated safety barrier around memory management with little to no configurable parameters. Go automatically handles the drudgery of bookkeeping for memory allocation and release using a runtime garbage collector. Pointer arithmetic is not permitted at runtime; therefore, developers cannot traverse memory blocks by adding to or subtracting from a base memory address.

Fast compilation

Another one of Go's attractions is its millisecond build-time for moderately-sized projects. This is made possible with features such as a simple syntax, conflict-free grammar, and a strict identifier resolution that forbids unused declared resources such as imported packages or variables. Furthermore, the build system resolves packages using transitivity information stored in the closest source node in the dependency tree. Again, this reduces the code-compile-run cycle to feel more like a dynamic language instead of a compiled language.

Testing and code coverage

While other languages usually rely on third-party tools for testing, Go includes both a built-in API and tools designed specifically for automated testing, benchmarking, and code coverage. Similar to other features in Go, the test tools use simple conventions to automatically inspect and instrument the test functions found in your code.

The following function is a simplistic implementation of the Euclidean division algorithm that returns a quotient and a remainder value (as variables q and r) for positive integers:

```go
func DivMod(dvdn, dvsr int) (q, r int) {
  r = dvdn
  for r >= dvsr {
    q += 1
    r = r - dvsr
  }
  return
}
```

golang.fyi/ch01/testexample/divide.go

In a separate source file, we can write a test function to validate the algorithm by checking the remainder value returned by the tested function using the Go test API as shown in the following code:

```go
package testexample
import "testing"
func TestDivide(t *testing.T) {
  dvnd := 40
    for dvsor := 1; dvsor < dvnd; dvsor++ {
      q, r := DivMod(dvnd, dvsor)
    if (dvnd % dvsor) != r {
      t.Fatalf("%d/%d q=%d, r=%d, bad remainder.", dvnd, dvsor, q, r)
      }
```

```
    }
}
```

To exercise the test source code, simply run Go's test tool as shown in the following example:

```
$> go test .
ok    github.com/vladimirvivien/learning-go/ch01/testexample  0.003s
```

The test tool reports a summary of the test result indicating the package that was tested and its pass/fail outcome. The Go Toolchain comes with many more features designed to help programmers create testable code, including:

- Automatically instrument code to gather coverage statistics during tests
- Generating HTML reports for covered code and tested paths
- A benchmark API that lets developers collect performance metrics from tests
- Benchmark reports with valuable metrics for detecting performance issues

You can read all about testing and its related tools in Chapter 12, *Code Testing*.

Documentation

Documentation is a first-class component in Go. Arguably, the language's popularity is in part due to its extensive documentation (see http://golang.org/pkg). Go comes with the Godoc tool, which makes it easy to extract documentation from comment text embedded directly in the source code. For example, to document the function from the previous section, we simply add comment lines directly above the DivMod function as shown in the following example:

```
// DivMod performs a Eucledan division producing a quotient and remainder.
// This version only works if dividend and divisor > 0.
func DivMod(dvdn, dvsr int) (q, r int) {
    ...
}
```

The Go documentation tool can automatically extract and create HTML-formatted pages. For instance, the following command will start the Godoc tool as a server on localhost port 6000:

```
$> godoc -http=":6001"
```

You can then access the documentation of your code directly from your web browser. For instance, the following figure shows the generated documentation snippet for the previous function located at
`http://localhost:6001/pkg/github.com/vladimirvivien/learning-go/ch01/te stexample/`:

```
func DivMod

func DivMod(dvdn, dvsr int) (q, r int)

DivMod performs a division/remainder operation.
This version only works if dividend and divisor > 0.
other conditions may cause panic or other unwanted
behavior
```

An extensive library

For its short existence, Go rapidly grew a collection of high-quality APIs as part of its standard library that are comparable to other popular and more established languages. The following, by no means exhaustive, lists some of the core APIs that programmers get out-of-the-box:

- Complete support for regular expressions with search and replace
- Powerful IO primitives for reading and writing bytes
- Full support for networking from socket, TCP/UDP, IPv4, and IPv6
- APIs for writing production-ready HTTP services and clients
- Support for traditional synchronization primitives (mutex, atomic, and so on)
- General-purpose template framework with HTML support
- Support for JSON/XML serializations
- RPC with multiple wire formats
- APIs for archive and compression algorithms: `tar`, `zip/gzip`, `zlib`, and so on
- Cryptography support for most major algorithms and hash functions
- Access to OS-level processes, environment info, signaling, and much more

The Go Toolchain

Before we end the chapter, one last aspect of Go that should be highlighted is its collection of tools. While some of these tools were already mentioned in previous sections, others are listed here for your awareness:

- `fmt`: Reformats source code to adhere to the standard
- `vet`: Reports improper usage of source code constructs
- `lint`: Another source code tool that reports flagrant style infractions
- `goimports`: Analyzes and fixes package import references in source code
- `godoc`: Generates and organizes source code documentation
- `generate`: Generates Go source code from directives stored in source code
- `get`: Remotely retrieves and installs packages and their dependencies
- `build`: Compiles code in a specified package and its dependencies
- `run`: Provides the convenience of compiling and running your Go program
- `test`: Performs unit tests with support for benchmark and coverage reports
- `oracle` static analysis tool: Queries source code structures and elements
- `cgo`: Generates source code for interoperability between Go and C

Summary

Within its relatively short existence, Go has won the hearts of many adopters who value simplicity as a way to write code that is exact and is able to scale in longevity. As you have seen from the previous sections in this chapter, it is easy to get started with your first Go program.

The chapter also exposed its readers to a high-level summary of the most essential features of Go including its simplified syntax, its emphasis on concurrency, and the tools that make Go a top choice for software engineers, creating systems for the age of data center computing. As you may imagine, this is just a taste of what's to come.

In the following chapters, the book will continue to explore in detail the syntactical elements and language concepts that make Go a great language to learn. Let's Go!

Go Language Essentials

2

In the previous chapter, we established the elemental characteristics that make Go a great language with which to create modern system programs. In this chapter, we dig deeper into the language's syntax to explore its components and features.

We will cover the following topics:

- The Go source file
- Identifiers
- Variables
- Constants
- Operators

The Go source file

We have seen, in Chapter 1, *A First Step in Go*, some examples of Go programs. In this section, we will examine the Go source file. Let us consider the following source code file (which prints "Hello World" greetings in different languages):

```go
package main

import "fmt"
import "math/rand"
import "time"

var greetings = [][]string{
    {"Hello, World!", "English"},
    {"Salut Monde", "French"},
    {"世界您好", "Simplified Chinese"},
    {"qo' vIvan", "Klingon"},
    {"हैलो वर्ल्ड", "Hindi"},
    {"안녕하세요", "Korean"},
    {"привет мир", "Russian"},
    {"Wapendwa Dunia", "Swahili"},
    {"Hola Mundo", "Spanish"},
    {"Merhaba Dünya", "Turkish"},
}

func greeting() [] string {
    seed := time.Now().UnixNano()
    rnd := rand.New(rand.NewSource(seed))
    return greetings[rnd.Intn(len(greetings))]
}

func main() {
    g := greeting()
    fmt.Printf("%s (%s)\n", g[0], g[1])
}
```

golang.fyi/ch02/helloworld2.go

A typical Go source file, such as the one listed earlier, can be divided into three main sections, illustrated as follows:

- The **Package Clause**:

  ```go
  //1 Package Clause
  package main
  ```

- The **Import Declaration**:

```
//2 Import Declaration
import "fmt"
import "math/rand"
import "time"
```

- The **Source Body**:

```
//3 Source Body
var greetings = [][]string{
  {"Hello, World!","English"},
  ...
}

func greeting() [] string {
  ...
}

func main() {
  ...
}
```

The **package** clause indicates the name of the package this source file belongs to (see Chapter 6, Go *Packages and Programs* for a detailed discussion on package organization). The **import** declaration lists any external package that the source code wishes to use. The Go compiler strictly enforces package declaration usage. It is considered an error (compilation) to include an unused package in your source file. The last portion of the source is considered the body of your source file. It is where you declare variables, constants, types, and functions.

All Go source files must end with the .go suffix. In general, you can name a Go source file whatever you want. Unlike Java, for instance, there is no direct association between a Go file name and the types it declared in its content. It is, however, considered good practice to name your file something indicative of its content.

Before we explore Go's syntax in greater detail, it is important to understand some basic structural elements of the language. While some of these elements are syntactically bolted into the language, others are simple idioms and conventions that you should be aware of to make your introduction to Go simple and enjoyable.

Optional semicolon

You may have noticed that Go does not require a semicolon as a statement separator. This is a trait borrowed from other lighter and interpreted languages. The following two programs are functionally equivalent. The first program uses idiomatic Go and omits the semicolons:

```go
package main
import "fmt"
func main() {
    fmt.Println("Hello, 世界")
}
```

The second version of the program, shown as follows, uses superfluous semicolons to explicitly terminate its statements. While the compiler may thank you for your help, this is not idiomatic in Go:

```go
package main;
import "fmt";

func main() {
    fmt.Println("Hello, 世界");
}
```

Although semicolons in Go are optional, Go's formal grammar still requires them as statement terminators. So, the Go compiler will insert semicolons at the end of source code lines that end with the following:

- An identifier
- A literal value for string, Boolean, numeric, or complex
- A control flow directive such as break, continue, or return
- A closing parenthesis or bracket such as), }, or]
- The increment ++ or the decrement -- operator

Due to these rules, the compiler enforces strict syntactical forms that heavily influence source code style in Go. For instance, all code blocks must start with an open curly { brace on the same line as its preceding statement. Otherwise, the compiler may insert the semicolon in a location that breaks the code, as shown in the following if statement:

```
func main() {
    if "a" == "a"
    {
        fmt.Println("Hello, World!")
    }
}
```

Moving the curly brace to the next line causes the compiler to insert the semicolon prematurely, which will result in the following syntax error:

```
$> ... missing condition in if statement ...
```

This is because the compiler inserted the semicolon after the if statement (if "a"=="a";), using the semicolon insertion rules discussed in this section. You can verify this by manually inserting a semicolon after the if condition statement; you will get the same error. This is an excellent place to transition into the next section, to discuss trailing commas in code blocks.

Multiple lines

Breaking up expressions into multiple lines must follow the semi-colon rules discussed in the previous section. Mainly, in a multi-line expression, each line must end with a token that prevents the premature insertion of a semi-colon, as illustrated in the following table. It should be noted that rows in the table with an invalid expression will not compile:

Expression	Valid
`lonStr := "Hello World! " +` `"How are you?"`	Yes, the + operator prevents a premature semi-colon from being inserted.
`lonStr := "Hello World! "` `+ "How are you?"`	No, a semi-colon will be inserted after the first line, semantically breaking the line.
`fmt.Printf("[%s] %d %d %v",` `str, num1, num2, nameMap)`	Yes, the comma properly breaks the expression.

`fmt.Printf("[%s] %d %d %v",`
`str,`
`num1,`
`num2,`
`nameMap)`
	Yes, the compiler inserts a semi-colon only after the last line.

`weekDays := []string{`
`"Mon", "Tue",`
`"Wed", "Thr",`
`"Fri"`
`}`
	No, the `Fri` line causes a premature semi-colon to be inserted.

`weekDays2 := []string{`
`"Mon", "Tue",`
`"Wed", "Thr",`
`"Fri",`
`}`
	Yes, the `Fri` line contains a trailing comma, which causes compiler to insert a semi-colon at the next line.

`weekDays1 := []string{`
`"Mon", "Tue",`
`"Wed", "Thr",`
`"Fri"}`
	Yes, the semi-colon is inserted after the line with the closing bracket.

You may wonder why the Go compiler puts the onus on the developer to provide line-break hints to indicate the end of a statement. Surely, Go designers could have devised an elaborate algorithm to figure this out automatically. Yes, they could have. However, by keeping the syntax simple and predictable, the compiler is able to quickly parse and compile Go source code.

> The Go toolchain includes the gofmt tool, which can be used to consistently apply proper formatting rules to your source code. There is also the `govet` tool, which goes much further by analyzing your code for structural problems with code elements.

Go identifiers

Go identifiers are used to name program elements including packages, variables, functions, and types. The following summarizes some attributes about identifiers in Go:

- Identifiers support the Unicode character set
- The first position of an identifier must be a letter or an underscore
- Idiomatic Go favors mixed caps (camel case) naming
- Package-level identifiers must be unique across a given package
- Identifiers must be unique within a code block (functions, control statements)

The blank identifier

The Go compiler is particularly strict about the use of declared identifiers for variables or packages. The basic rule is: *you declare it, you must use it*. If you attempt to compile code with unused identifiers such as variables or named packages, the compilers will not be pleased and will fail compilation.

Go allows you to turn off this behavior using the blank identifier, represented by the _ (underscore) character. Any declaration or assignment that uses the blank identifier is not bound to any value and is ignored at compile time. The blank identifier is usually used in two contexts, as listed in the following subsections.

Muting package imports

When a package declaration is preceded by an underscore, the compiler allows the package to be declared without any further referenced usage:

```
import "fmt"
import "path/filepath"
import _ "log"
```

In the previous code snippet, the package `log` will be muted without any further reference in the code. This can be a handy feature during active development of new code, where developers may want to try new ideas without constantly having to comment out or delete the declarations. Although a package with a blank identifier is not bound to any reference, the Go runtime will still initialize it. `Chapter 6`, *Go Packages and Programs*, discusses the package initialization lifecycle.

Muting unwanted function results

When a Go function call returns multiple values, each value in the return list must be assigned to a variable identifier. In some cases, however, it may be desirable to mute unwanted results from the return list while keeping others, as shown in the following call:

```
_, execFile := filepath.Split("/opt/data/bigdata.txt")
```

The previous call to the function `filepath.Split("/opt/data/bigdata.txt")` takes a path and returns two values: the first is the parent path (`/opt/data`) and the second is the file name (`bigdata.txt`). The first value is assigned to the blank identifier and is, therefore, unbounded to a named identifier, which causes it to be ignored by the compiler. In future discussions, we will explore other uses of this idiom's other contexts, such as error-handling and `for` loops.

Built-in identifiers

Go comes with a number of built-in identifiers. They fall into different categories, including types, values, and built-in function.

Types

The following identifiers are used for Go's built-in types:

Category	Identifier
Numeric	byte, int, int8, int16, int32, int64, rune, uint, uint8, uint16, uint32, uint64, float32, float64, complex64, complex128, uintptr
String	string
Boolean	bool
Error	error

Values

These identifiers have preassigned values:

Category	Identifier
Boolean constants	`true`, `false`
Constant counter	`iota`
Uninitialized value	`nil`

Functions

The following functions are available as part of Go's built-in pre-declared identifiers:

Category	Identifier
Initialization	`make()`, `new()`
Collections	`append()`, `cap()`, `copy()`, `delete()`
Complex numbers	`complex()`, `imag()`, `real()`
Error Handling	`panic()`, `recover()`

Go variables

Go is a strictly typed language, which implies that all variables are named elements that are bound to both a value and a type. As you will see, the simplicity and flexibility of its syntax make declaring and initializing variables in Go feel more like a dynamically-typed language.

Variable declaration

Before you can use a variable in Go, it must be declared with a named identifier for future reference in the code. The long form of a variable declaration in Go follows the format shown here:

```
var <identifier list> <type>
```

The `var` keyword is used to declare one or more variable identifiers followed by the type of the variables. The following source code snippet shows an abbreviated program with several variables declared outside of the function `main()`:

```
package main

import "fmt"

var name, desc string
var radius int32
var mass float64
var active bool
var satellites []string

func main() {
  name = "Sun"
  desc = "Star"
  radius = 685800
  mass = 1.989E+30
  active = true
  satellites = []string{
    "Mercury",
    "Venus",
    "Earth",
    "Mars",
    "Jupiter",
    "Saturn",
    "Uranus",
    "Neptune",
  }
  fmt.Println(name)
  fmt.Println(desc)
  fmt.Println("Radius (km)", radius)
  fmt.Println("Mass (kg)", mass)
  fmt.Println("Satellites", satellites)
}
```

golang.fyi/ch02/vardec1.go

The zero-value

The previous source code shows several examples of variables being declared with a variety of types. Then the variables are assigned a value inside the function `main()`. At first glance, it would appear that these declared variables do not have an assigned value when they are declared. This would contradict our previous assertion that all Go variables are bound to a type and a value.

How can we declare a variable and not bind a value to it? During declaration of a variable, if a value is not provided, Go will automatically bind a default value (or a zero-value) to the variable for proper memory initialization (we see how to do both declaration and initialization in one expression later).

The following table shows Go types and their default zero-values:

Type	Zero-Value
`string`	`""` (empty string)
Numeric – Integers: `byte`, `int`, `int8`, `int16`, `int32`, `int64`, `rune`, `uint`, `uint8`, `uint16`, `uint32`, `uint64`, `uintptr`	0
Numeric – Floating point: `float32`, `float64`	0.0
`bool`	false
`Array`	Each index position has a zero-value corresponding to the array's element type.
`Struct`	An empty `struct` with each member having its respective zero-value.
Other types: Interface, function, channel, slice, map, and pointer	nil

Initialized declaration

As hinted earlier, Go also supports the combination of both variable declaration and initialization as one expression using the following format:

var <identifier list> <type> = <value list or initializer expressions>

This declaration format has the following properties:

- An identifier list provided on the left-hand side of the equal sign (followed by a type)
- A matching comma-separated value list on the right-hand side
- Assignment occurs in the respective order of identifiers and values
- Initializer expressions must yield a matching list of values

The following abbreviated example shows the declaration and initialization combination at work:

```
var name, desc string = "Earth", "Planet"
var radius int32 = 6378
var mass float64 = 5.972E+24
var active bool = true
var satellites = []string{
  "Moon",
}
```

golang.fyi/ch02/vardec2.go

Omitting variable types

So far, we have discussed what is called the long form of Go's variable declaration and initialization. To make the language feel closer to its dynamically-typed cousins, the type specification can be omitted, as shown in the following declaration format:

var <identifier list> = <value list or initializer expressions>

During compilation, the compiler infers the type of the variable based on the assigned value or the initializer expression on the right-hand side of the equal sign, as shown in the following example.

```
var name, desc = "Mars", "Planet"
var radius = 6755
var mass = 641693000000000.0
var active = true
var satellites = []string{
  "Phobos",
  "Deimos",
}
```

golang.fyi/ch02/vardec3.go

As stated earlier, when a variable is assigned a value, it must receive a type along with that value. When the type of the variable is omitted, the type information is deduced from the assigned value or the returned value of an expression. The following table shows the type that is inferred given a literal value:

Literal value	Inferred type

Double- or single-quoted (raw) text:
`"Planet Mars"`
`"All planets revolve around the Sun."`
	`string`

Integers:
`-76`
`0`
`1244`
`1840`
	`int`

Decimals:
`-0.25`
`4.0`
`3.1e4`
`7e-12`
	`float64`

Complex numbers:
`-5.0i`
`3i`
`(0+4i)`
	`complex128`

Booleans:
`true`
`false`
	`bool`

Array values: `[2]int{-76, 8080}`	The `array` type defined in the literal value. In this case it is: `[2]int`

Map values:
`map[string]int{`
`    "Sun": 685800,`
`    "Earth": 6378,`
`    "Mars": 3396,`
`}`
	The map type defined in the literal value. In this case it is: `map[string]int`

Slice values: `[]int{-76, 0, 1244, 1840}`	The `slice` type defined in the literal value: `[]int`

Struct values:
``
struct{
   name string
   diameter int}
{
   "Mars", 3396,
}
``
	A `struct` type as defined in the literal value. In this case the type is:
	``
	struct{name string; diameter int}
	``

Function values:
``
var sqr = func (v int)   int {
   return v * v
}
``
	The function type defined in the function definition literal. In this `case`, variable `sqr` will have type:
	``
	func (v int) int
	``

Short variable declaration

Go can further reduce the variable declaration syntax using the *short variable declaration* format. In this format, the declaration loses the var keyword and the type specification, and uses an assignment operator := (colon-equal), as shown:

<identifier list> := <value list or initializer expressions>

This is a simple and uncluttered idiom that is commonly used when declaring variables in Go. The following code sample shows usage of the short variable declarations:

```
func main() {
    name := "Neptune"
    desc := "Planet"
    radius := 24764
    mass := 1.024e26
    active := true
    satellites := []string{
        "Naiad", "Thalassa", "Despina", "Galatea", "Larissa",
     "S/2004 N 1", "Proteus", "Triton", "Nereid", "Halimede",
        "Sao", "Laomedeia", "Neso", "Psamathe",
    }
...
}
```

golang.fyi/ch02/vardec4.go

Notice the keyword `var` and variable types have been omitted in the declaration. Short variable declaration uses the same mechanism to infer the type of the variable discussed earlier.

Restrictions for short variable declaration

For convenience, the short form of the variable declaration does come with several restrictions that you should be aware of to avoid confusion:

- Firstly, it can only be used within a function block
- The assignment operator `:=`, declares variable and assign values
- `:=` cannot be used to update a previously declared variable
- Updates to variables must be done with an equal sign

While these restrictions may have their justifications rooted in the simplicity of Go's grammar, they are generally viewed as a source of confusion for newcomers to the language. For instance, the colon-equal operator cannot be used with package-level variables assignments. Developers learning Go may find it compelling to use the assignment operator as a way to update a variable, but that would cause a compilation error.

Variable scope and visibility

Go uses lexical scoping based on code blocks to determine the visibility of variables within a package. Depending on the location where a variable is declared, within the source text, will determine its scope. As a general rule, a variable is only accessible from within the block where it is declared and visible to all nested sub-blocks.

The following screenshot illustrates the scope of several variables declared within a source text. Each variable declaration is marked with its scope (`package`, `function`, `for` loop, and `if...else` block):

```go
import (
    "bytes"
    ...
    "strconv"
)

var mapFile string = "./nummap.txt"
var numbersFile = "./nums.txt"
var fileMode = 4000
var nums bytes.Buffer

func loadNumberMap() error {
    data, err := ioutil.ReadFile(mapFile)
    if err != nil {
        return err
    }
    for i, b := range data {
        if rune(b) == '1' {
            nums.WriteString(strconv.Itoa(i))
            nums.WriteRune('\n')
        }
    }
    fmt.Println("Loaded all mapped values.")
    return nil
}
```

Package

Function Block

For-Loop Block

As explained earlier, variable visibility works top-down. Variables with package scope, such as `mapFile` and `numbersFile`, are globally visible to all other elements in the package. Moving down the scope ladder, function-block variables such as `data` and `err` are visible to all elements in the function and including sub-blocks. Variables `i` and `b` in the inner `for` loop block are only visible within that block. Once the loop is done, `i` and `b` would go out of scope.

One source of confusion to newcomers to Go is the visibility of package-scoped variables. When a variable is declared at package level (outside of a function or method block), it is globally visible to the entire package, not just to the source file where the variable is declared. This means a package-scoped variable identifier can only be declared once in a group of files that make up a package, a fact that may not be obvious to developers starting out with Go. Refer to `Chapter 6`, *Go Packages and Programs*, for details on package organization.

Variable declaration block

Go's syntax allows the declaration of top-level variables to be grouped together into blocks for greater readability and code organization. The following example shows a rewrite of one of the previous examples using the variable declaration block:

```go
var (
  name string = "Earth"
  desc string = "Planet"
  radius int32 = 6378
  mass float64 = 5.972E+24
  active bool = true
  satellites []string
)
```

golang.fyi/ch02/vardec5.go

Go constants

In Go, a constant is a value with a literal representation such as a string of text, Boolean, or numbers. The value for a constant is static and cannot be changed after initial assignment. While the concept they represent is simple, constants, however, have some interesting properties that make them useful, especially when working with numeric values.

Constant literals

Constants are values that can be represented by a text literal in the language. One of the most interesting properties of constants is that their literal representations can either be treated as typed or untyped values. Unlike variables, which are intrinsically bound to a type, constants can be stored as untyped values in memory space. Without that type constraint, numeric constant values, for instance, can be stored with great precision.

The followings are examples of valid constant literal values that can be expressed in Go:

```go
"Mastering Go"
'G'
false
111009
2.71828
943144834575133743475585575724555574926671352 1e+500
5.0i
```

Typed constants

Go constant values can be bound to named identifiers using a constant declaration. Similar to a variable declaration, Go uses the `const` keyword to indicate the declaration of a constant. Unlike variables, however, the declaration must include the literal value to be bound to the identifier, as shown in the following format:

const <identifier list> type = <value list or initializer expressions>

Constants cannot have any dependency that requires runtime resolution. The compiler must be able to resolve the value of a constant at compile time. This means all constants must be declared and initialized with a value literal (or an expression that results to a constant value).

The following snippet shows some typed constants being declared:

```
const a1, a2 string = "Mastering", "Go"
const b rune = 'G'
const c bool = false
const d int32 = 111009
const e float32 = 2.71828
const f float64 = math.Pi * 2.0e+3
const g complex64 = 5.0i
const h time.Duration = 4 * time.Second
```

golang.fyi/ch02/const.go

Notice in the previous source snippet that each declared constant identifier is explicitly given a type. As you would expect, this implies that the constant identifier can only be used in contexts that are compatible with its types. However, the next section explains how this works differently when the type is omitted in the constant declaration.

Untyped constants

Constants are even more interesting when they are untyped. An untyped constant is declared as follows:

const <identifier list> = <value list or initializer expression>

As before, the keyword `const` is used to declare a list of identifiers as constants along with their respective bounded values. However, in this format, the type specification is omitted in the declaration. As an untyped entity, a constant is merely a blob of bytes in memory without any type precision restrictions imposed. The following shows some sample declarations of untyped constants:

```
const i = "G is" + " for Go "
const j = 'V'
const k1, k2 = true, !k1
const l = 111*100000 + 9
const m1 = math.Pi / 3.141592
const m2 = 1.4142135623730950488016887242096980785696719875376...
const m3 = m2 * m2
const m4 = m3 * 1.0e+400
const n = -5.0i * 3
const o = time.Millisecond * 5
```

golang.fyi/ch02/const.go

From the previous code snippet, the untyped constant `m2` is assigned a long decimal value (truncated to fit on the printed page as it goes another 17 digits). Constant `m4` is assigned a much larger number of `m3` x `1.0e+400`. The entire value of the resulting constant is stored in memory without any loss in precision. This can be an extremely useful tool for developers interested in computations where a high level of precision is important.

Assigning untyped constants

Untyped constant values are of limited use until they are assigned to variables, used as function parameters, or are part of an expression assigned to a variable. In a strongly-typed language like Go, this means there is a potential for some type adjustment to ensure that the value stored in the constant can be properly assigned to the target variable. One advantage of using untyped constants is that the type system relaxes the strict application of type checking. An untyped constant can be assigned to different, though compatible, types of different precision without any complaint from the compiler, as shown in the following example:

```
const m2 = 1.4142135623730950488016887242096980785696719875376...
var u1 float32 = m2
var u2 float64 = m2
u3 := m2
```

The previous snippet shows the untyped constant m2 being assigned to two variables of different floating-point precisions, u1 and u2, and to an untyped variable, u3. This is possible because constant m2 is stored as a raw untyped value and can therefore be assigned to any variable compatible with its representation (a floating point).

While the type system will accommodate the assignment of m2 to variables of different precision, the resulting assignment is adjusted to fit the variable type, as noted in the following:

```
u1 = 1.4142135        //float32
u2 = 1.4142135623730951    //float64
```

What about variable u3, which is itself an untyped variable? Since u3 does not have a specified type, it will rely on type inference from the constant value to receive a type assignment. Recall from the discussion in the section *Omitting Variable Types* earlier, that constant literals are mapped to basic Go types based on their textual representations. Since constant m2 represents a decimal value, the compiler will infer its default to be a float64, which will be automatically assigned to variable u3, as shown:

```
U3 = 1.4142135623730951   //float64
```

As you can see, Go's treatment of untyped raw constant literals increases the language's usability by automatically applying some simple, but effective, type inference rules without sacrificing type-safety. Unlike other languages, developers do not have to explicitly specify the type in the value literal or perform some sort of typecast to make this work.

Constant declaration block

As you may have guessed, constant declarations, can be organized as code blocks to increase readability. The previous example can be rewritten as follows:

```
const (
    a1, a2 string        = "Mastering", "Go"
    b      rune          = 'G'
    c      bool          = false
    d      int32         = 111009
    e      float32       = 2.71828
    f      float64       = math.Pi * 2.0e+3
    g      complex64     = 5.0i
    h      time.Duration = 4 * time.Second
    ...
)
```

golang.fyi/ch02/const2.go

Constant enumeration

One interesting usage of constants is to create enumerated values. Using the declaration block format (shown in the preceding section), you can easily create numerically increasing enumerated integer values. Simply assign the pre-declared constant value `iota` to a constant identifier in the declaration block, as shown in the following code sample:

```
const (
    StarHyperGiant = iota
    StarSuperGiant
    StarBrightGiant
    StarGiant
    StarSubGiant
    StarDwarf
    StarSubDwarf
    StarWhiteDwarf
    StarRedDwarf
    StarBrownDwarf
)
```

golang.fyi/ch02/enum0.go

The compiler will then automatically do the following:

- Declare each member in the block as an untyped integer constant value
- Initialize `iota` with a value of zero
- Assign `iota`, or zero, to the first constant member (`StarHyperGiant`)
- Each subsequent constant is assigned an `int` value increased by one

So the previous list of constants would be assigned a sequence of values going from zero to nine. Whenever `const` appears as a declaration block, it resets the counter to zero. In the following snippet, each set of constants is enumerated from zero to four separately:

```
const (
    StarHyperGiant = iota
    StarSuperGiant
    StarBrightGiant
    StarGiant
    StarSubGiant
)
const (
    StarDwarf = iota
    StarSubDwarf
    StarWhiteDwarf
    StarRedDwarf
```

```
    StarBrownDwarf
)
```

golang.fyi/ch02/enum1.go

Overriding the default enumeration type

By default, an enumerated constant is declared as an untyped integer value. However, you can override the default type of the enumerated values by providing an explicit numeric type for your enumerated constants, as shown in the following code sample:

```
const (
    StarDwarf byte = iota
    StarSubDwarf
    StarWhiteDwarf
    StarRedDwarf
    StarBrownDwarf
)
```

You can specify any numeric type that can represent integers or floating point values. For instance, in the preceding code sample, each constant will be declared as type `byte`.

Using iota in expressions

When `iota` appears in an expression, the same mechanism works as expected. The compiler will apply the expression for each successive increasing value of `iota`. The following example assigns even numbers to the enumerated members of the constant declaration block:

```
const (
    StarHyperGiant = 2.0*iota
    StarSuperGiant
    StarBrightGiant
    StarGiant
    StarSubGiant
)
```

golang.fyi/ch02/enum2.go

As you may expect, the previous example assigns an even value to each enumerated constants, starting with 0, as shown in the following output:

```
StarHyperGiant = 0      [float64]
```

```
StarSuperGiant = 2      [float64]
StarBrightGiant = 4     [float64]
StarGiant = 6           [float64]
StarSubGiant = 8        [float64]
```

Skipping enumerated values

When working with enumerated constants, you may want to throw away certain values that should not be part of the enumeration. This can be accomplished by assigning iota to the blank identifier at the desired position in the enumeration. For instance, the following skips the values 0 and 64:

```
_                   = iota      // value 0
StarHyperGiant = 1 << iota
StarSuperGiant
StarBrightGiant
StarGiant
StarSubGiant
_               // value 64
StarDwarf
StarSubDwarf
StarWhiteDwarf
StarRedDwarf
StarBrownDwarf
```

golang.fyi/ch02/enum3.go

Since we skip iota position 0, the first assigned constant value is at position 1. This results in expression 1 << iota resolving to 1 << 1 = 2. The same is done at the sixth position, where expression 1 << iota returns 64. That value will be skipped and not assigned to any constant, as shown in the following output:

```
StarHyperGiant = 2
StarSuperGiant = 4
StarBrightGiant = 8
StarGiant = 16
StarSubGiant = 32
StarDwarf = 128
StarSubDwarf = 256
StarWhiteDwarf = 512
StarRedDwarf = 1024
StarBrownDwarf = 2048
```

Go operators

Staying true to its simplistic nature, operators in Go do exactly what you would expect, mainly, they allow operands to be combined into expressions. There are no hidden surprise behaviors with Go operators as there is no support for operator-overloading as found in C++ or Scala. This was a deliberate decision from the designers to keep the semantics of the language simple and predictable.

This section explores the most common operators that you will encounter as you start with Go. Other operators are covered throughout other chapters of the book.

Arithmetic operators

The following table summarizes the arithmetic operators supported in Go.

Operator	Operation	Compatible types
*, /, –	Multiplication, division, and subtraction	Integers, floating points, and complex numbers
%	Remainder	Integers
+	Addition	Integers, floating points, complex numbers, and strings (concatenation)

Note that the addition operator, +, can be applied to strings such as in the expression `var i = "G is" + " for Go"`. The two string operands are concatenated to create a new string that is assigned to variable `i`.

The increment and decrement operators

As with other C-like languages, Go supports the ++ (increment) and the –– (decrement) operators. When applied, these operators increase, or decrease, the operand's value by one, respectively. The following shows a function that uses the decrement operator to traverse the letters in string s in the reverse order:

```
func reverse(s string) {
  for i := len(s) - 1; i >= 0; {
    fmt.Print(string(s[i]))
    i--
  }
}
```

It is important to note that the increment and decrement operators are statements, not expressions, as shown in the following snippets:

```
nextChar := i++        // syntax error
fmt.Println("Current char", i--)    // syntax error
nextChar++        // OK
```

In the preceding examples, it is worth noting that the increment and decrement statements only support the postfix notation. The following snippet would not compile because of statement −i:

```
for i := len(s) - 1; i >= 0; {
    fmt.Print(string(s[i]))
    --i    //syntax error
}
```

Go assignment operators

Operator	Description
=	The simple assignment works as expected. It updates the left operand with the value of the right.
:=	The colon-equal operator declares a new variable, the left-side operator, and assigns it the value (and type) of the operand on the right.
+= , −= , *= , /= , %=	Apply the indicated operation using the left and the right operator and store the result in the left operator. For instance, a *= 8 implies a = a * 8.

Bitwise operators

Go includes full support for manipulating values at their most elemental forms. The following summarizes bitwise operators supported by Go:

Operator	Description
&	Bitwise AND
|	Bitwise OR
a ^ b	Bitwise XOR

&^	Bitwise AND NOT
^a	Unary bitwise complement
<<	Left-shift
>>	Right-shift

The right operand, in a shift operation, must be an unsigned integer or be able to be converted to an unsigned value. When the left operand is an untyped constant value, the compiler must be able to derive a signed integer type from its value or it will fail compilation.

The shift operators in Go also support both arithmetic and logical shifts. If the left operand is unsigned, Go automatically applies logical shift, whereas if it is signed, Go will apply an arithmetic shift.

Logical Operators

The following is a list of Go logical operations on Boolean values:

Operator	Operation
&&	Logical AND
||	Logical OR
!	Logical NOT

Comparison operators

All Go types can be tested for equality, including basic and composite types. However, only string, integer, and floating-point values can be compared using ordering operators, as is summarized in the following table:

Operator	Operation	Supported type
==	Equal	String, numeric, Boolean, interface, pointer, and struct types
!=	Not Equal	String, numeric, Boolean, interface, pointer, and struct types

< , <= , > , >=	Ordering operators	String, integers, and floating points

Operator precedence

Since Go has fewer operators than are found in its counterparts such as C or Java, its operator precedence rules are far simpler. The following table lists Go's operator precedence echelon, starting with the highest:

Operation	Precedence
Multiplicative	*, /, %, <<, >>, &, &^
Additive	+, -, |, ^
Comparative	==, !=, <, <=, >, >=
Logical AND	&&
Logical OR	||

Summary

This chapter covered a lot of ground around the basic constructs of the Go language. It started with the structure of Go's source code text file and progressed to cover variable identifiers, declarations, and initializations. The chapter also provided extensive coverage of Go constants, constant declaration, and operators.

At this point, you may feel a bit overwhelmed by so much pedestrian information about the language and its syntax. The good news is that you don't have to know all of these details to be productive with the language. In the following chapters, we will continue to explore some of the more interesting bits about Go, including data types, functions, and packages.

3
Go Control Flow

Go borrows several of its control flow syntax from the C-family of languages. It supports all of the expected control structures, including `if...else`, `switch`, `for` loop, and even `goto`. Conspicuously absent, though, are `while` or `do...while` statements. The following topics in this chapter examine Go's control flow elements, some of which you may already be familiar with, and others that bring a new set of functionalities not found in other languages:

- The `if` statement
- The `switch` statement
- The type `Switch`
- The `for` statement

The if statement

The `if` statement, in Go, borrows its basic structural form from other C-like languages. The statement conditionally executes a code block when the Boolean expression that follows the `if` keyword evaluates to `true`, as illustrated in the following abbreviated program, which displays information about world currencies:

```
import "fmt"

type Currency struct {
  Name    string
  Country string
  Number  int
}

var CAD = Currency{
```

```
        Name: "Canadian Dollar",
        Country: "Canada",
        Number: 124}

    var FJD = Currency{
        Name: "Fiji Dollar",
        Country: "Fiji",
        Number: 242}

    var JMD = Currency{
        Name: "Jamaican Dollar",
        Country: "Jamaica",
        Number: 388}

    var USD = Currency{
        Name: "US Dollar",
        Country: "USA",
        Number: 840}

    func main() {
      num0 := 242
      if num0 > 100 || num0 < 900 {
        fmt.Println("Currency: ", num0)
        printCurr(num0)
      } else {
        fmt.Println("Currency unknown")
      }

      if num1 := 388; num1 > 100 || num1 < 900 {
        fmt.Println("Currency:", num1)
        printCurr(num1)
      }
    }

    func printCurr(number int) {
      if CAD.Number == number {
        fmt.Printf("Found: %+v\n", CAD)
      } else if FJD.Number == number {
        fmt.Printf("Found: %+v\n", FJD)
      } else if JMD.Number == number {
        fmt.Printf("Found: %+v\n", JMD)
      } else if USD.Number == number {
        fmt.Printf("Found: %+v\n", USD)
      } else {
        fmt.Println("No currency found with number", number)
      }
    }
```

The `if` statement in Go looks similar to other languages. However, it sheds a few syntactic rules, while enforcing new ones:

- The parentheses around the test expression are not necessary. While the following `if` statement will compile, it is not idiomatic:

```
if (num0 > 100 || num0 < 900) {
    fmt.Println("Currency: ", num0)
    printCurr(num0)
}
```

- Use the following instead:

```
if num0 > 100 || num0 < 900 {
    fmt.Println("Currency: ", num0)
    printCurr(num0)
}
```

- The curly braces for the code block are always required. The following snippet will not compile:

```
if num0 > 100 || num0 < 900 printCurr(num0)
```

- However, this will compile:

```
if num0 > 100 || num0 < 900 {printCurr(num0)}
```

- It is idiomatic, however, to write the `if` statement on multiple lines (no matter how simple the statement block may be). This encourages good style and clarity. The following snippet will compile with no issues:

```
if num0 > 100 || num0 < 900 {printCurr(num0)}
```

- However, the preferred idiomatic layout for the statement is to use multiple lines, as follows:

```
if num0 > 100 || num0 < 900 {
    printCurr(num0)
}
```

- The `if` statement may include an optional `else` block, which is executed when the expression in the `if` block evaluates to `false`. The code in the `else` block must be wrapped in curly braces using multiple lines, as shown in the following snippet:

```
if num0 > 100 || num0 < 900 {
    fmt.Println("Currency: ", num0)
    printCurr(num0)
} else {
    fmt.Println("Currency unknown")
}
```

- The `else` keyword may be immediately followed by another `if` statement forming an `if...else...if` chain, as used in the function `printCurr()` from the source code listed earlier:

```
if CAD.Number == number {
    fmt.Printf("Found: %+v\n", CAD)
} else if FJD.Number == number {
    fmt.Printf("Found: %+v\n", FJD)
}
```

The `if...else...if` statement chain can grow as long as needed and may be terminated by an optional `else` statement to express all other untested conditions. Again, this is done in the `printCurr()` function, which tests four conditions using the `if...else...if` blocks. Lastly, it includes an `else` statement block to catch any other untested conditions:

```
func printCurr(number int) {
    if CAD.Number == number {
        fmt.Printf("Found: %+v\n", CAD)
    } else if FJD.Number == number {
        fmt.Printf("Found: %+v\n", FJD)
    } else if JMD.Number == number {
        fmt.Printf("Found: %+v\n", JMD)
    } else if USD.Number == number {
        fmt.Printf("Found: %+v\n", USD)
    } else {
        fmt.Println("No currency found with number", number)
    }
}
```

In Go, however, the idiomatic, and cleaner, way to write such a deep `if...else...if` code block is to use an expressionless `switch` statement. This is covered later, in the *Switch statement* section.

The if statement initialization

The `if` statement supports a composite syntax where the tested expression is preceded by an initialization statement. At runtime, the initialization is executed before the test expression is evaluated, as illustrated in this code snippet (from the program listed earlier):

```
if num1 := 388; num1 > 100 || num1 < 900 {
    fmt.Println("Currency:", num1)
    printCurr(num1)
}
```

The initialization statement follows normal variable declaration and initialization rules. The scope of the initialized variables is bound to the `if` statement block, beyond which they become unreachable. This is a commonly used idiom in Go and is supported in other flow control constructs covered in this chapter.

Switch statements

Go also supports a `switch` statement similar to that found in other languages such as, C or Java. The `switch` statement in Go achieves multi-way branching by evaluating values or expressions from `case` clauses, as shown in the following, abbreviated, source code:

```
import "fmt"

type Curr struct {
    Currency string
    Name     string
    Country  string
    Number   int
}

var currencies = []Curr{
    Curr{"DZD", "Algerian Dinar", "Algeria", 12},
    Curr{"AUD", "Australian Dollar", "Australia", 36},
    Curr{"EUR", "Euro", "Belgium", 978},
    Curr{"CLP", "Chilean Peso", "Chile", 152},
    Curr{"EUR", "Euro", "Greece", 978},
    Curr{"HTG", "Gourde", "Haiti", 332},
    ...
}

func isDollar(curr Curr) bool {
    var bool result
    switch curr {
```

```
    default:
      result = false
    case Curr{"AUD", "Australian Dollar", "Australia", 36}:
      result = true
    case Curr{"HKD", "Hong Kong Dollar", "Hong Koong", 344}:
      result = true
    case Curr{"USD", "US Dollar", "United States", 840}:
      result = true
    }
    return result
}
func isDollar2(curr Curr) bool {
    dollars := []Curr{currencies[2], currencies[6], currencies[9]}
    switch curr {
    default:
      return false
    case dollars[0]:
      fallthrough
    case dollars[1]:
      fallthrough
    case dollars[2]:
      return true
    }
    return false
}

func isEuro(curr Curr) bool {
    switch curr {
    case currencies[2], currencies[4], currencies[10]:
      return true
    default:
      return false
    }
}

func main() {
    curr := Curr{"EUR", "Euro", "Italy", 978}
    if isDollar(curr) {
      fmt.Printf("%+v is Dollar currency\n", curr)
    } else if isEuro(curr) {
      fmt.Printf("%+v is Euro currency\n", curr)
    } else {
      fmt.Println("Currency is not Dollar or Euro")
    }
    dol := Curr{"HKD", "Hong Kong Dollar", "Hong Koong", 344}
    if isDollar2(dol) {
      fmt.Println("Dollar currency found:", dol)
    }
```

```
}
```

golang.fyi/ch03/switchstmt.go

The switch statement in Go has some interesting properties and rules that make it easy to use and reason about:

- Semantically, Go's switch statement can be used in two contexts:
  - An expression switch statement
  - A type switch statement
- The break statement can be used to escape out of a switch code block early.
- The switch statement can include a default case when no other case expressions evaluate to a match. There can only be one default case and it may be placed anywhere within the switch block.

Using expression switches

Expression switches are flexible and can be used in many contexts where control flow of a program needs to follow multiple path. An expression switch supports many attributes, as outlined in the following bullets:

- Expression switches can test values of any types. For instance, the following code snippet (from the previous program listing) tests variable Curr of type struct:

```go
func isDollar(curr Curr) bool {
  var bool result
  switch curr {
    default:
    result = false
    case Curr{"AUD", "Australian Dollar", "Australia", 36}:
    result = true
    case Curr{"HKD", "Hong Kong Dollar", "Hong Koong", 344}:
    result = true
    case Curr{"USD", "US Dollar", "United States", 840}:
    result = true
  }
  return result
}
```

- The expressions in `case` clauses are evaluated from left to right, top to bottom, until a value (or expression) is found that is equal to that of the `switch` expression.
- Upon encountering the first case that matches the `switch` expression, the program will execute the statements for the `case` block and then immediately exit the `switch` block. Unlike other languages, the Go `case` statement does not need to use a break to avoid falling through the next case (see the *Fallthrough cases* section). For instance, calling `isDollar(Curr{"HKD", "Hong Kong Dollar", "Hong Kong", 344})` will match the second `case` statement in the preceding function. The code will set the result to `true` and exit the `switch` code block immediately.
- Case clauses can have multiple values (or expressions) separated by commas with a logical OR operator implied between them. For instance, in the following snippet, the `switch` expression `curr` is tested against values `currencies[2]`, `currencies[4]`, or `currencies[10]`, using one case clause until a match is found:

```
func isEuro(curr Curr) bool {
  switch curr {
    case currencies[2], currencies[4], currencies[10]:
    return true
    default:
    return false
  }
}
```

- The `switch` statement is the cleaner and preferred idiomatic approach to writing complex conditional statements in Go. This is evident when the preceding snippet is compared to the following, which does the same comparison using `if` statements:

```
func isEuro(curr Curr) bool {
  if curr == currencies[2] || curr == currencies[4],
  curr == currencies[10]{
    return true
  }else{
    return false
  }
}
```

The fallthrough cases

There is no automatic *fall through* in Go's `case` clause as there is in the C or Java `switch` statements. Recall that a `switch` block will exit after executing its first matching case. The code must explicitly place the `fallthrough` keyword, as the last statement in a `case` block, to force the execution flow to fall through the successive `case` block. The following code snippet shows a `switch` statement with a `fallthrough` in each case block:

```
func isDollar2(curr Curr) bool {
  switch curr {
  case Curr{"AUD", "Australian Dollar", "Australia", 36}:
    fallthrough
  case Curr{"HKD", "Hong Kong Dollar", "Hong Kong", 344}:
    fallthrough
  case Curr{"USD", "US Dollar", "United States", 840}:
    return true
  default:
    return false
  }
}
```

golang.fyi/ch03/switchstmt.go

When a case is matched, the `fallthrough` statements cascade down to the first statement of the successive `case` block. So, if `curr = Curr{"AUD", "Australian Dollar", "Australia", 36}`, the first case will be matched. Then the flow cascades down to the first statement of the second case block, which is also a `fallthrough` statement. This causes the first statement, to return `true`, of the third case block to execute. This is functionally equivalent to the following snippet:

```
switch curr {
case Curr{"AUD", "Australian Dollar", "Australia", 36},
     Curr{"HKD", "Hong Kong Dollar", "Hong Kong", 344},
     Curr{"USD", "US Dollar", "United States", 840}:
  return true
default:
  return false
}
```

Expressionless switches

Go supports a form of the `switch` statement that does not specify an expression. In this format, each `case` expression must evaluate to a Boolean value `true`. The following abbreviated source code illustrates the uses of an expressionless `switch` statement, as listed in function `find()`. The function loops through the slice of `Curr` values to search for a match based on field values in the `struct` function that's passed in:

```go
import (
  "fmt"
  "strings"
)
type Curr struct {
  Currency string
  Name     string
  Country  string
  Number   int
}

var currencies = []Curr{
  Curr{"DZD", "Algerian Dinar", "Algeria", 12},
  Curr{"AUD", "Australian Dollar", "Australia", 36},
  Curr{"EUR", "Euro", "Belgium", 978},
  Curr{"CLP", "Chilean Peso", "Chile", 152},
  ...
}

func find(name string) {
  for i := 0; i < 10; i++ {
    c := currencies[i]
    switch {
    case strings.Contains(c.Currency, name),
      strings.Contains(c.Name, name),
      strings.Contains(c.Country, name):
      fmt.Println("Found", c)
    }
  }
}
```

golang.fyi/ch03/switchstmt2.go

Notice in the previous example, the `switch` statement in function `find()` does not include an expression. Each `case` expression is separated by a comma and must be evaluated to a Boolean value with an implied OR operator between each. The previous `switch` statement is equivalent to the following use of an `if` statement to achieve the same logic:

```
func find(name string) {
  for I := 0; i < 10; i++ {
    c := currencies[i]
    if strings.Contains(c.Currency, name) ||
      strings.Contains(c.Name, name) ||
      strings.Contains(c.Country, name){
      fmt.Println""Foun"", c)
    }
  }
}
```

Switch initializer

The `switch` keyword may be immediately followed by a simple initialization statement where variables, local to the `switch` code block, may be declared and initialized. This convenient syntax uses a semi-colon between the initializer statement and the `switch` expression to declare variables, which may appear anywhere in the `switch` code block. The following code sample shows how this is done by initializing two variables, `name` and `curr`, as part of the `switch` declaration:

```
func assertEuro(c Curr) bool {
  switch name, curr := "Euro", "EUR"; {
  case c.Name == name:
    return true
  case c.Currency == curr:
    return true
  }
  return false
}
```

golang.fyi/ch03/switchstmt2.go

The previous code snippet uses an expressionless `switch` statement with an initializer. Notice the trailing semi-colon to indicate the separation between the initialization statement and the expression area for the switch. In the example, however, the `switch` expression is empty.

Type switches

Given Go's strong type support, it should be of little surprise that the language supports the ability to query type information. The type `switch` is a statement that uses the Go interface type to compare the underlying type information of values (or expressions). A full discussion on interface types and type assertion is beyond the scope of this section. You can find more details on the subject in `Chapter 8`, *Methods, Interfaces, and Objects*.

Nevertheless, for the sake of completeness, a short discussion on type switches is provided here. For now, all you need to know is that Go offers the type `interface{}`, or empty interface, as a super type that is implemented by all other types in the type system. When a value is assigned type `interface{}`, it can be queried using the type `switch`, as shown in function `findAny()` in the following code snippet, to query information about its underlying type:

```go
func find(name string) {
   for i := 0; i < 10; i++ {
     c := currencies[i]
     switch {
     case strings.Contains(c.Currency, name),
       strings.Contains(c.Name, name),
       strings.Contains(c.Country, name):
       fmt.Println("Found", c)
     }
   }
}

func findNumber(num int) {
   for _, curr := range currencies {
     if curr.Number == num {
       fmt.Println("Found", curr)
     }
   }
}

func findAny(val interface{}) {
   switch i := val.(type) {
   case int:
     findNumber(i)
```

```
    case string:
        find(i)
    default:
        fmt.Printf("Unable to search with type %T\n", val)
    }
}

func main() {
findAny("Peso")
    findAny(404)
    findAny(978)
    findAny(false)
}
```

golang.fyi/ch03/switchstmt2.go

The function `findAny()` takes an `interface{}` as its parameter. The type `switch` is used to determine the underlying type and value of the variable `val` using the type assertion expression:

```
switch i := val.(type)
```

Notice the use of the keyword `type` in the preceding type assertion expression. Each case clause will be tested against the type information queried from `val.(type)`. Variable `i` will be assigned the actual value of the underlying type and is used to invoke a function with the respective value. The default block is invoked to guard against any unexpected type assigned to the parameter `val` parameter. Function `findAny` may then be invoked with values of diverse types, as shown in the following code snippet:

```
findAny("Peso")
findAny(404)
findAny(978)
findAny(false)
```

The for statements

As a language related to the C-family, Go also supports `for` loop style control structures. However, as you may have come to expect by now, Go's `for` statements work interestingly differently and simply. The `for` statement in Go supports four distinct idioms, as summarized in the following table:

For Statement	Usage
For condition	Used to semantically replace `while` and `do...while` loops: ```for x < 10 { ... }```
Infinite loop	The conditional expression may be omitted to create an infinite loop: ```for { ... }```
Traditional	This is the traditional form of the C-family `for` loop with the initializer, test, and update clauses: ```for x:=0; x < 10; x++ { ... }```
For range	Used to iterate over an expression representing a collection of items stored in an array, string (array of rune), slice, map, and channel: ```for i, val := range values { ... }```

Notice, as with all other control statements in Go, the `for` statements do not use parentheses around their expressions. All statements for the loop code block must be enclosed within curly brackets or the compiler will produce an error.

For condition

The `for` condition uses a construct that is semantically equivalent to the `while` loop found in other languages. It uses the keyword `for`, followed by a Boolean expression that allows the loop to proceed as long as it is evaluated to true. The following abbreviated source listing shows an example of this form of the `for` loop:

```
type Curr struct {
  Currency string
```

```
     Name       string
     Country    string
     Number     int
 }
 var currencies = []Curr{
     Curr{"KES", "Kenyan Shilling", "Kenya", 404},
     Curr{"AUD", "Australian Dollar", "Australia", 36},
     ...
 }

 func listCurrs(howlong int) {
     i := 0
     for i < len(currencies) {
         fmt.Println(currencies[i])
         i++
     }
 }
```

golang.fyi/ch03/forstmt.go

The `for` statement, in function `listCurrs()`, iterates as long as the conditional expression `i < len(currencies)` returns `true`. Care must be taken to ensure the value of `i` is updated with each iteration to avoid creating an accidental infinite loop.

Infinite loop

When the Boolean expression is omitted in the `for` statement, the loop runs indefinitely, as shown the following example:

```
for {
    // statements here
}
```

This is equivalent to the `for(;;)` or the `while (true)` found in other languages, such as C or Java.

The traditional for statement

Go also supports the traditional form of the `for` statement, which includes an initialization statement, a conditional expression, and an update statement, all separated by a semi-colon. This is the form of the statement that is traditionally found in other C-like languages. The following source snippet illustrates the use of a traditional for statement in the function `sortByNumber`:

```go
type Curr struct {
   Currency string
   Name     string
   Country  string
   Number   int
}

var currencies = []Curr{
   Curr{"KES", "Kenyan Shilling", "Kenya", 404},
   Curr{"AUD", "Australian Dollar", "Australia", 36},
   ...
}

func sortByNumber() {
  N := len(currencies)
  for i := 0; i < N-1; i++ {
     currMin := i
     for k := i + 1; k < N; k++ {
     if currencies[k].Number < currencies[currMin].Number {
        currMin = k
     }
      }
     // swap
     if currMin != i {
        temp := currencies[i]
     currencies[i] = currencies[currMin]
     currencies[currMin] = temp
      }
   }
  }
```

golang.fyi/ch03/forstmt.go

The previous example implements a selection sort that sorts the `slice` currencies by comparing the `Number` field of each `struct` value. The different sections of the `for` statement are highlighted using the following snippet of code (from the preceding function):

```
for k := i + 1; k < N; k++ {
    if currencies[k].Number < currencies[currMin].Number {
        currMin = k
    }
}
```

It turns out that the traditional `for` statement is a superset of the other forms of the loop discussed so far, as summarized in the following table:

For statement	Description

`k:=initialize()`
`for ; k < 10;`
`++{`
`...`
`}`
	The initialization statement is omitted. Variable k is initialized outside of the `for` statement. The idiomatic way, however, is to initialize your variables with the `for` statement.

`for k:=0; k < 10;{`
`...`
`}`
	The `update` statement (after the last semi-colon) is omitted here. The developer must provide update logic elsewhere or you risk creating an infinite loop.

`for ; k < 10;{`
`...`
`}`
	This is equivalent to the `for` condition form (discussed earlier) `for k < 10 { ... }`. Again, the variable k is expected to be declared prior to the loop. Care must be taken to update k or you risk creating an infinite loop.

`for k:=0; ;k++{`
`...`
`}`
	Here, the conditional expression is omitted. As before, this evaluates the conditional to `true`, which will produce an infinite loop if proper termination logic is not introduced in the loop.

`for ; ;{ ... }`	This is equivalent to the form `for{ ... }` and produces an infinite loop.

The initialization and the `update` statements, in the `for` loop, are regular Go statements. As such, they can be used to initialize and update multiple variables, as is supported by Go. To illustrate this point, the next example initializes and updates two variables, `w1` and `w2`, at the same time in the statement clauses:

```
import (
    "fmt"
    "math/rand"
)

var list1 = []string{
```

```
    "break", "lake", "go",
    "right", "strong",
    "kite", "hello"}

var list2 = []string{
    "fix", "river", "stop",
    "left", "weak", "flight",
    "bye"}

func main() {
    rand.Seed(31)
    for w1, w2:= nextPair();
    w1 != "go" && w2 != "stop";
    w1, w2 = nextPair() {

        fmt.Printf("Word Pair -> [%s, %s]\n", w1, w2)
    }
}

func nextPair() (w1, w2 string) {
    pos := rand.Intn(len(list1))
    return list1[pos], list2[pos]
}
```

golang.fyi/ch03/forstmt2.go

The initialization statements initialize variables w1 and w2 by calling the function
nextPair(). The condition uses a compound logical expression that will keep the loop
running as long as it is evaluated to true. Lastly, variables w1 and w2 are both updated with
each iteration of the loop by calling nextPair().

The for range

Lastly, the for statement supports one additional form that uses the keyword range to
iterate over an expression that evaluates to an array, slice, map, string, or channel. The for-
range loop has this generic form:

for [<identifier-list> :=] range <expression> { ... }

Depending on the type produced by the `range` expression, there can be up to two variables emitted by each iteration, as summarized in the following table:

Range Expression	Range Variables

Loop over array or slice:
`for i, v := range`
`[]V{1,2,3} {`
`...`
`}`
	The range produces two values, where `i` is the loop index and `v` is the value `v[i]` from the collection. Further discussions on array and slice are covered in Chapter 7, *Composite Types*.

Loop over string value:
`for i, v := range`
`"Hello" {`
`...`
`}`
	The range produces two values, where `i` is the index of byte in the string and `v` is the value of the UTF-8 encoded byte at `v[i]` returned as a rune. Further discussion on the string type is covered in in Chapter 4, *Data Types*.

Loop over map:
`for k, v := range`
`map[K]V {`
`...`
`}`
	The `range` produces two values, where `k` is assigned the value of the map key of type K and `v` gets stored at `map[k]` of type V. Further discussion on map is covered in Chapter 7, *Composite Types*.

Loop on channel values:
`var ch chan T`
`for c := range ch`
`{`
`...`
`}`
	An adequate discussion of channels is covered in Chapter 9, *Concurrency*. A channel is a two-way conduit able to receive and emit values. The `for...range` statement assigns each value received from the channel to variable `c` with each iteration.

You should be aware that the value emitted with each iteration is a copy of the original item stored in the source. For instance, in the following program, the values in the slice do not get updated after the loop completes:

```
import "fmt"

func main() {
  vals := []int{4, 2, 6}
  for _, v := range vals {
    v--
  }
  fmt.Println(vals)
}
```

To update the original value using the `for...range` loop, use the index expression to access the original value, as illustrated in the following.

```go
func main() {
  vals := []int{4, 2, 6}
  for i, v := range vals {
    vals[i] = v - 1
  }
  fmt.Println(vals)
}
```

In the previous example, value `i` is used in a slice index expression `vals[i]` to update the original value stored in the slice. It is possible to omit the iteration value (the second variable in the assignment) if you only need access to the index value of an array, slice, or string (or key for a map). For instance, in the following example, the `for...range` statement only emits the current index value with each iteration:

```go
func printCurrencies() {
  for i := range currencies {
    fmt.Printf("%d: %v\n", i, currencies[i])
  }
}
```

golang.fyi/ch03/for-range-stmt.go

Finally, there are some situations where you may not be interested in any of the values generated by the iteration, but rather the iteration mechanic itself. The next form of the for statement was introduced (as of Version 1.4 of Go) to express a for range without any variable declaration as shown in the following code snippet:

```go
func main() {
  for range []int{1,1,1,1} {
    fmt.Println("Looping")
  }
}
```

The previous code will print `"Looping"` four times on the standard output. This form of the `for...range` loop is used sometimes when the range expression is over a channel. It is used to simply notify of the presence of a value in the channel.

The break, continue, and goto statements

Go supports a group of statements designed specifically to exit abruptly out of a running code block, such as switch and for statement, and transfer control to a different section of the code. All three statements can accept a label identifier that specifies a targeted location in the code where control is to be transferred.

The label identifier

Before diving into the core of this section, it is worthwhile to look at the label used by these statements. Declaring a label in Go requires an identifier followed by a colon, as shown in the following snippet:

```
DoSearch:
```

Naming your label is a matter of style. However, one should follow the identifier naming guidelines covered in the previous chapter. A label must be enclosed within a function. The Go compiler will not allow unused labels to dangle in the code. Similar to variables, if a label is declared, it must be referenced in the code.

The break statement

As in other C-like languages, the Go `break` statement terminates and exits the innermost enclosing `switch` or `for` statement code block and transfers control to another part of the running program. The `break` statement can accept an optional label identifier specifying a labeled location, in the enclosing function, where the flow of the program will resume. Here are some attributes of the label for the `break` statement to remember:

- The label must be declared within the same running function where the `break` statement is located
- A declared label must be followed immediately by the enclosing control statement (a `for` loop or `switch` statement) where the break is nested

If a `break` statement is followed by a label, control is transferred, not to the location where the label is, but rather to the statement immediately following the labeled block. If a label is not provided, the `break` statement abruptly exits and transfers control to the next statement following its enclosing `for` statement (or `switch` statement) block.

The following code is an overly exaggerated linear search that illustrates the working of the break statement. It does a word search and exits once the first instance of the word is found in the slice:

```
import (
  "fmt"
)

var words = [][]string{
  {"break", "lake", "go", "right", "strong", "kite", "hello"},
  {"fix", "river", "stop", "left", "weak", "flight", "bye"},
  {"fix", "lake", "slow", "middle", "sturdy", "high", "hello"},
}

func search(w string) {
DoSearch:
  for i := 0; i < len(words); i++ {
    for k := 0; k < len(words[i]); k++ {
      if words[i][k] == w {
        fmt.Println("Found", w)
        break DoSearch
      }
    }
  }
}
```

golang.fyi/ch03/breakstmt.go

In the previous code snippet, the break DoSearch statement will essentially exit out of the innermost for loop and cause the execution flow to continue after the outermost labeled for statement, which in this example, will simply end the program.

The continue statement

The continue statement causes the control flow to immediately terminate the current iteration of the enclosing for loop and jump to the next iteration. The continue statement can take an optional label as well. The label has similar properties to that of the break statement:

- The label must be declared within the same running function where the continue statement is located
- The declared label must be followed immediately by an enclosing for loop statement where the continue statement is nested

When present, the `continue` statement is reached within a `for` statement block, the `for` loop will be abruptly terminated and control will be transferred to the outermost labeled `for` loop block for continuation. If a label is not specified, the `continue` statement will simply transfer control to the start of its enclosing `for` loop block for continuation of the next iteration.

To illustrate, let us revisit the previous example of word search. This version uses a `continue` statement, which causes the search to find multiple occurrences of the searched word in the slice:

```
func search(w string) {
DoSearch:
  for i := 0; i < len(words); i++ {
    for k := 0; k < len(words[i]); k++ {
      if words[i][k] == w {
        fmt.Println("Found", w)
        continue DoSearch
      }
    }
  }
}
```

golang.fyi/ch03/breakstmt2.go

The `continue DoSearch` statement causes the current iteration of the innermost loop to stop and transfer control to the labeled outer loop, causing it to continue with the next iteration.

The goto statement

The `goto` statement is more flexible, in that it allows flow control to be transferred to an arbitrary location, inside a function, where a target label is defined. The `goto` statement causes an abrupt transfer of control to the label referenced by the `goto` statement. The following shows Go's `goto` statement in action in a simple, but functional example:

```
import "fmt"

func main() {
  var a string
Start:
  for {
    switch {
    case a < "aaa":
      goto A
```

```
        case a >= "aaa" && a < "aaabbb":
            goto B
        case a == "aaabbb":
            break Start
        }
    A:
        a += "a"
        continue Start
    B:
        a += "b"
        continue Start
    }
    fmt.Println(a)
}
```

golang.fyi/ch03/gotostmt.go

The code uses the `goto` statement to jump to different sections of the `main()` function. Notice that the `goto` statement can target labels defined anywhere in the code. The superfluous usage of the `Start:` label is left in the code for completeness and is not necessary in this context (since continue, without the label, would have the same effect). The following provides some guidance when using the `goto` statement:

- Avoid using the `goto` statement unless the logic being implemented can only be achieved using `goto` branching. This is because overuse of the `goto` statement can make code harder to reason about and debug.
- Place `goto` statements and their targeted label within the same enclosing code block when possible.
- Avoid placing labels where a `goto` statement will cause the flow to skip new variable declarations or cause them to be re-declared.
- Go will let you jump from inner to outer enclosing code blocks.
- It is a compilation error if you try to jump to a peer or to an enclosing code block.

Summary

This chapter provided a walkthrough of the mechanism of control flow in Go, including `if`, `switch`, and `for` statements. While Go's flow control constructs appear simple and easy to use, they are powerful and implement all branching primitives expected of a modern language. Readers are introduced to each concept with ample detail and examples to ensure clarity of the topics. The next chapter continues our look into Go fundamentals by introducing the reader to the Go type systems.

4
Data Types

Go is a strongly-typed language, which means any language element that stores (or expression that produces) a value has a type associated with it. In this chapter, readers will learn about the features of the type system as they explore the common data types supported by the language as outlined in the following:

- Go types
- Numeric types
- Boolean type
- Pointers
- Type declaration
- Type conversion

Go types

To help launch the conversation about types, let us take a peek at the types available. Go implements a simple type system that provides programmers direct control over how memory is allocated and laid out. When a program declares a variable, two things must take place:

- The variable must receive a type
- The variable will also be bound to a value (even when none is assigned)

This allows the type system to allocate the number of bytes necessary to store the declared value. The memory layout for declared variables maps directly to their declared types. There is no type boxing or automatic type conversion that takes place. The space you expect to be allocated is actually what gets reserved in memory.

To demonstrate this fact, the following program uses a special package called `unsafe` to circumvent the type system and extract memory size information for declared variables. It is important to note that this is purely illustrative as most programs do not commonly make use of the `unsafe` package.

```go
package main
import (
    "fmt"
    "unsafe"
)

var (
    a uint8   = 72
    b int32   = 240
    c uint64  = 1234564321
    d float32 = 12432345.232
    e int64   = -1233453443434
    f float64 = -1.43555622362467
    g int16   = 32000
    h [5]rune = [5]rune{'O', 'n', 'T', 'o', 'p'}
)

func main() {
    fmt.Printf("a = %v [%T, %d bits]\n", a, a, unsafe.Sizeof(a)*8)
    fmt.Printf("b = %v [%T, %d bits]\n", b, b, unsafe.Sizeof(b)*8)
    fmt.Printf("c = %v [%T, %d bits]\n", c, c, unsafe.Sizeof(c)*8)
    fmt.Printf("d = %v [%T, %d bits]\n", d, d, unsafe.Sizeof(d)*8)
    fmt.Printf("e = %v [%T, %d bits]\n", e, e, unsafe.Sizeof(e)*8)
    fmt.Printf("f = %v [%T, %d bits]\n", f, f, unsafe.Sizeof(f)*8)
    fmt.Printf("g = %v [%T, %d bits]\n", g, g, unsafe.Sizeof(g)*8)
    fmt.Printf("h = %v [%T, %d bits]\n", h, h, unsafe.Sizeof(h)*8)
}
```

golang.fyi/ch04/alloc.go

When the program is executed, it prints out the amount of memory (in bits) consumed by each declared variable:

```
$>go run alloc.go
a = 72 [uint8, 8 bits]
b = 240 [int32, 32 bits]
c = 1234564321 [uint64, 64 bits]
d = 1.2432345e+07 [float32, 32 bits]
e = -1233453443434 [int64, 64 bits]
f = -1.43555622362467 [float64, 64 bits]
g = 32000 [int16, 16 bits]
h = [79 110 84 111 112] [[5]int32, 160 bits]
```

From the preceding output, we can see that variable a (of type uint8) will be stored using eight bits (or one byte), variable b using 32 bits (or four bytes), and so on. With the ability to influence memory consumption coupled with Go's support for pointer types, programmers are able to strongly control how memory is allocated and consumed in their programs.

This chapter will cover the types listed in the following table. They include basic types such as numeric, Boolean, and strings:

Type	Description
string	Type for storing text values
rune	An integer type (int32) used to represent characters.
byte, int, int8, int16, int32, int64, rune, uint, uint8, uint16, uint32, uint64, uintptr	Types for storing integral values.
float32, float64	Types for storing floating point decimal values.
complex64, complex128	Types that can represent complex numbers with both real and imaginary parts.
bool	Type for Boolean values.
*T, pointer to type T	A type that represents a memory address where a value of type T is stored.

The remaining types supported by Go, such as those listed in the following table, include composite, interface, function, and channels. They are covered later in chapters dedicated to their respective topics.

Type	Description
Array [n]T	An ordered collection of fixed size n of numerically indexed sequence of elements of a type T.
Slice []T	A collection of unspecified size of numerically indexed sequence of elements of type T.
struct{}	A structure is a composite type composed of elements known as fields (think of an object).
map[K]T	An unordered sequence of elements of type T indexed by a key of arbitrary type K.

`interface{}`	A named set of function declarations that define a set of operations that can be implemented by other types.
`func (T) R`	A type that represents all functions with a given parameter type `T` and return type `R`.
`chan T`	A type for an internal communication channel to send or receive values of type `T`.

Numeric types

Go's numeric types include support for integral and decimal values with a variety of sizes ranging from 8 to 64 bits. Each numeric type has its own layout in memory and is considered unique by the type system. As a way of enforcing this, and to avoid any sort of confusion when porting Go on different platforms, the name of a numeric type reflects its size requirement. For instance, type *int16* indicates an integer type that uses 16 bits for internal storage. This means that numberic values must be explicitly be converted when crossing type boundaries in assignments, expressions, and operations.

The following program is not all that functional, since all values are assigned to the blank identifier. However, it illustrates all of the numeric data types supported in Go.

```
package main
import (
    "math"
    "unsafe"
)

var _ int8 = 12
var _ int16 = -400
var _ int32 = 12022
var _ int64 = 1 << 33
var _ int = 3 + 1415

var _ uint8 = 18
var _ uint16 = 44
var _ uint32 = 133121
var i uint64 = 23113233
var _ uint = 7542
var _ byte = 255
var _ uintptr = unsafe.Sizeof(i)

var _ float32 = 0.5772156649
var _ float64 = math.Pi
```

```
var _ complex64 = 3.5 + 2i
var _ complex128 = -5.0i

func main() {
    fmt.Println("all types declared!")
}
```

golang.fyi/ch04/nums.go

Unsigned integer types

The following table lists all available types that can represent unsigned integers and their storage requirements in Go:

Type	Size	Description
uint8	Unsigned 8-bit	Range 0 – 255
uint16	Unsigned 16-bit	Range 0 – 65535
uint32	Unsigned 32-bit	Range 0 – 4294967295
uint64	Unsigned 64-bit	Range 0 – 18446744073709551615
uint	Implementation specific	A pre-declared type designed to represent either the 32 or 64-bit integers. As of version 1.x of Go, uint represents a 32-bit unsigned integer.
byte	Unsigned 8-bit	Alias for the unit8 type.
uintptr	Unsigned	An unsigned integer type designed to store pointers (memory addresses) for the underlying machine architecture.

Signed integer types

The following table lists all available types that can represent signed integers and their storage requirements in Go:

Type	Size	Description
int8	Signed 8-bit	Range -128 – 127
int16	Signed 16-bit	Range -32768 – 32767

int32	Signed 32-bit	Range -2147483648 – 2147483647
int64	Signed 64-bit	Range -9223372036854775808 – 9223372036854775807
int	Implementati specific	A pre-declared type designed to represent either the 32 or 64-bit integers. As of version 1.x of Go, int represents a 32-bit signed integer.

Floating point types

Go supports the following types for representation of decimal values using IEEE standards:

Type	Size	Description
float32	Signed 32-bit	IEEE-754 standard representation of single precision floating point values.
float64	Signed 64-bit	IEEE-754 standard representation of double-precision floating point values.

Complex number types

Go also supports representation of complex numbers with both imaginary and real parts as shown by the following table:

Type	Size	Description
complex64	float32	Represents complex numbers with real and imaginary parts stored as float32 values.
complex128	float64	Represents complex numbers with real and imaginary parts stored as float64 values.

Numeric literals

Go supports the natural representation of integer values using a sequence of digits with a combination of a sign and decimal point (as seen in the previous example). Optionally, Go integer literals can also represent hexadecimal and octal numbers as illustrated in the following program:

```
package main
import "fmt"
```

```
func main() {
    vals := []int{
        1024,
        0x0FF1CE,
        0x8BADF00D,
        0xBEEF,
        0777,
    }
    for _, i := range vals {
        if i == 0xBEEF {
            fmt.Printf("Got %d\n", i)
            break
        }
    }
}
```

golang.fyi/ch04/intslit.go

Hexadecimal values are prepended with the 0x or (0X) prefix while octal values start with the number 0 as shown in the previous example. Floating point values can be represented using both decimal and exponential notations as shown in the following examples:

```
package main

import "fmt"

func main() {
    p := 3.1415926535
    e := .5772156649
    x := 7.2E-5
    y := 1.616199e-35
    z := .416833e32

    fmt.Println(p, e, x, y, z)
}
```

golang.fyi/ch04/floats.go

The previous program shows several representations of floating point literals in Go. Numbers can include an optional exponent portion indicated by e (or E) at the end of the number. For instance, 1.616199e-35 in the code represents numerical value 1.616199 x 10^{-35}. Lastly, Go supports literals for expressing complex numbers as shown in the following example:

```
package main
import "fmt"
```

```
func main() {
    a := -3.5 + 2i
    fmt.Printf("%v\n", a)
    fmt.Printf("%+g, %+g\n", real(a), imag(a))
}
```

golang.fyi/ch04/complex.go

In the previous example, variable a is assigned a complex number with both a real and an imaginary part. The imaginary literal is a floating point number followed by the letter i. Notice that Go also offers two built-in functions, real() and imag(), to deconstruct complex numbers into their real and imaginary parts respectively.

Boolean type

In Go, Boolean binary values are stored using the bool type. Although a variable of type bool is stored as a 1-byte value, it is not, however, an alias for a numeric value. Go provides two pre-declared literals, true and false, to represent Boolean values as shown in the following example:

```
package main
import "fmt"

func main() {
    var readyToGo bool = false
    if !readyToGo {
        fmt.Println("Come on")
    } else {
        fmt.Println("Let's go!")
    }
}
```

golang.fyi/ch04/bool.go

Rune and string types

In order to start our discussion about the rune and string types, some background context is in order. Go can treat character and string literal constants in its source code as Unicode. It is a global standard whose goal is to catalog symbols for known writing systems by assigning a numerical value (known as code point) to each character.

By default, Go inherently supports UTF-8 which is an efficient way of encoding and storing Unicode numerical values. That is all the background needed to continue with this subject. No further detail will be discussed as it is beyond the scope of this book.

The rune

So, what exactly does the rune type have to do with Unicode? The rune is an alias for the *int32* type. It is specifically intended to store Unicode integer values encoded as UTF-8. Let us take a look at some rune literals in the following program:

```go
package main
import (
    "fmt"
)

var (
    bksp = '\b'
    tab  = '\t'
    nwln = '\n'
    char1 = 'ɸ'
    char2 = 'আ'
    char3 = '語'
    char4 = '\u0369'
    char5 = '\xFA'
    char6 = '\045'
)

func main() {
    fmt.Println(bksp)
    fmt.Println(tab)
    fmt.Println(nwln)
    fmt.Println(char1)
    fmt.Println(char2)
    fmt.Println(char3)
    fmt.Println(char4)
    fmt.Println(char5)
    fmt.Println(char6)
}
```

golang.fyi/ch04/rune.go

Each variable in the previous program stores a Unicode character as a `rune` value. In Go, the `rune` may be specified as a string literal constant surrounded by single quotes. The literal may be one of the following:

- A printable character (as shown with variables `char1`, `char2`, and `char3`)
- A single character escaped with backslash for non-printable control values as tab, linefeed, newline, and so on
- \u followed by Unicode values directly (\u0369)
- \x followed by two hex digits
- A backslash followed by three octal digits (\045)

Regardless of the `rune` literal value within the single quotes, the compiler compiles and assigns an integer value as shown by the printout of the previous variables:

```
$>go run runes.go
8
9
10
632
2438
35486
873
250
37
```

The string

In Go, a string is implemented as a slice of immutable byte values. Once a string value is assigned to a variable, the value of that string is never changed. Typically, string values are represented as constant literals enclosed within double quotes as shown in the following example:

```
package main
import "fmt"

var (
    txt  = "水 and 火"
    txt2 = "\u6C34\x20brings\x20\x6c\x69\x66\x65."
    txt3 = `
\u6C34\x20
brings\x20
\x6c\x69\x66\x65.
`
)

func main() {
    fmt.Printf("%s (%d)\n", txt, len(txt))
    for i := 0; i < len(txt); i++ {
        fmt.Printf("%U ", txt[i])
    }
    fmt.Println()
    fmt.Println(txt2)
    fmt.Println(txt3)
}
```

golang.fyi/ch04/string.go

The previous snippet shows variable txt being assigned a string literal containing seven characters including two embedded Chinese characters. As referenced earlier, the Go compiler will automatically interpret string literal values as Unicode characters and encode them using UTF-8. This means that under the cover, each literal character is stored as a rune and may end up taking more than one byte for storage per visible character. In fact, when the program is executed, it prints the length of txt as 11, instead of the expected seven characters for the string, accounting for the additional bytes used for the Chinese symbols.

Interpreted and raw string literals

The following snippet (from the previous example) includes two string literals assigned to variable txt2 and txt3 respectively. As you can see, these two literals have the exact same content, however, the compiler will treat them differently:

```
var (
    txt2 = "\u6C34\x20brings\x20\x6c\x69\x66\x65."
    txt3 = `
\u6C34\x20
brings\x20
```

```
\x6c\x69\x66\x65.
`
)
```

golang.fyi/ch04/string.go

The literal value assigned to variable txt2 is enclosed in double quotes. This is known as an interpreted string. An interpreted string may contain normal printable characters as well as backslash-escaped values which are parsed and interpreted as rune literals. So, when txt2 is printed, the escape values are translated as the following string:

```
水 brings life.
```

Each symbol, in the interpreted string, corresponds to an escape value or a printable symbol as summarized in the following table:

水	<space>	brings	<space>	life	.
\u6C34	\x20	brings	\x20	\x6c\x69\x66\x65	.

On the other hand, the literal value assigned to variable txt3 is surrounded by the grave accent characters ` `. This creates what is known as a raw string in Go. Raw string values are uninterpreted where escape sequences are ignored and all valid characters are encoded as they appear in the literal.

When variable txt3 is printed, it produces the following output:

```
\u6C34\x20brings\x20\x6c\x69\x66\x65.
```

Notice that the printed string contains all the backslash-escaped values as they appear in the original string literal. Uninterpreted string literals are a great way to embed large multi-line textual content within the body of a source code without breaking its syntax.

Pointers

In Go, when a piece of data is stored in memory, the value for that data may be accessed directly or a pointer may be used to reference the memory address where the data is located. As with other C-family languages, pointers in Go provide a level of indirection that let programmers process data more efficiently without having to copy the actual data value every time it is needed.

Unlike C, however, the Go runtime maintains control of the management of pointers at runtime. A programmer cannot add an arbitrary integer value to the pointer to generate a new pointer address (a practice known as pointer arithmetic). Once an area of memory is referenced by a pointer, the data in that area will remain reachable until it is no longer referenced any pointer variable. At that point, the unreferenced value becomes eligible for garbage collection.

The pointer type

Similar to C/C++, Go uses the * operator to designate a type as a pointer. The following snippet shows several pointers with different underlying types:

```
package main
import "fmt"

var valPtr *float32
var countPtr *int
var person *struct {
    name string
    age  int
}
var matrix *[1024]int
var row []*int64

func main() {
    fmt.Println(valPtr, countPtr, person, matrix, row)
}
```

golang.fyi/ch04/pointers.go

Given a variable of type T, Go uses expression *T as its pointer type. The type system considers T and *T as distinct and are not fungible. The zero value of a pointer, when it is not pointing to anything, is the address 0, represented by the literal *constant* nil.

The address operator

Pointer values can only be assigned addresses of their declared types. One way you can do so in Go is to use the address operator &(ampersand) to obtain the address value of a variable as shown in the following example:

```
package main
import "fmt"
```

```
func main() {
    var a int = 1024
    var aptr *int = &a

    fmt.Printf("a=%v\n", a)
    fmt.Printf("aptr=%v\n", aptr)
}
```

golang.fyi/ch04/pointers.go

Variable `aptr`, of pointer type `*int`, is initialized and assigned the address value of variable `a` using expression `&a` as listed here:

```
var a int = 1024
var aptr *int = &a
```

While variable `a` stores the actual value, we say that `aptr` points to `a`. The following shows the output of the program with the value of variable `a` and its memory location assigned to `aptr`:

```
a=1024
aptr=0xc208000150
```

The assigned address value will always be the same (always pointing to `a`) regardless of where `aptr` may be accessed in the code. It is also worth noting that Go does not allow the use of the address operator with literal constant for numeric, string, and bool types. Therefore, the following will not compile:

```
var aptr *int = &1024
fmt.Printf("a ptr1 = %v\n", aptr)
```

There is a syntactical exception to this rule, however, when initializing composite types such as struct and array with literal constants. The following program illustrates such scenarios:

```
package main
import "fmt"

func main() {
    structPtr := &struct{ x, y int }{44, 55}
    pairPtr := &[2]string{"A", "B"}

    fmt.Printf("struct=%#v, type=%T\n", structPtr, structPtr)
    fmt.Printf("pairPtr=%#v, type=%T\n", pairPtr, pairPtr)
}
```

golang.fyi/ch04/address2.go

In the previous code snippet, the address operator is used directly with composite literal `&struct{ x, y int }{44, 55}` and `&[2]string{"A", "B"}` to return pointer types `*struct { x int; y int }` and `*[2]string` respectively. This is a bit of syntactic sugar that eliminates the intermediary step of assigning the values to a variable, then retrieving their assigned addresses.

The new() function

The built-in function *new(<type>)* can also be used to initialize a pointer value. It first allocates the appropriate memory for a zero-value of the specified type. The function then returns the address for the newly created value. The following program uses the `new()` function to initialize variables `intptr` and `p`:

```
package main
import "fmt"

func main() {
    intptr := new(int)
    *intptr = 44

    p := new(struct{ first, last string })
    p.first = "Samuel"
    p.last = "Pierre"

    fmt.Printf("Value %d, type %T\n", *intptr, intptr)
    fmt.Printf("Person %+v\n", p)
}
```

golang.fyi/ch04/newptr.go

Variable `intptr` is initialized as `*int` and p as `*struct{first, last string}`. Once initialized, both values are updated accordingly later in the code. You can use the `new()` function to initialize pointer variables with zero values when the actual values are not available at the time of initialization.

Pointer indirection – accessing referenced values

If all you have is an address, you can access the value to which it points by applying the *
operator to the pointer value itself (or dereferencing). The following program illustrates this
idea in functions `double()` and `cap()`:

```
package main
import (
    "fmt"
    "strings"
)

func main() {
    a := 3
    double(&a)
    fmt.Println(a)
    p := &struct{ first, last string }{"Max", "Planck"}
    cap(p)
    fmt.Println(p)
}

func double(x *int) {
    *x = *x * 2
}

func cap(p *struct{ first, last string }) {
    p.first = strings.ToUpper(p.first)
    p.last = strings.ToUpper(p.last)
}
```

golang.fyi/ch04/derefptr.go

In the preceding code, the expression *x = *x * 2, in function `double()`, can be
decomposed as follows to understand how it works:

Expression	Step
*x * 2	Original expression where x is of type *int.
*(*x) * 2	Dereferencing pointers by applying * to address values.
3 * 2 = 6	Dereferenced value of *(*x) = 3.
*(*x) = 6	The right side of this expression dereferences the value of x. It is updated with the result 6.

In function `cap()`, a similar approach is used to access and update fields in composite variable p of type `struct{first, last string}`. However, when dealing with composites, the idiom is more forgiving. It is not necessary to write `*p.first` to access the pointer's field value. We can drop the `*` and just use `p.first = strings.ToUpper(p.first)`.

Type declaration

In Go, it is possible to bind a type to an identifier to create a new named type that can be referenced and used wherever the type is needed. Declaring a type takes the general format as follows:

type <name identifier> <underlying type name>

The type declaration starts with the keyword `type` followed by a *name identifier* and the name of an existing *underlying type*. The underlying type can be a built-in named type such as one of the numeric types, a Boolean, or a string type as shown in the following snippet of type declarations:

```
type truth bool
type quart float64
type gallon float64
type node string
```

 A type declaration can also use a composite *type literal* as its underlying type. Composite types include array, slice, map, and struct. This section focuses on non-composite types. For further details on composite types, refer to `Chapter 7, Composite Types`.

The following sample illustrates how named types work in their most basic forms. The code in the example converts temperature values. Each temperature unit is represented by a declared type including `fahrenheit`, `celsius`, and `kelvin`.

```
package main
import "fmt"

type fahrenheit float64
type celsius float64
type kelvin float64

func fharToCel(f fahrenheit) celsius {
    return celsius((f - 32) * 5 / 9)
}
```

```
func fharToKel(f fahrenheit) celsius {
    return celsius((f-32)*5/9 + 273.15)
}

func celToFahr(c celsius) fahrenheit {
    return fahrenheit(c*5/9 + 32)
}

func celToKel(c celsius) kelvin {
    return kelvin(c + 273.15)
}

func main() {
    var c celsius = 32.0
    f := fahrenheit(122)
    fmt.Printf("%.2f \u00b0C = %.2f \u00b0K\n", c, celToKel(c))
    fmt.Printf("%.2f \u00b0F = %.2f \u00b0C\n", f, fharToCel(f))
}
```

golang.fyi/ch04/typedef.go

In the preceding code snippet, the new declared types are all based on the underlying built-in numeric type `float64`. Once the new type has been declared, it can be assigned to variables and participate in expressions just like its underlying type. The newly declared type will have the same zero-value and can be converted to and from its underlying type.

Type conversion

In general, Go considers each type to be different. This means under normal circumstances, values of different types are not fungible in assignment, function parameters, and expression contexts. This is true for built-in and declared types. For instance, the following will cause a build error due to type mismatch:

```
package main
import "fmt"

type signal int

func main() {
    var count int32
    var actual int
    var test int64 = actual + count

    var sig signal
    var event int = sig
```

```
    fmt.Println(test)
    fmt.Println(event)
}
```

golang.fyi/ch04/type_conv.go

The expression `actual + count` causes a build time error because both variables are of different types. Even though variables `actual` and `count` are of numeric types and `int32` and `int` have the same memory representation, the compiler still rejects the expression.

The same is true for declared named types and their underlying types. The compiler will reject assignment `var event int = sig` because type `signal` is considered to be different from type `int`. This is true even though `signal` uses `int` as its underlying type.

To cross type boundaries, Go supports a type conversion expression that converts value from one type to another. Type conversion is done using the following format:

<target_type>(<value or expression>)

The following code snippet fixes the previous example by converting the variables to the proper types:

```
type signal int
func main() {
    var count int32
    var actual int
    var test int32 = int32(actual) + count

    var sig signal
    var event int = int(sig)
}
```

golang.fyi/ch04/type_conv2.go

Note that in the previous snippet assignment expression `var test int32 = int32(actual) + count` converts variable `actual` to the proper type to match the rest of the expression. Similarly, expression `var event int = int(sig)` converts variable `sig` to match the target type `int` in the assignment.

The conversion expressions satisfy the assignment by explicitly changing the type of the enclosing values. Obviously, not all types can be converted from one to another. The following table summarizes common scenarios when type conversion is appropriate and allowed:

Description	Code

The target type and converted value are both simple numeric types.	`var i int`
	`var i2 int32 = int32(i)`
	`var re float64 = float64(i +   int(i2))`

The target type and the converted value are both complex numeric types.	`var cn64 complex64` `var cn128 complex128 =   complex128(cn64)`

The target type and converted value have the same underlying types.	`type signal int`
	`var sig signal`
	`var event int = int(sig)`

The target type is a string and the converted value is a valid integer type.	`a := string(72)`
	`b := string(int32(101))`
	`c := string(rune(108))`

The target type is string and the converted value is a slice of bytes, int32, or runes.	`msg0 := string([]byte{'H','i'})` `msg1 := string([]rune{'Y','o','u','!'})`
The target type is a slice of byte, int32, or rune values and the converted value is a string.	`data0 := []byte("Hello")` `data0 := []int32("World!")`

Additionally, the conversion rules also work when the target type and converted value are pointers that reference the same types. Besides these scenarios in the previous table, Go types cannot be explicitly converted. Any attempt to do so will result in a compilation error.

Summary

This chapter presented its readers with an introduction the Go type system. The chapter opened with an overview of types and dove into a comprehensive exploration of the basic built-in types such as numeric, Boolean, string, and pointer types. The discussion continued by exposing the reader to other important topics such as named type definition. The chapter closed with coverage of the mechanics of type conversion. In coming chapters, you will get a chance to learn more about other types such as composite, function, and interface.

5

Functions in Go

One of Go's syntactical *tour de force* is via its support for higher-order functions as is found in dynamic languages such as Python or Ruby. As we will see in this chapter, a function is also a typed entity with a value that can be assigned to a variable. In this chapter, we are going to explore functions in Go covering the following topics:

- Go functions
- Passing parameter values
- Anonymous functions and closures
- Higher-order functions
- Error signaling handling
- Deferring function calls
- Function panic and recovery

Go functions

In Go, functions are first-class, typed programming elements. A declared function literal always has a type and a value (the defined function itself) and can optionally be bound to a named identifier. Because functions can be used as data, they can be assigned to variables or passed around as parameters of other functions.

Function declaration

Declaring a function in Go takes the general form illustrated in the following figure. This canonical form is used to declare named and anonymous functions.

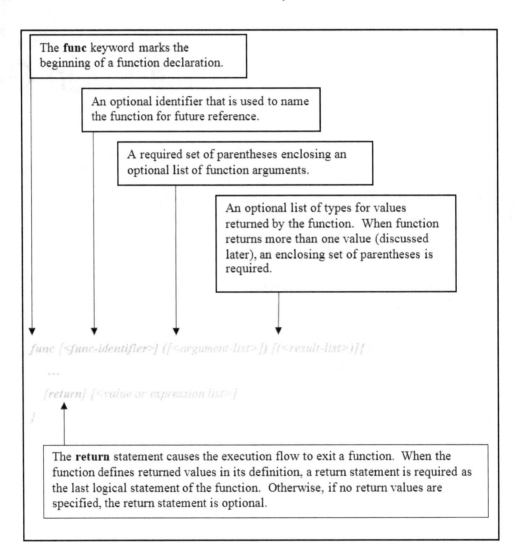

The **func** keyword marks the beginning of a function declaration.

An optional identifier that is used to name the function for future reference.

A required set of parentheses enclosing an optional list of function arguments.

An optional list of types for values returned by the function. When function returns more than one value (discussed later), an enclosing set of parentheses is required.

```
func [<func-identifier>] ([<argument-list>]) [(<result-list>)]{
    ...
    [return] [<value or expression list>]
}
```

The **return** statement causes the execution flow to exit a function. When the function defines returned values in its definition, a return statement is required as the last logical statement of the function. Otherwise, if no return values are specified, the return statement is optional.

The most common form of function definition in Go includes the function's assigned identifier in the function literal. To illustrate this, the following table shows the source code of several programs with definitions of named functions with different combinations of parameters and return types.

Code	Description
```package main import ("fmt" "math") func printPi() { fmt.Printf("printPi() %v\n", math.Pi) } func main() { printPi() } ("fmt" "math") func printPi() { fmt.Printf("printPi() %v\n", math.Pi) } func main() { printPi() }``` golang.fyi/ch05/func0.go	A function with the name identifier `printPi`. It takes no parameter and returns no values. Notice when there is nothing to return, the `return` statement is optional.
```package main import "fmt" func avogadro() float64 { return 6.02214129e23 } func main() { fmt.Printf("avogadro() = %e 1/mol\n", avogadro()) }``` golang.fyi/ch05/func1.go	A function named `avogadro`. It takes no parameter but returns a value of type `float64`. Notice the `return` statement is required when a return value is declared as part of the function's signature.

``go
package main
import "fmt"
func fib(n int) {
  fmt.Printf("fib(%d):
  [", n)
  var p0, p1 uint64 = 0,
  1
  fmt.Printf("%d %d ",
  p0, p1)
  for i := 2; i <= n; i++
  {
    p0, p1 = p1, p0+p1
    fmt.Printf("%d ",p1)
  }
  fmt.Println("]")
}
func main() {
  fib(41)
}
``
golang.fyi/ch05/func2.go
	This defines the function `fib`. It takes parameter n of type `int` and prints the Fibonacci sequence for up to n. Again, nothing to return, therefore the `return` statement is omitted.

``go
package main
import (
  "fmt"
  "math"
)
func isPrime(n int) bool {
  lim :=
  int(math.Sqrt
  (float64(n)))
  for p := 2; p <= lim;
  p++ {
    if (n % p) == 0 {
      return false
    } }
  return true
}
func main() {
  prime := 37
  fmt.Printf
  ("isPrime(%d) =
  %v\n", prime,
  isPrime(prime))
}
``
golang.fyi/ch05/func3.go
	The last example defines the `isPrime` function. It takes a parameter of type `int` and returns a value of type `bool`. Since the function is declared to return a value of type `bool`, the last logical statement in the execution flow must be a `return` statement that returns a value of the declared type.

Function signature
The set of specified parameter types, result types, and the order in which those types are declared is known as the signature of the function. It is another unique characteristic that help identify a function. Two functions may have the same number of parameters and result values; however, if the order of those elements are different, then the functions have different signatures.

The function type

Normally, the name identifier, declared in a function literal, is used to invoke the function using an invocation expression whereby the function identifier is followed by a parameter list. This is what we have seen throughout the book so far and it is illustrated in the following example calling the `fib` function:

```
func main() {
    fib(41)
}
```

When, however, a function's identifier appears without parentheses, it is treated as a regular variable with a type and a value as shown in the following program:

```
package main
import "fmt"

func add(op0 int, op1 int) int {
    return op0 + op1
}

func sub(op0, op1 int) int {
    return op0 - op1
}

func main() {
    var opAdd func(int, int) int = add
    opSub := sub
    fmt.Printf("op0(12,44)=%d\n", opAdd(12, 44))
    fmt.Printf("sub(99,13)=%d\n", opSub(99, 13))
}
```

golang.fyi/ch05/functype.go

The type of a function is determined by its signature. Functions are considered to be of the same type when they have the same number of arguments with the same types in the same order. In the previous example the `opAdd` variable is declared having the type `func (int, int) int` . This is the same signature as the declared functions `add` and `sub`. Therefore, the `opAdd` variable is assigned the `add` function variable. This allows `opAdd` to be invoked as you would invoke the `add` function.

The same is done for the `opSub` variable. It is assigned the value represented by the function identifier `sub` and type `func (int, int)`. Therefore, `opSub(99,13)` invokes the second function, which returns the result of a subtraction.

Variadic parameters

The last parameter of a function can be declared as **variadic (variable length arguments)** by affixing ellipses (...) before the parameter's type. This indicates that zero or more values of that type may be passed to the function when it is called.

The following example implements two functions that accept variadic parameters. The first function calculates the average of the passed values and the second function sums up the numbers passed in as arguments:

```
package main
import "fmt"

func avg(nums ...float64) float64 {
    n := len(nums)
    t := 0.0
    for _, v := range nums {
        t += v
    }
    return t / float64(n)
}

func sum(nums ...float64) float64 {
    var sum float64
    for _, v := range nums {
        sum += v
    }
    return sum
}

func main() {
    fmt.Printf("avg([1, 2.5, 3.75]) =%.2f\n", avg(1, 2.5, 3.75))
    points := []float64{9, 4, 3.7, 7.1, 7.9, 9.2, 10}
```

```
        fmt.Printf("sum(%v) = %.2f\n", points, sum(points...))
    }
```

golang.fyi/ch05/funcvariadic.go

The compiler resolves the variadic parameter as a slice of type `[]float64` in both the preceding functions. The parameter values can then be accessed using a slice expression as shown in the previous example. To invoke functions with variadic arguments, simply provide a comma-separated list of values that matches the specified type as shown in the following snippet:

```
    fmt.Printf("avg([1, 2.5, 3.75]) =%.2f\n", avg(1, 2.5, 3.75)))
```

When no parameters are provided, the function receives an empty slice. The astute reader may be wondering, "Is it possible to pass in an existing slice of values as variadic arguments?" Thankfully, Go provides an easy idiom to handle such a case. Let's examine the call to the sum function in the following code snippet:

```
    points := []float64{9, 4, 3.7, 7.1, 7.9, 9.2, 10}
    fmt.Printf("sum(%v) = %f\n", points, sum(points...))
```

A slice of floating-point values is declared and stored in variable points. The slice can be passed as a variadic parameter by adding ellipses to the parameter in the sum(points...) function call.

Function result parameters

Go functions can be defined to return one or more result values. So far in the book, most of the functions we have encountered have been defined to return a single result value. In general, a function is able to return a list of result values, with diverse types, separated by a comma (see the previous section, *Function declaration*).

To illustrate this concept, let us examine the following simple program which defines a function that implements an Euclidian division algorithm (see http://en.wikipedia.org/wiki/Division_algorithm). The div function returns both the quotient and the remainder values as its result:

```
    package main
    import "fmt"

    func div(op0, op1 int) (int, int) {
        r := op0
        q := 0
        for r >= op1 {
```

```
            q++
            r = r - op1
        }
    return q, r
}

func main() {
    q, r := div(71, 5)
    fmt.Printf("div(71,5) -> q = %d, r = %d\n", q, r)
}
```

The **return** keyword is followed by the number of result values matching (respectively) the declared results in the function's signature. In the previous example, the signature of the div function specifies two int values to be returned as result values. Internally, the function defines int variables p and r that are returned as result values upon completion of the function. Those returned values must match the types defined in the function's signature or risk compilation errors.

Functions with multiple result values must be invoked in the proper context:

- They must be assigned to a list of identifiers of the same types respectively
- They can only be included in expressions that expect the same number of returned values

This is illustrated in the following source snippet:

```
q, r := div(71, 5)
fmt.Printf("div(71,5) -> q = %d, r = %d\n", q, r)
```

Named result parameters

In general, the result list of a function's signature can be specified using variable identifiers along with their types. When using named identifiers, they are passed to the function as regular declared variables and can be accessed and modified as needed. Upon encountering a return statement, the last assigned result values are returned. This is illustrated in the following source snippet, which is a rewrite of the previous program:

```
func div(dvdn, dvsr int) (q, r int) {
    r = dvdn
    for r >= dvsr {
        q++
        r = r - dvsr
    }
```

```
    return
}
```

Notice the `return` statement is naked; it omits all identifiers. As stated earlier, the values assigned in q and r will be returned to the caller. For readability, consistency, or style, you may elect not to use a naked `return` statement. It is perfectly legal to attach the identifier's name with the `return` statement (such as `return q, r`) as before.

Passing parameter values

In Go, all parameters passed to a function are done so by value. This means a local copy of the passed values is created inside the called function. There is no inherent concept of passing parameter values by reference. The following code illustrates this mechanism by modifying the value of the passed parameter, val, inside the dbl function:

```
package main
import (
    "fmt"
    "math"
)

func dbl(val float64) {
    val = 2 * val // update param
    fmt.Printf("dbl()=%.5f\n", val)
}

func main() {
    p := math.Pi
    fmt.Printf("before dbl() p = %.5f\n", p)
    dbl(p)
    fmt.Printf("after dbl() p = %.5f\n", p)
}
```

When the program runs, it produces the following output that chronicles the state of the p variable before it is passed to the dbl function. The update is made locally to the passed parameter variable inside the dbl function, and lastly the value of the p variable after the dbl function is called:

```
$> go run funcpassbyval.go
before dbl() p = 3.14159
```

```
dbl()=6.28319
after dbl() p = 3.14159
```

The preceding output shows that the original value assigned to variable p remains variable unchanged, even after it is passed to a function that seems to update its value internally. This is because the val parameter in the dbl function receives a local copy of the passed parameter.

Achieving pass-by-reference

While the pass-by-value is appropriate in many cases, it is important to note that Go can achieve pass-by-reference semantics using pointer parameter values. This allows a called function to reach outside of its lexical scope and change the value stored at the location referenced by the pointer parameter as is done in the half function in the following example:

```go
package main
import "fmt"

func half(val *float64) {
    fmt.Printf("call half(%f)\n", *val)
    *val = *val / 2
}

func main() {
    num := 2.807770
    fmt.Printf("num=%f\n", num)
    half(&num)
    fmt.Printf("half(num)=%f\n", num)
}
```

golang.fyi/ch05/funcpassbyref.go

In the previous example, the call to the half(&num) function in main() updates, in place, the original value referenced by its num parameter. So, when the code is executed, it shows the original value of num and its value after the call to the half function:

```
$> go run funcpassbyref.go
num=2.807770
call half(2.807770)
half(num)=1.403885
```

As was stated earlier, Go function parameters are passed by value. This is true even when the function takes a pointer value as its parameter. Go still creates and passes in a local copy of the pointer value. In the previous example, the `half` function receives a copy of the pointer value it receives via the `val` parameter. The code uses pointer operator (*) to dereference and manipulate, in place, the value referenced by `val`. When the `half` function exits and goes out of scope, its changes are accessible by calling the `main` function.

Anonymous Functions and Closures

Functions can be written as literals without a named identifier. These are known as anonymous functions and can be assigned to a variable to be invoked later as shown in the following example:

```
package main
import "fmt"

var (
    mul = func(op0, op1 int) int {
        return op0 * op1
    }

    sqr = func(val int) int {
        return mul(val, val)
    }
)

func main() {
    fmt.Printf("mul(25,7) = %d\n", mul(25, 7))
    fmt.Printf("sqr(13) = %d\n", sqr(13))
}
```

golang.fyi/ch05/funcs.go

The previous program shows two anonymous functions declared and bound to the `mul` and `sqr` variables. In both cases, the functions take in parameters and return a value. Later in `main()`, the variables are used to invoke the function code bound to them.

Invoking anonymous function literals

It is worth noting that an anonymous function does not have to be bound to an identifier. The function literal can be evaluated, in place, as an expression that returns the function's result. This is done by ending the function literal with a list of argument values, enclosed in parentheses, as shown in the following program:

```
package main
import "fmt"

func main() {
    fmt.Printf(
            "94 (°F) = %.2f (°C)\n",
            func(f float64) float64 {
                    return (f - 32.0) * (5.0 / 9.0)
            }(94),
    )
}
```

golang.fyi/ch05/funcs.go

The literal format not only defines the anonymous function, but also invokes it. For instance, in the following snippet (from the previous program), the anonymous function literal is nested as a parameter to `fmt.Printf()`. The function itself is defined to accept a parameter and returns a value of type `float64`.

```
fmt.Printf(
    "94 (°F) = %.2f (°C)\n",
    func(f float64) float64 {
            return (f - 32.0) * (5.0 / 9.0)
    }(94),
)
```

Since the function literal ends with a parameter list enclosed within parentheses, the function is invoked as an expression.

Closures

Go function literals are closures. This means they have lexical visibility to non-local variables declared outside of their enclosing code block. The following example illustrates this fact:

```
package main
import (
    "fmt"
```

```go
    "math"
)

func main() {
    for i := 0.0; i < 360.0; i += 45.0 {
        rad := func() float64 {
            return i * math.Pi / 180
        }()
        fmt.Printf("%.2f Deg = %.2f Rad\n", i, rad)
    }
}
```

github.com/vladimirvivien/learning-go/ch05/funcs.go

In the previous program, the function literal code block, `func() float64 {return deg * math.Pi / 180}()`, is defined as an expression that converts degrees to radians. With each iteration of the loop, a closure is formed between the enclosed function literal and the outer non-local variable, `i`. This provides a simpler idiom where the function naturally accesses non-local values without resorting to other means such as pointers.

 In Go, lexically closed values can remain bounded to their closures long after the outer function that created the closure has gone out of scope. The garbage collector will handle cleanups as these closed values become unbounded.

Higher-order functions

We have already established that Go functions are values bound to a type. So, it should not be a surprise that a Go function can take another function as a parameter and also return a function as a result value. This describes the notion known as a higher-order function, which is a concept adopted from mathematics. While types such as `struct` let programmers abstract data, higher-order functions provide a mechanism to encapsulate and abstract behaviors that can be composed together to form more complex behaviors.

To make this concept clearer, let us examine the following program, which uses a higher-order function, `apply`, to do three things. It accepts a slice of integers and a function as parameters. It applies the specified function to each element in the slice. Lastly, the `apply` function also returns a function as its result:

```go
package main
import "fmt"

func apply(nums []int, f func(int) int) func() {
```

```go
    for i, v := range nums {
        nums[i] = f(v)
    }
    return func() {
        fmt.Println(nums)
    }
}

func main() {
    nums := []int{4, 32, 11, 77, 556, 3, 19, 88, 422}
    result := apply(nums, func(i int) int {
        return i / 2
    })
    result()
}
```

golang.fyi/ch05/funchighorder.go

In the program, the `apply` function is invoked with an anonymous function that halves each element in the slice as highlighted in the following snippet:

```go
nums := []int{4, 32, 11, 77, 556, 3, 19, 88, 422}
result := apply(nums, func(i int) int {
    return i / 2
})
result()
```

As a higher-order function, `apply` abstracts the transformation logic which can be provided by any function of type `func(i int) int`, as shown next. Since the `apply` function returns a function, the variable `result` can be invoked as shown in the previous snippet.

As you explore this book, and the Go language, you will continue to encounter usage of higher-order functions. It is a popular idiom that is used heavily in the standard libraries. You will also find higher-order functions used in some concurrency patterns to distribute workloads (see `Chapter 9`, *Concurrency*).

Error signaling and handling

At this point, let us address how to idiomatically signal and handle errors when you make a function call. If you have worked with languages such as Python, Java, or C#, you may be familiar with interrupting the flow of your executing code by throwing an exception when an undesirable state arises.

As we will explore in this section, Go has a simplified approach to error signaling and error handling that puts the onus on the programmer to handle possible errors immediately after a called function returns. Go discourages the notion of interrupting an execution by indiscriminately short-circuiting the executing program with an exception in the hope that it will be properly handled further up the call stack. In Go, the traditional way of signaling errors is to return a value of type `error` when something goes wrong during the execution of your function. So let us take a closer look how this is done.

Signaling errors

To better understand what has been described in the previous paragraph, let us start with an example. The following source code implements an anagram program, as described in Column 2 from Jon Bentley's popular *Programming Pearls* book (second edition). The code reads a dictionary file (`dict.txt`) and groups all words with the same anagram. If the code does not quite make sense, please see `golang.fyi/ch05/anagram1.go` for an annotated explanation of how each part of the program works.

```
package main

import (
    "bufio"
    "bytes"
    "fmt"
    "os"
    "errors"
)

// sorts letters in a word (i.e. "morning" -> "gimnnor")
func sortRunes(str string) string {
    runes := bytes.Runes([]byte(str))
    var temp rune
    for i := 0; i < len(runes); i++ {
            for j := i + 1; j < len(runes); j++ {
                    if runes[j] < runes[i] {
                            temp = runes[i]
                            runes[i], runes[j] = runes[j], temp
                    }

            }
    }
    return string(runes)
}

// load loads content of file fname into memory as []string
```

```go
func load(fname string) ([]string, error) {
    if fname == "" {
        return nil, errors.New(
            "Dictionary file name cannot be empty.")
    }

    file, err := os.Open(fname)
    if err != nil {
        return nil, err
    }
    defer file.Close()

    var lines []string
    scanner := bufio.NewScanner(file)
    scanner.Split(bufio.ScanLines)
    for scanner.Scan() {
        lines = append(lines, scanner.Text())
    }
    return lines, scanner.Err()
}

func main() {
    words, err := load("dict.txt")
    if err != nil {
        fmt.Println("Unable to load file:", err)
        os.Exit(1)
    }

    anagrams := make(map[string][]string)
    for _, word := range words {
        wordSig := sortRunes(word)
        anagrams[wordSig] = append(anagrams[wordSig], word)
    }

    for k, v := range anagrams {
        fmt.Println(k, "->", v)
    }
}
```

golang.fyiy/ch05/anagram1.go

Again, if you want a more detail explanation of the previous program, take a look at the link supplied earlier. The focus here is on error signaling used in the previous program. As a convention, Go code uses the built-in type `error` to signal when an error occurred during execution of a function. Therefore, a function must return a value of type error to indicate to its caller that something went wrong. This is illustrated in the following snippet of the `load` function (extracted from the previous example):

```
func load(fname string) ([]string, error) {
    if fname == "" {
        return nil, errors.New(
            "Dictionary file name cannot be empty.")
    }

    file, err := os.Open(fname)
    if err != nil {
            return nil, err
    }
    ...
}
```

Notice that the `load` function returns multiple result parameters. One is for the expected value, in this case `[]string`, and the other is the error value. Idiomatic Go dictates that the programmer returns a non-nil value for result of type `error` to indicate that something abnormal occurred during the execution of the function. In the previous snippet, the `load` function signals an error occurrence to its callers in two possible instances:

- when the expected filename (`fname`) is empty
- when the call to `os.Open()` fails (for example, permission error, or otherwise)

In the first case, when a filename is not provided, the code returns an error using `errors.New()` to create a value of type `error` to exit the function. In the second case, the `os.Open` function returns a pointer representing the file and an error assigned to the `file` and `err` variables respectively. If `err` is not `nil` (meaning an error was generated), the execution of the `load` function is halted prematurely and the value of `err` is returned to be handled by the calling function further up the call stack.

When returning an error for a function with multiple result parameters, it is customary to return the zero-value for the other (non-error type) parameters. In the example, a value of `nil` is returned for the result of type `[]string`. While not necessary, it simplifies error handling and avoids any confusion for function callers.

Error handling

As described previously, signaling of an erroneous state is as simple as returning a non-nil value, of type error, during execution of a function. The caller may choose to handle the error or return it for further evaluation up the call stack as was done in the load function. This idiom forces errors to propagate upwards until they are handled at some point. The next snippet shows how the error generated by the load function is handled in the main function:

```
func main() {
    words, err := load("dict.txt")
    if err != nil {
        fmt.Println("Unable to load file:", err)
        os.Exit(1)
    }
    ...
}
```

Since the main function is the topmost caller in the call stack, it handles the error by terminating the entire program.

This is all there is to the mechanics of error handling in Go. The language forces the programmer to always test for an erroneous state on every function call that returns a value of the type error. The if...not...nil error handling idiom may seem excessive and verbose to some, especially if you are coming from a language with formal exception mechanisms. However, the gain here is that the program can construct a robust execution flow where programmers always know where errors may come from and handle them appropriately.

The error type

The error type is a built-in interface and, therefore must be implemented before it can be used. Fortunately, the Go standard library comes with implementations ready to be used. We have already used one of the implementation from the package, errors:

```
errors.New("Dictionary file name cannot be empty.")
```

You can also create parameterized error values using the fmt.Errorf function as shown in the following snippet:

```
func load(fname string) ([]string, error) {
    if fname == "" {
        return nil, errors.New(
```

```
                "Dictionary file name cannot be emtpy.")
        }

        file, err := os.Open(fname)
        if err != nil {
                return nil, fmt.Errorf(
                        "Unable to open file %s: %s", fname, err)
        }
        ...
}
```

It is also idiomatic to assign error values to high-level variables so they can be reused throughout a program as needed. The following snippet pulled from http://golang.org/src/os/error.go shows the declaration of reusable errors associated with OS file operations:

```
var (
    ErrInvalid    = errors.New("invalid argument")
    ErrPermission = errors.New("permission denied")
    ErrExist      = errors.New("file already exists")
    ErrNotExist   = errors.New("file does not exist")
)
```

```
          http://golang.org/src/os/error.go
```

You can also create your own implementation of the error interface to create custom errors. This topic is revisited in Chapter 7, *Methods, Interfaces, and Objects* where the book discusses the notion of extending types.

Deferring function calls

Go supports the notion of deferring a function call. Placing the keyword defer before a function call has the interesting effect of pushing the function unto an internal stack, delaying its execution right before the enclosing function returns. To better explain this, let us start with the following simple program that illustrates the use of defer:

```
package main
import "fmt"

func do(steps ...string) {
    defer fmt.Println("All done!")
    for _, s := range steps {
```

```
        defer fmt.Println(s)
    }

    fmt.Println("Starting")
}

func main() {
    do(
        "Find key",
        "Aplly break",
        "Put key in ignition",
        "Start car",
    )
}
```

golang.fyi/ch05/defer1.go

The previous example defines the do function that takes variadic parameter steps. The function defers the statement with defer fmt.Println("All done!"). Next, the function loops through slice steps and defers the output of each element with defer fmt.Println(s). The last statement in the function do is a non-deferred call to fmt.Println("Starting"). Notice the order of the printed string values when the program is executed, as shown in the following output:

```
$> go run defer1.go
Starting
Start car
Put key in ignition
Aplly break
Find key
All done!
```

There are a couple facts that explain the reverse order of the printout. First, recall that deferred functions are executed right before their enclosing function returns. Therefore, the first value printed is generated by the last non-deferred method call. Next, as stated earlier, deferred statements are pushed into a stack. Therefore, deferred calls are executed using a last-in-first-out order. That is why "All done!" is the last string value printed in the output.

Using defer

The `defer` keyword modifies the execution flow of a program by delaying function calls. One idiomatic usage for this feature is to do a resource cleanup. Since defer will always get executed when the surrounding function returns, it is a good place to attach cleanup code such as:

- Closing open files
- Releasing network resources
- Closing the Go channel
- Committing database transactions
- And do on

To illustrate, let us return to our anagram example from earlier. The following code snippet shows a version of the code where defer is used to close the file after it has been loaded. The `load` function calls `file.Close()` right before it returns:

```
func load(fname string) ([]string, error) {
...
   file, err := os.Open(fname)
   if err != nil {
        return nil, err
   }
   defer file.Close()
...
}
```

golang.fyi/ch05/anagram2.go

The pattern of opening-defer-closing resources is widely used in Go. By placing the deferred intent immediately after opening or creating a resource allows the code to read naturally and reduces the likeliness of creating a resource leakage.

Function panic and recovery

Earlier in the chapter, it was stated that Go does not have the traditional exception mechanism offered by other languages. Nevertheless, in Go, there is a way to abruptly exit an executing function known as function panic. Conversely, when a program is panicking, Go provides a way of recovering and regaining control of the execution flow.

Function panic

During execution, a function may panic because of any one of following:

- Explicitly calling the **panic** built-in function
- Using a source code package that panics due to an abnormal state
- Accessing a nil value or an out-of-bound array element
- Concurrency deadlock

When a function panics, it aborts and executes its deferred calls. Then its caller panics, causing a chain reaction as illustrated in the following figure:

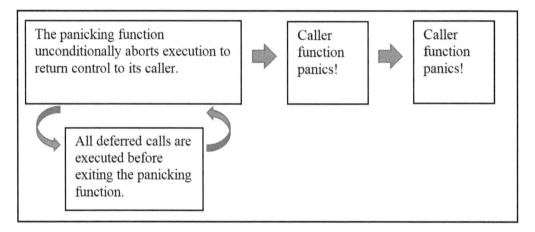

The panic sequence continues all the way up the call stack until the `main` function is reached and the program exits (crashes). The following source code snippet shows a version of the anagram program that will cause an explicit panic if an output anagram file already exists when it tries to create one. This is done illustratively to cause the `write` function to panic when there is a file error:

```
package main
...
func write(fname string, anagrams map[string][]string) {
    file, err := os.OpenFile(
            fname,
            os.O_WRONLY+os.O_CREATE+os.O_EXCL,
            0644,
    )
    if err != nil {
            msg := fmt.Sprintf(
                    "Unable to create output file: %v", err,
```

```
        )
        panic(msg)
    }
    ...
}

func main() {
    words, err := load("dict.txt")
    if err != nil {
        fmt.Println("Unable to load file:", err)
        os.Exit(1)
    }
    anagrams := mapWords(words)
    write("out.txt", anagrams)
}
```

golang.fyi/ch05/anagram2.go

In the preceding snippet, the `write` function calls the `panic` function if `os.OpenFile()` method errors out. When the program calls the `main` function, if there is an output file already in the working directory, the program will panic and crash as shown in the following stack trace, indicating the sequence of calls that caused the crash:

```
> go run anagram2.go
panic: Unable to create output file: open out.txt: file exists
goroutine 1 [running]:
main.write(0x4e7b30, 0x7, 0xc2080382a0)
/Go/src/github.com/vladimirvivien/learning-go/ch05/anagram2.go:72 +0x1a3
main.main()
Go/src/github.com/vladimirvivien/learning-go/ch05/anagram2.go:103 +0x1e9
exit status 2
```

Function panic recovery

When a function panics, as explained earlier, it can crash an entire program. That may be the desired outcome depending on your requirements. It is possible, however, to regain control after a panic sequence has started. To do this, Go offers the built-in function called `recover`.

Recover works in tandem with panic. A call to function recover returns the value that was passed as an argument to panic. The following code shows how to recover from the panic call that was introduced in the previous example. In this version, the write function is moved inside `makeAnagram()` for clarity. When the `write` function is invoked from `makeAnagram()` and fails to open a file, it will panic. However, additional code is now added to recover:

```go
package main
...
func write(fname string, anagrams map[string][]string) {
    file, err := os.OpenFile(
            fname,
            os.O_WRONLY+os.O_CREATE+os.O_EXCL,
            0644,
    )
    if err != nil {
            msg := fmt.Sprintf(
                    "Unable to create output file: %v", err,
            )
            panic(msg)
    }
    ...
}

func makeAnagrams(words []string, fname string) {
    defer func() {
            if r := recover(); r != nil {
                    fmt.Println("Failed to make anagram:", r)
            }
    }()

    anagrams := mapWords(words)
    write(fname, anagrams)
}
func main() {
    words, err := load("")
    if err != nil {
            fmt.Println("Unable to load file:", err)
            os.Exit(1)
    }
    makeAnagrams(words, "")
}
```

golang.fyi/ch05/anagram3.go

To be able to recover from an unwinding panic sequence, the code must make a deferred call to the recover function. In the previous code, this is done in the makeAnagrams function by wrapping recover() inside an anonymous function literal, as highlighted in the following snippet:

```
defer func() {
    if r := recover(); r != nil {
        fmt.Println("Failed to make anagram:", r)
    }
}()
```

When the deferred recover function is executed, the program has an opportunity to regain control and prevent the panic from crashing the running program. If recover() returns nil, it means there is no current panic unwinding up the call stack or the panic was already handled downstream.

So, now when the program is executed, instead of crashing with a stack trace, the program recovers and gracefully displays the issue as shown in the following output:

```
> go run anagram3.go
Failed to make anagram: Unable to open output file for creation: open
out.txt: file exists
```

You may be wondering why we are using a nil to test the value returned by the recover function when a string was passed inside the call to panic. This is because both panic and recover take an empty interface type. As you will learn, the empty interface type is a generic type with the ability to represent any type in Go's type system. We will learn more about the empty interface in Chapter 7, *Methods, Interfaces and Objects* during discussions about interfaces.

Summary

This chapter presented its reader with an exploration of Go functions. It started with an overview of named function declarations, followed by a discussion on function parameters. The chapter delved into a discussion of function types and function values. The last portion of the chapter discussed the semantics of error handling, panic, and recovery. The next chapter continues the discussion of functions; however, it does so within the context of Go packages. It explains the role of a package as a logical grouping of Go functions (and other code elements) to form sharable and callable code modules.

6

Go Packages and Programs

Chapter 5, *Functions in Go* covered functions, the elementary level of abstraction for code organization that makes code addressable and reusable. This chapter continues up the ladder of abstraction with a discussion centered around Go packages. As will be covered in detail here, a package is a logical grouping of language elements stored in source code files that can be shared and reused, as covered in the following topics:

- The Go package
- Creating packages
- Building packages
- Package visibility
- Importing packages
- Package initialization
- Creating programs
- Remote packages

The Go package

Similar to other languages, Go source code files are grouped into compilable and sharable units known as packages. However, all Go source files must belong to a package (there is no such notion as a default package). This strict approach allows Go to keep its compilation rules and package resolution rules simple by favoring convention over configuration. Let us take a deep dive into the fundamentals of packages, their creation, use, and recommended practice.

Understanding the Go package

Before we dive into package creation and use, it is crucial to take a high-level view of the concept of packages to help steer the discussion later. A Go package is both a physical and a logical unit of code organization used to encapsulate related concepts that can be reused. By convention, a group of source files stored in the same directory are considered to be part of the same package. The following illustrates a simple directory tree, where each directory represents a package containing some source code:

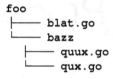

golang.fyi/ch06-foo

While not a requirement, it is a recommended convention to set a package's name, in each source file, to match the name of the directory where the file is located. For instance, source file `blat.go` is declared to be part of package `foo`, as shown in the following code, because it is stored in directory named `foo`:

```
package foo

import (
    "fmt"
    "foo/bar/bazz"
)

func fooIt() {
    fmt.Println("Foo!")
    bazz.Qux()
}
```

golang.fyi/ch06-foo/foo/blat.go

Files `quux.go` and `qux.go` are both part of package`bazz` since they are located in a directory with that name, as shown in the following code snippets:

``
package bazz
import "fmt"
func Qux() {
   fmt.Println("bazz.Qux")
}
``
golang.fyi/ch06-foo/foo/bazz/quux.go
	``
	package bazz
	import "fmt"
	func Quux() {
	   Qux() fmt.Println("gazz.Quux")
	}
	``
	golang.fyi/ch06-foo/foo/bazz/qux.go

The workspace

Another important concept to understand when discussing packages is that of the *Go workspace*. The workspace is simply an arbitrary directory that serves as a namespace used to resolved packages during certain tasks such as compilation. By convention, Go tools expect three specifically named subdirectories in a workspace directory: `src`, `pkg`, and `bin`. These subdirectories store Go source files along with all built package artifacts respectively.

Establishing a static directory location where Go packages are kept together has the following advantages:

- Simple setup with near-zero configuration
- Fast compilation by reducing code search to a known location
- Tools can easily create source graph of code and package artifacts
- Automatic inference and resolution of transitive dependencies from source
- Project setup can be made portable and easily distributable

The following is a partial (and simplified) tree layout of my Go workspace on my laptop with the three subdirectories, bin, pkg, and src, highlighted:

```
/home/vladimir/Go/
├──── bin
│     ├──── circ
│     ├──── golint
│     ...
├──── pkg
│     └──── linux_amd64
│           ├──── github.com
│           │     ├──── golang
│           │     │     └──── lint.a
│           │     └──── vladimirvivien
│           │           └──── learning-go
│           │                 └──── ch06
│           │                       ├──── current.a
│           ...         ...
└──── src
      ├──── github.com
      │     ├──── golang
      │     │     └──── lint
      │     │           ├──── golint
      │     │           │     ├──── golint.go
      │     ...         ...  ...
      │     └──── vladimirvivien
      │           └──── learning-go
      │                 ├──── ch01
      │                 ...
      │                 ├──── ch06
      │                 │     ├──── current
      │                 │     │     ├──── doc.go
      │                 │     │     └──── lib.go
      ...               ...
```

Sample workspace directory

- bin: This is an auto-generated directory that stores compiled Go executable artifacts (also known as programs or commands). When Go tools compile and install executable packages, they are placed in this directory. The previous sample workspace shows two binaries listed circ and golint. It is a recommended practice to add this directory to your operating system's PATH environment variable to make your command available locally.

- `pkg`: This directory is also auto-generated to store built package artifacts. When the Go tools build and install non-executable packages, they are stored as object files (with `.a` suffix) in subdirectories with name patterns based on the targeted operating system and architecture. In the sample workspace, the object files are placed under subdirectory `linux_amd64`, which indicates that the object files in this directory were compiled for the Linux operating system running on a 64-bit architecture.
- `src`: This is a user-created directory where the Go source code files are stored. Each subdirectory under `src` is mapped to a package. *src* is the root directory from which all import paths are resolved. The Go tools search that directory to resolve packages referenced in your code during compilation or other activities that depend on the source path. The sample workspace in the previous figure shows two packages: `github.com/golang/lint/golint/` and `github.com/vladimirvivien/learning-go/ch06/current`.

You may be wondering about the `github.com` prefix in the package path shown in the workspace example. It is worth noting there are no naming requirements for the package directories (see the *Naming packages* section). A package can have any arbitrary name. However, Go recommends certain conventions that help with global namespace resolution and package organization.

Creating a workspace

Creating a workspace is as simple as setting an operating system environment named `GOPATH` and assigning to it the root path of the location of the workspace directory. On a Linux machine, for instance, where the root directory for the workspace is `/home/username/Go`, the workspace would be set as:

```
$> export GOPATH=/home/username/Go
```

When setting up the `GOPATH` environment variable, it is possible to specify multiple locations where packages are stored. Each directory is separated by an OS-dependent path delimiter character (in other words, colon for Linux/Unix, semi-colon for Windows) as shown below:

```
$> export GOPATH=/home/myaccount/Go;/home/myaccount/poc/Go
```

The Go tools will search all listed locations in the GOPATH when resolving package names. The Go compiler will, however, only store compiled artifacts, such as object and binary files, in the first directory location assigned to GOPATH.

The ability to configure your workspace by simply setting an OS environmental variable has tremendous advantages. It gives developers the ability to dynamically set the workspace at compile time to meet certain workflow requirements. For instance, a developer may want to test an unverified branch of code prior to merging it. He or she may want to set up a temporary workspace to build that code as follows (Linux): $> GOPATH=/temporary/go/workspace/path go build

The import path

Before moving on to the detail of setting up and using packages, one last important concept to cover is the notion of an *import path*. The relative path of each package, under workspace path $GOPATH/src, constitutes a global identifier known as the package's import path. This implies that no two packages can have the same import path values in a given workspace.

Let us go back to our simplified directory tree from earlier. For instance, if we set the workspace to some arbitrary path value such as GOPATH=/home/username/Go:

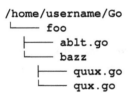

From the sample workspace illustrated above, the directory path of the packages is mapped to their respective import paths as shown in the following table:

Directory Path	Import Path
/home/username/Go/foo	"foo"
/home/username/Go/foo/bar	"foo/bar"
/home/username/Go/foo/bar/bazz	"foo/bar/bazz"

Creating packages

Until now, the chapter has covered the rudimentary concepts of the Go package; now it is time to dive deeper and look at the creation of Go code contained in packages. One of the main purposes of a Go package is to abstract out and aggregate common logic into sharable code units. Earlier in the chapter, it was mentioned that a group of Go source files in a directory is considered to be a package. While this is technically true, there is more to the concept of a Go package than just shoving a bunch of files in a directory.

To help illustrate the creation of our first packages, we will enlist the use of example source code found in `github.com/vladimirvivien/learning-go/ch06`. The code in that directory defines a set of functions to help calculate electrical values using *Ohm's Law*. The following shows the layout of the directories that make up the packages for the example (assuming they are saved in some workspace directory `$GOPATH/src`):

```
github.com/vladimirvivien/learning-go/ch06
├── current
│   ├── curr.go
│   └── doc.go
├── power
│   ├── doc.go
│   ├── ir
│   │   └── power.go
│   ├── powlib.go
│   └── vr
│       └── power.go
├── resistor
│   ├── doc.go
│   ├── lib.go
│   ├── res_equivalence.go
│   ├── res.go
│   └── res_power.go
└── volt
    ├── doc.go
    └── volt.go
```

Package layout for Ohm's Law example

Each directory, in the previous tree, contains one or more Go source code files that define and implement the functions, and other source code elements, that will be arranged into packages and be made reusable. The following table summarizes the import paths and package information extracted from preceding workspace layout:

Import Path	Package
"github.com/vladimirvivien/learning-go/ch06/**current**"	`current`
"github.com/vladimirvivien/learning-go/ch06/**power**"	`power`
"github.com/vladimirvivien/learning-go/ch06/**power/ir**"	`ir`
"github.com/vladimirvivien/learning-go/ch06/**power/vr**"	`vr`
"github.com/vladimirvivien/learning-go/ch06/**resistor**"	`resistor`
"github.com/vladimirvivien/learning-go/ch06/**volt**"	`volt`

While there are no naming requirements, it is sensible to name package directories to reflect their respective purposes. From the previous table, each package in the example is named to represent an electrical concept, such as current, power, resistor, and volt. The *Naming packages* section will go into further detail about package naming conventions.

Declaring the package

Go source files must declare themselves to be part of a package. This is done using the `package` clause, as the first legal statement in a Go source file. The declared package consists of the `package` keyword followed by a name identifier. The following shows source file `volt.go` from the `volt` package:

```
package volt

func V(i, r float64) float64 {
    return i * r
}

func Vser(volts ...float64) (Vtotal float64) {
    for _, v := range volts {
        Vtotal = Vtotal + v
    }
    return
}

func Vpi(p, i float64) float64 {
    return p / i
```

```
}
```

golang.fyi/ch06/volt/volt.go

The package identifier in the source file can be set to any arbitrary value. Unlike, say, Java, the name of the package does not reflect the directory structure where the source file is located. While there are no requirements for the package name, it is an accepted convention to name the package identifier the same as the directory where the file is located. In our previous source listing, the package is declared with identifier `volt` because the file is stored inside the *volt* directory.

Multi-File packages

The logical content of a package (source code elements such as types, functions, variables, and constants) can physically scale across multiple Go source files. A package directory can contain one or more Go source files. For instance, in the following example, package `resistor` is unnecessarily split among several Go source files to illustrate this point:

```
package resistor
func recip(val float64) float64 {
    return 1 / val
}
```
golang.fyi/ch06/resistor/lib.go

```
package resistor
func Rser(resists ...float64) (Rtotal float64) {
    for _, r := range resists {
        Rtotal = Rtotal + r
    }
    return
}
func Rpara(resists ...float64) (Rtotal float64) {
    for _, r := range resists {
        Rtotal = Rtotal + recip(r)
    }
    return
}
```
golang.fyi/ch06/resistor/res_equivalance.go

```
package resistor
func R(v, i float64) float64 {
    return v / i
}
```
golang.fyi/ch06/resistor/res.go

```
package resistor
func Rvp(v, p float64) float64 {
    return (v * v) / p
}
```
golang.fyi/ch06/resistor/res_power.go

Each file in the package must have a package declaration with the same name identifier (in this case `resistor`). The Go compiler will stitch all elements from all of the source files together to form one logical unit within a single scope that can be used by other packages.

It is important to point out that compilation will fail if the package declaration is not identical across all source files in a given directory. This is understandable, as the compiler expects all files in a directory to be part of the same package.

Naming packages

As mentioned earlier, Go expects each package in a workspace to have a unique fully qualified import path. Your program may have as many packages as you want and your package structure can be as deep as you like in the workspace. However, idiomatic Go prescribes some **rules** for the naming and organization of your packages to make creating and using packages simple.

Use globally unique namespaces

Firstly, it is a good idea to fully qualify the import path of your packages in a global context, especially if you plan to share your code with others. Consider starting the name of your import path with a namespace scheme that uniquely identifies you or your organization. For instance, company *Acme, Inc.* may choose to start all of their Go package names with `acme.com/apps`. So a fully qualified import path for a package would be `"acme.com/apps/foo/bar"`.

Later in this chapter, we will see how package import paths can be used when integrating Go with source code repository services such as GitHub.

Add context to path

Next, as you devise a naming scheme for your package, use the package's path to add context to the name of your package name. The context in the name should start generic and get more specific from left to right. As an example, let us refer to the import paths for the power package (from the example earlier). The calculation of power values is split among three sub-packages shown as follows:

- `github.com/vladimirvivien/learning-go/ch06/`**power**
- `github.com/vladimirvivien/learning-go/ch06/`**power/ir**
- `github.com/vladimirvivien/learning-go/ch06/`**power/vr**

The parent path `power` contains package members with broader context. The sub-packages `ir` and `vr` contain members that are more specific with narrower contexts. This naming pattern is used heavily in Go, including the built-in packages such as the following:

- `crypto/md5`
- `net/http`
- `net/http/httputil`
- `reflect`

Note a package depth of one is a perfectly legitimate package name (see `reflect`) as long as it captures both context and the essence of what it does. Again, keep things simple. Avoid the temptation of nesting your packages beyond a depth of more than three inside your namespace. This temptation will be especially strong if you are a Java developer used to long nested package names.

Use short names

When reviewing the names of built-in Go packages, one thing you will notice is the brevity of the names compared to other languages. In Go, a package is considered to be a collection of code that implements a specific set of closely related functionalities. As such, the import paths of your packages should be succinct and reflect what they do without being excessively long. Our example source code exemplifies this by naming the package directory with short names such as volt, power, resistance, current. In their respective contexts, each directory name states exactly what the package does.

The short name rule is rigorously applied in the built-in packages of Go. For instance, following are several package names from Go's built-in packages: `log`, `http`, `xml`, and `zip`. Each name readily identifies the purpose of the package.

Short package names have the advantage of reducing keystrokes in larger code bases. However, having short and generic package names also has the disadvantage of being prone to import path clashes where developers in a large project (or developers of open source libraries) may end up using the same popular names (in other words, log, util, db, and so on) in their code. As we will see later in the chapter, this can be handled using named import paths.

Building packages

The Go tools reduce the complexity of compiling your code by applying certain conventions and sensible defaults. Although a full discussion of Go's build tool is beyond the scope of this section (or chapter), it is useful to understand the purpose and use of the build and install tools. In general, the use of the build and install tools is as follows:

$> go build [<package import path>]

The import path can be explicitly provided or omitted altogether. The build tool accepts the import path expressed as either fully qualified or relative paths. Given a properly setup workspace, the following are all equivalent ways to compile package volt, from the earlier example:

```
$> cd $GOPATH/src/github.com/vladimirvivien/learning-go
$> go build ./ch06/volt
$> cd $GOPATH/src/github.com/vladimirvivien/learning-go/ch06
$> go build ./volt
$> cd $GOPATH/src/github.com/vladimirvivien/learning-go/ch06/volt
$> go build .
$> cd $GOPATH/src/
$> go build github.com/vladimirvivien/learning-go/ch06/current /volt
```

The go build command above will compile all Go source files and their dependencies found in directory volt. Furthermore, it is also possible to build all of your packages and sub-packages in a given directory using the wildcard parameter appended to an import path shown as follows:

```
$> cd $GOPATH/src/github.com/vladimirvivien/learning-go/ch06
$> go build ./...
```

The previous will build all packages and sub-packages found in the directory $GOPATH/src/github.com/vladimirvivien/learning-go/ch06.

Installing a package

By default, the build command outputs its results into a tool-generated temporary directory that is lost after the build process completes. To actually generate a usable artifact, you must use the `install` tool to keep a copy of the compiled object files.

The `install` tool has the exact semantics as the build tool:

```
$> cd $GOPATH/src/github.com/vladimirvivien/learning-go/ch06
$> go install ./volt
```

In addition to compiling the code, it also saves and outputs the result to workspace location `$GOPATH/pkg` as shown in the following:

```
$GOPATH/pkg/linux_amd64/github.com/vladimirvivien/learning-go/
└── ch06
    └── volt.a
```

The generated object files (with the `.a` extension) allow the package to be reused and linked against other packages in the workspace. Later in the chapter, we will examine how to compile executable programs.

Package visibility

Regardless of the number of source files declared to be part of a package, all source code elements (types, variables, constants, and functions), declared at a package level, share a common scope. Therefore, the compiler will not allow an element identifier to be re-declared more than once in the entire package. Let us use the following code snippets to illustrate this point, assuming both source files are part of the same package `$GOPATH/src/foo`:

```
package foo                package foo
var (                      var bar struct{
   bar int = 12               x, y int
)                          }
func qux () {              func quux() {
   bar += bar                 bar = bar * bar
}                          }
foo/file1.go               foo/file2.go
```

Illegal variable identifier re-declaration

Although they are in two separate files, the declaration of variables with identifier `bar` is illegal in Go. Since the files are part of the same package, both identifiers have the same scope and therefore clash.

The same is true for function identifiers. Go does not support the overloading of function names within the same scope. Therefore, it is illegal to have a function identifier used more than once, regardless of the function's signature. If we assume the following code appears in two different source files within the same package, the following snippet would be illegal:

``
package foo
var (
   bar int = 12
)
func qux () {
   bar += bar
}
``
foo/file1.go
	``
	package foo
	var (
	   fooVal int = 12
	)
	func qux (inc int) int {
	   return fooVal += inc
	}
	``
	foo/file1.go

Illegal function identifier re-declaration

In the previous code snippets, function name identifier `qux` is used twice. The compiler will fail the compilation even though both functions have different signatures. The only way to fix this is to change the name.

Package member visibility

The usefulness of a package is its ability to expose its source elements to other packages. Controlling the visibility of elements of a package is simple and follows this rule: *capitalized identifiers are exported automatically*. This means any type, variable, constant, or function with capitalized identifiers is automatically visible from outside of the package where it is declared.

Referring to the Ohm's Law example, described earlier, the following illustrates this functionality from the package `resistor` (found in `github.com/vladimirvivien/learning-go/ch06/resistor`):

Code	Description

``
package resistor
func R(v, i float64)
float64 {
   return v / i
}
``
	Function R is automatically exported and can be accessed from other packages as: `resistor.R()`

``
package resistor
func recip(val
float64) float64 {
    return 1 / val
}
``
	Function identifier `recip` is in all lowercase and therefore is not exported. Though accessible within its own scope, the function will not be visible from within other packages.

It is worth restating that members within the same package are always visible to each other. In Go, there are no complicated visibility structures of private, friend, default, and so on, as is found in other languages. This frees the developer to concentrate on the solution being implemented rather than modeling visibility hierarchies.

Importing package

At this point, you should have a good understanding of what a package is, what it does, and how to create one. Now, let us see how to use a package to import and reuse its members. As you will find in several other languages, the keyword `import` is used to import source code elements from an external package. It allows the importing source to access exported elements found in the imported package (see the *Package scope and visibility* section earlier in the chapter). The general format for the import clause is as follows:

import [package name identifier] "<import path>"

Notice that the import path must be enclosed within double quotes. The `import` statement also supports an optional package identifier that can be used to explicitly name the imported package (discussed later). The import statement can also be written as an import block, as shown in the following format. This is useful where there are two or more import packages listed:

import (

[package name identifier] "<import path>"

)

The following source code snippet shows the import declaration block in the Ohm's Law examples introduced earlier:

```
import (
    "flag"
    "fmt"
    "os"

    "github.com/vladimirvivien/learning-go/ch06/current"
    "github.com/vladimirvivien/learning-go/ch06/power"
    "github.com/vladimirvivien/learning-go/ch06/power/ir"
    "github.com/vladimirvivien/learning-go/ch06/power/vr"
        "github.com/vladimirvivien/learning-go/ch06/volt"
)
```

golang.fyi/ch06/main.go

Often the name identifiers of imported packages are omitted, as done above. Go then applies the name of the last directory of the import path as the name identifier for the imported package, as shown, for some packages, in the following table:

Import Path	Package name
flag	flag
github.com/vladimirvivien/learning-go/ch06/current	current
github.com/vladimirvivien/learning-go/ch06/power/ir	ir
github.com/vladimirvivien/learning-go/ch06/volt	volt

The dot notation is used to access exported members of an imported package. In the following source code snippet, for instance, method `volt.V()` is invoked from imported package `"github.com/vladimirvivien/learning-go/ch06/volt"`:

```
...
import "github.com/vladimirvivien/learning-go/ch06/volt"
func main() {
    ...
    switch op {
    case "V", "v":
        val := volt.V(i, r)
    ...
}
```

golang.fyi/ch06/main.go

Specifying package identifiers

As was mentioned, an `import` declaration may explicitly declare a name identifier for the import, as shown in the following import snippet:

```
import res "github.com/vladimirvivien/learning-go/ch06/resistor"
```

Following the format described earlier, the name identifier is placed before the import path as shown in the preceding snippet. A named package can be used as a way to shorten or customize the name of a package. For instance, in a large source file with numerous usage of a certain package, this can be a welcome feature to reduce keystrokes.

Assigning a name to a package is also a way to avoid package identifier collisions in a given source file. It is conceivable to import two or more packages, with different import paths, that resolve to the same package names. As an example, you may need to log information with two different logging systems from different libraries, as illustrated in the following code snippet:

```
package foo
import (
    flog "github.com/woom/bat/logger"
    hlog "foo/bar/util/logger"
)

func main() {
    flog.Info("Programm started")
    err := doSomething()
    if err != nil {
      hlog.SubmitError("Error - unable to do something")
    }
}
```

As depicted in the previous snippet, both logging packages will resolve to the same name identifier of `"logger"` by default. To resolve this, at least one of the imported packages must be assigned a name identifier to resolve the name clash. In the previous example, both import paths were named with a meaningful name to help with code comprehension.

The dot identifier

A package can optionally be assigned a dot (period) as its identifier. When an `import` statement uses the dot identifier (`.`) for an import path, it causes members of the imported package to be merged in scope with that of the importing package. Therefore, imported members may be referenced without additional qualifiers. So if package `logger` is imported with the dot identifier in the following source code snippet, when accessing exported member function `SubmitError` from the logger package, the package name is omitted:

```
package foo

import (
    . "foo/bar/util/logger"
)

func main() {
    err := doSomething()
    if err != nil {
        SubmitError("Error - unable to do something")
    }
}
```

While this feature can help reduce repetitive keystrokes, it not an encouraged practice. By merging the scope of your packages, it becomes more likely to run into identifier collisions.

The blank identifier

When a package is imported, it is a requirement that one of its members be referenced in the importing code at least once. Failure to do so will result in a compilation error. While this feature helps simplify package dependency resolution, it can be cumbersome, especially in the early phase of a developing code.

Using the blank identifier (similar to variable declarations) causes the compiler to bypass this requirement. For instance, the following snippet imports the built-in package `fmt`; however, it never uses it in the subsequent source code:

```
package foo
import (
    _ "fmt"
    "foo/bar/util/logger"
)

func main() {
```

```
    err := doSomething()
    if err != nil {
        logger.Submit("Error - unable to do something")
    }
  }
}
```

A common idiom for the blank identifier is to load packages for their side effects. This relies on the initialization sequence of packages when they are imported (see the following *Package initialization* section). Using the blank identifier will cause an imported package to be initialized even when none of its members can referenced. This is used in contexts where the code is needed to silently run certain initialization sequences.

Package initialization

When a package is imported, it goes through a series of initialization sequences before its members are ready to be used. Package-level variables are initialized using dependency analysis that relies on lexical scope resolution, meaning variables are initialized based on their declaration order and their resolved transitive references to each other. For instance, in the following snippet, the resolved variable declaration order in package foo will be a, y, b, and x:

```
package foo
var x = a + b(a)
var a = 2
var b = func(i int) int {return y * i}
var y = 3
```

Go also makes use of a special function named init that takes no arguments and returns no result values. It is used to encapsulate custom initialization logic that is invoked when the package is imported. For instance, the following source code shows an init function used in the resistor package to initialize function variable Rpi:

```
package resistor

var Rpi func(float64, float64) float64

func init() {
    Rpi = func(p, i float64) float64 {
        return p / (i * i)
    }
}

func Rvp(v, p float64) float64 {
    return (v * v) / p
```

```
    }
```

golang.fyi/ch06/resistor/res_power.go

In the preceding code, the `init` function is invoked after the package-level variables are initialized. Therefore, the code in the `init` function can safely rely on the declared variable values to be in a stable state. The `init` function is special in the following ways:

- A package can have more than one `init` functions defined
- You cannot directly access declared `init` functions at runtime
- They are executed in the lexical order they appear within each source file
- The `init` function is a great way to inject logic into a package that gets executed prior to any other functions or methods.

Creating programs

So far in the book, you have learned how to create and bundle Go code as reusable packages. A package, however, cannot be executed as a standalone program. To create a program (also known as a command), you take a package and define an entry point of execution as follows:

- Declare (at least one) source file to be part of a special package called `main`
- Declare one function name `main()` to be used as the entry point of the program

The function `main` takes no argument nor returns any value. The following shows the abbreviated source code for the `main` package used in the Ohm's Law example (from earlier). It uses the package `flag`, from Go's standard library, to parse program arguments formatted as `flag`:

```
package main
import (
    "flag"
    "fmt"
    "os"

    "github.com/vladimirvivien/learning-go/ch06/current"
    "github.com/vladimirvivien/learning-go/ch06/power"
    "github.com/vladimirvivien/learning-go/ch06/power/ir"
    "github.com/vladimirvivien/learning-go/ch06/power/vr"
    res "github.com/vladimirvivien/learning-go/ch06/resistor"
    "github.com/vladimirvivien/learning-go/ch06/volt"
)
```

```go
var (
    op string
    v float64
    r float64
    i float64
    p float64

    usage = "Usage: ./circ <command> [arguments]\n" +
      "Valid command { V | Vpi | R | Rvp | I | Ivp |"+
     "P | Pir | Pvr }"
)

func init() {
    flag.Float64Var(&v, "v", 0.0, "Voltage value (volt)")
    flag.Float64Var(&r, "r", 0.0, "Resistance value (ohms)")
    flag.Float64Var(&i, "i", 0.0, "Current value (amp)")
    flag.Float64Var(&p, "p", 0.0, "Electrical power (watt)")
    flag.StringVar(&op, "op", "V", "Command - one of { V | Vpi |"+
     " R | Rvp | I | Ivp | P | Pir | Pvr }")
}

func main() {
    flag.Parse()
    // execute operation
    switch op {
    case "V", "v":
     val := volt.V(i, r)
     fmt.Printf("V = %0.2f * %0.2f = %0.2f volts\n", i, r, val)
    case "Vpi", "vpi":
    val := volt.Vpi(p, i)
     fmt.Printf("Vpi = %0.2f / %0.2f = %0.2f volts\n", p, i, val)
    case "R", "r":
    val := res.R(v, i))
     fmt.Printf("R = %0.2f / %0.2f = %0.2f Ohms\n", v, i, val)
    case "I", "i":
    val := current.I(v, r))
     fmt.Printf("I = %0.2f / %0.2f = %0.2f amps\n", v, r, val)
    ...
    default:
        fmt.Println(usage)
        os.Exit(1)
    }
}
```

golang.fyi/ch06/main.go

The previous listing shows the source code of the main package and the implementation of the function main which gets executed when the program runs. The Ohm's Law program accepts command-line arguments that specify which electrical operation to execute (see the following *Accessing program arguments* section). The function init is used to initialize parsing of the program flag values. The function main is set up as a big switch statement block to select the proper operation to execute based on the selected flags.

Accessing program arguments

When a program is executed, the Go runtime makes all command-line arguments available as a slice via package variable os.Args. For instance, when the following program is executed, it prints all command-line arguments passed to the program:

```
package main
import (
    "fmt"
    "os"
)

func main() {
    for _, arg := range os.Args {
        fmt.Println(arg)
    }
}
```

golang.fyi/ch06-args/hello.go

The following is the output of the program when it is invoked with the shown arguments:

```
$> go run hello.go hello world how are you?
/var/folders/.../exe/hello
hello
world
how
are
you?
```

Note that the command-line argument "hello world how are you?", placed after the program's name, is split as a space-delimited string. Position 0 in slice os.Args holds the fully qualified name of the program's binary path. The rest of the slice stores each item in the string respectively.

The `flag` package, from Go's standard library, uses this mechanism internally to provide processing of structured command-line arguments known as flags. In the Ohm's Law example listed earlier, the `flag` package is used to parse several flags, as listed in the following source snippet (extracted from the full listing earlier):

```
var (
    op string
    v float64
    r float64
    i float64
    p float64
)

func init() {
    flag.Float64Var(&v, "v", 0.0, "Voltage value (volt)")
    flag.Float64Var(&r, "r", 0.0, "Resistance value (ohms)")
    flag.Float64Var(&i, "i", 0.0, "Current value (amp)")
    flag.Float64Var(&p, "p", 0.0, "Electrical power (watt)")
    flag.StringVar(&op, "op", "V", "Command - one of { V | Vpi |"+
    " R | Rvp | I | Ivp | P | Pir | Pvr }")
}
func main(){
    flag.Parse()
    ...
}
```

The snippet shows function `init` used to parse and initialize expected flags `"v"`, `"i"`, `"p"`, and `"op"` (at runtime, each flag is prefixed with a minus sign). The initialization functions in package `flag` sets up the expected type, the default value, a flag description, and where to store the parsed value for the flag. The flag package also supports the special flag "help", used to provide helpful hints about each flag.

`flag.Parse()`, in the function `main`, is used to start the process of parsing any flags provided as command-line. For instance, to calculate the current of a circuit with 12 volts and 300 ohms, the program takes three flags and produces the shown output:

```
$> go run main.go -op I -v 12 -r 300
I = 12.00 / 300.00 = 0.04 amps
```

Building and installing programs

Building and installing Go programs follow the exact same procedures as building a regular package (as was discussed earlier in the *Building and installing packages* section). When you build source files of an executable Go program, the compiler will generate an executable binary file by transitively linking all the decencies declared in the `main` package. The build tool will name the output binary, by default the same name as the directory where the Go program source files are located.

For instance, in the Ohm's Law example, the file `main.go`, which is located in the directory `github.com/vladimirvivien/learning-go/ch06`, is declared to be part of the `main` package. The program can be built as shown in the following:

```
$> cd $GOPATH/src/github.com/vladimirvivien/learning-go/ch06
$> go build .
```

When the `main.go` source file is built, the build tool will generate a binary named `ch06` because the source code for the program is located in a directory with that name. You can control the name of the binary using the output flag `-o`. In the following example, the build tool creates a binary file named `ohms`.

```
$> cd $GOPATH/src/github.com/vladimirvivien/learning-go/ch06
$> go build -o ohms
```

Lastly, installing a Go program is done in exactly the same way as installing a regular package using the Go `install` command:

```
$> cd $GOPATH/src/github.com/vladimirvivien/learning-go/ch06
$> go install .
```

When a program is installed using the Go install command, it will be built, if necessary, and its generated binary will be saved in the `$GOPAHT/bin` directory. Adding the workspace `bin` directory to your OS's `$PATH` environment variable will make your Go program available for execution.

 Go-generated programs are statically linked binaries. They require no additional dependencies to be satisfied to run. However, Go-compiled binaries include the Go runtime. This is the set of operations that handle functionalities such as garbage collection, type information, reflection, goroutines scheduling, and panic management. While a comparable C program would be order of magnitudes smaller, Go's runtime comes with the tools that make Go enjoyable.

Remote packages

One of the tools that is shipped with Go allows programmers to retrieve packages directly from remote source code repositories. Go, by default, readily supports integration with version control systems including the following:

- Git (`git`, `http://git-scm.com/`)
- Mercurial (`hg`, `http://mercurial.selenic.com/`)
- Subversion (`svn`, `http://subversion.apache.org/`)
- Bazaar (`bzr`, `http://bazaar.canonical.com/`)

 In order for Go to pull package source code from a remote repository, you must have a client for that version control system installed as a command on your operating system's execution path. Under the cover, Go launches the client to interact with the source code repository server.

The `get` command-line tool allows programmers to retrieve remote packages using a fully qualified project path as the import path for the package. Once the package is downloaded, it can be imported for use in local source files. For instance, if you wanted to include one of the packages from the Ohm's Law example from preceding snippet, you would issue the following command from the command-line:

```
$> go get github.com/vladimirvivien/learning-go/ch06/volt
```

The `go get` tool will download the specified import path along with all referenced dependencies. The tool will then build and install the package artifacts in `$GOPATH/pkg`. If the `import` path happens to be a program, go get will generate the binary in `$GOPATH/bin` as well as any referenced packages in `$GOPATH/pkg`.

Summary

This chapter presented an extensive look into the notion of source code organization and packages. Readers learned about the Go workspace and the import path. Readers were also introduced to the creation of packages and how to import packages to achieve code reusability. The chapter introduced mechanisms such as visibility of imported members and package initialization. The last portion of the chapter discussed the steps that are necessary to create an executable Go program from packaged code.

This was a lengthy chapter, and deservedly so to do justice to such a broad topic as package creation and management in Go. The next chapter returns to the Go types discussion with a detailed treatment of the composite types, such as array, slice, struct, and map.

7
Composite Types

In prior chapters, you may have caught glimpses of the use of composite types such as arrays, slices, maps, and structs in some of the sample code. While early exposure to these types may have left you curious, rest assured in this chapter you will get a chance to learn all about these composite types. This chapter continues what started in `Chapter 4`, *Data Types*, with discussions covering the following topics:

- The array type
- The slice type
- The map type
- The struct type

The array type

As you would find in other languages, Go arrays are containers for storing sequenced values of the same type that are numerically indexed. The following code snippet shows samples of variables that are assigned array types:

```
var val [100]int
var days [7]string
var truth [256]bool
var histogram [5]map[string]int
```

golang.fyi/ch07/arrtypes.go

Notice the types that are assigned to each variable in the previous example are specified using the following type format:

[<length>]<element_type>

The type definition of an array is composed of its length, enclosed within brackets, followed by the type of its stored elements. For instance, the `days` variable is assigned a type `[7]string`. This is an important distinction as Go's type system considers two arrays, storing the same type of elements but with different lengths, to be of different types. The following code illustrates this situation:

```
var days [7]string
var weekdays [5]string
```

Even though both variables are arrays with elements of type `string`, the type system considers the `days` and `weekdays` variables as different types.

 Later in the chapter, you will see how this type restriction is mitigated with the use of the slice type instead of arrays.

Array types can be defined to be multi-dimensions. This is done by combining and nesting the definition of one-dimensional array types as shown in the following snippet:

```
var board [4][2]int
var matrix [2][2][2][2] byte
```

golang.fyi/ch07/arrtypes.go

Go does not have a separate type for multi-dimensional arrays. An array with more than one dimension is composed of one-dimensional arrays that are nested within each other. The next section covers how single and multi-dimensional arrays are initialized.

Array initialization

When an array variable is not explicitly initialized, all of its elements will be assigned the zero-value for the declared type of the elements. An array can be initialized with a composite literal value with the following general format:

<array_type>{<comma-separated list of element values>}

The literal value for an array is composed of the array type definition (discussed in the previous section) followed by a set of comma-separated values, enclosed in curly brackets, as illustrated by the following code snippet, which shows several arrays being declared and initialized:

```
var val [100]int = [100]int{44,72,12,55,64,1,4,90,13,54}
var days [7]string = [7]string{
    "Monday",
    "Tuesday",
    "Wednesday",
    "Thursday",
    "Friday",
    "Saturday",
    "Sunday",
}
var truth = [256]bool{true}
var histogram = [5]map[string]int {
    map[string]int{"A":12,"B":1, "D":15},
    map[string]int{"man":1344,"women":844, "children":577,...},
}
```

golang.fyi/ch07/arrinit.go

The number of elements in the literal must be less than or equal to the size declared in the array type. If the array defined is multi-dimensional, it can be initialized using literal values by nesting each dimension within the enclosing brackets of another, as shown in the following example snippets:

```
var board = [4][2]int{
    {33, 23},
    {62, 2},
    {23, 4},
    {51, 88},
}
var matrix = [2][2][2][2]byte{
    {{{4, 4}, {3, 5}}, {{55, 12}, {22, 4}}},
    {{{2, 2}, {7, 9}}, {{43, 0}, {88, 7}}},
}
```

golang.fyi/ch07/arrinit.go

The following snippet shows two additional ways that array literals can be specified. The length of an array may be omitted and replaced by ellipses during initialization. The following will assign type [5]string to variable weekdays:

```
var weekdays = [...]string{
    "Monday",
    "Tuesday",
    "Wednesday",
    "Thursday",
    "Friday",
}
```

The literal value of an array can also be indexed. This is useful if you want to initialize only certain array elements while allowing others to be initialized with their natural zero-value. The following specifies the initial values for elements at positions 0, 2, 4, 6, 8. The remaining elements will be assigned the empty string:

```
var msg = [12]rune{0: 'H', 2: 'E', 4: 'L', 6: 'O', 8: '!'}
```

Declaring named array types

The type of an array can become awkward for reuse. For each declaration, it becomes necessary to repeat the declaration, which can be error prone. The way to handle this idiomatically is to alias array types using type declarations. To illustrate how this works, the following code snippet declares a new named type, matrix, using a multi-dimension array as its underlying type:

```
type matrix [2][2][2][2]byte

func main() {
    var mat1 matrix
    mat1 = initMat()
    fmt.Println(mat1)
}

func initMat() matrix {
    return matrix{
            {{{4, 4}, {3, 5}}, {{55, 12}, {22, 4}}},
            {{{2, 2}, {7, 9}}, {{43, 0}, {88, 7}}},
    }
}
```

golang.fyi/ch07/arrtype_dec.go

The declared named type, `matrix`, can be used in all contexts where its underlying array type is used. This allows a simplified syntax that promotes reuse of the complex array type.

Using arrays

Arrays are static entities that cannot grow or shrink in size once they are declared with a specified length. Arrays are a great option when a program needs to allocate a block of sequential memory of a predefined size. When a variable of an array type is declared, it is ready to be used without any further allocation semantics.

So the following declaration of the `image` variable would allocate a memory block composed of 256 adjacent `int` values initialized with zeroes, as shown in the following figure:

```
var image [256]byte
```

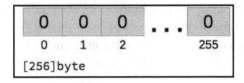

Similar to C and Java, Go uses the square brackets index expression to access values stored in an array variable. This is done by specifying the variable identifier followed by an index of the element enclosed within the square brackets, as shown in the following code sample:

```
p := [5]int{122,6,23,44,6}
p[4] = 82
fmt.Println(p[0])
```

The previous code updates the fifth element and prints the first element in the array.

Array length and capacity

The built-in `len` function returns the declared length of an array type. The built-in `cap` function can be used on an array to return its capacity. For instance, in the following source snippet, the array `seven` of type `[7]string` will return 7 as its length and capacity:

```go
func main() {
    seven := [7]string{"grumpy", "sleepy", "bashful"}
    fmt.Println(len(seven), cap(seven))
}
```

For arrays, the `cap()` function always returns the same value as `len()`. This is because the maximum capacity of an array value is its declared length. The capacity function is better suited for use with the slice type (discussed later in the chapter).

Array traversal

Array traversal can be done using the traditional `for` statement or with the more idiomatic `for...range` statement. The following snippet of code shows array traversal done with both the `for` statement, to initialize an array with random numbers in `init()`, and the `for range` statement used to realize the `max()` function:

```go
const size = 1000
var nums [size]int

func init() {
    rand.Seed(time.Now().UnixNano())
    for i := 0; i < size; i++ {
        nums[i] = rand.Intn(10000)
    }
}

func max(nums [size]int) int {
    temp := nums[0]
    for _, val := range nums {
        if val > temp {
            temp = val
        }
    }
    return temp
}
```

golang.fyi/ch07/arrmax_iter.go

In the traditional `for` statement, the loop's index variable `i` is used to access the value of the array using the index expression `num[i]`. In the `for...range` statement, in the `max` function, the iterated value is stored in the `val` variable with each pass of the loop and the index is ignored (assigned to the blank identifier). If you do not understand how *for* statements work, refer to `Chapter 3`, *Go Control Flow,* for a thorough explanation of the mechanics of loops in Go.

Array as parameters

Arrays values are treated as a single unit. An array variable is not a pointer to a location in memory, but rather represents the entire block of memory containing the array elements. This has the implications of creating a new copy of an array value when the array variable is reassigned or passed in as a function parameter.

This could have unwanted side effects on memory consumption for a program. One fix for is to use pointer types to reference array values. In the following example, a named type, `numbers`, is declared to represent array type `[1024 * 1024]]int`. Instead of taking the array value directly as parameters, functions `initialize()` and `max()` receive a pointer of type `*numbers`, as shown in the following source snippet:

```
type numbers [1024 * 1024]int
func initialize(nums *numbers) {
    rand.Seed(time.Now().UnixNano())
    for i := 0; i < size; i++ {
        nums[i] = rand.Intn(10000)
    }
}
func max(nums *numbers) int {
    temp := nums[0]
    for _, val := range nums {
        if val > temp {
            temp = val
        }
    }
    return temp
}
func main() {
    var nums *numbers = new(numbers)
    initialize(nums)
}
```

golang.fyi/ch07/arrptr.go

The previous code uses the built-in function `new(numbers)` to initialize the array elements with their zero values and obtain a pointer to that array as shown in `main()`. So when the functions `initialize` and `max` are invoked, they will receive the address (a copy of it) of the array instead of the entire 100K-sized array.

Before changing the subject, it should be noted that a composite literal array value can be initialized with the address operator `&` to initialize and return a pointer for the array, as shown in the following example. In the snippet, composite literal `&galaxies{...}` returns pointer `*galaxies`, initialized with the specified element values:

```
type galaxies [14]string
func main() {
    namedGalaxies = &galaxies{
        "Andromeda",
        "Black Eye",
        "Bode's",
        ...
    }
    printGalaxies(namedGalaxies)
}
```

golang.fyi/ch07/arraddr.go

The array type is a low-level storage construct in Go. Arrays, for instance, are usually used as the basis for storage primitives, where there are strict memory allocation requirements to minimize space consumption. In more common cases however, the slice, covered in the next section, is often used as the more idiomatic way of working with sequenced indexed collections.

The slice type

The slice type is commonly used as the idiomatic construct for indexed data in Go. The slice is more flexible and has many more interesting characteristics than arrays. The slice itself is a composite type with semantics similar to arrays. In fact, a slice uses an array as its underlying data storage mechanism. The general form of a slice type is given as follows:

[ ]<element_type>

The one obvious difference between a slice and an array type is omission of the size in the type declaration, as shown in the following examples:

```
var (
    image []byte
```

```
    ids []string
    vector []float64
    months []string
    q1 []string
    histogram []map[string]int // slice of map (see map later)
)
```

golang.fyi/ch07/slicetypes.go

The missing size attribute in the slice type indicates the following:

- Unlike arrays, the size of a slice is not fixed
- A slice type represents all sets of the specified element type

This means a slice can theoretically grow unbounded (though in practice this is not true as the slice is backed by an underlying bounded array). A slice of a given element type is considered to be the same type regardless of its underlying size. This removes the restriction found in arrays where the size determines the type.

For instance, the following variables, `months` and `q1`, have the same type of `[]string` and will compile with no problem:

```
var (
    months []string
    q1 []string
)
func print(strs []string){ ... }
func main() {
    print(months)
    print(q1)
}
```

golang.fyi/ch07/slicetypes.go

Similar to arrays, slice types may be nested to create multi-dimensional slices, as shown in the following code snippet. Each dimension can independently have its own size and must be initialized individually:

```
var(
    board [][]int
    graph [][][][]int
)
```

Slice initialization

A slice is represented by the type system as a value (the next section explores the internal representation of a slice). However, unlike the array type, an uninitialized slice has a zero value of *nil*, which means any attempt to access elements of an uninitialized slice will cause a program to panic.

One of the simplest ways to initialize a slice is with a composite literal value using the following format (similar to an array):

<slice_type>{<comma-separated list of element values>}

The literal value for a slice is composed of the slice type followed by a set of comma-separated values, enclosed in curly brackets, that are assigned to the elements of the slice. The following code snippet illustrates several slice variables initialized with composite literal values:

```
var (
    ids []string = []string{"fe225", "ac144", "3b12c"}
    vector = []float64{12.4, 44, 126, 2, 11.5}
    months = []string {
        "Jan", "Feb", "Mar", "Apr",
        "May", "Jun", "Jul", "Aug",
        "Sep", "Oct", "Nov", "Dec",
    }
    // slice of map type (maps are covered later)
    tables = []map[string][]int {
        {
            "age":{53, 13, 5, 55, 45, 62, 34, 7},
            "pay":{124, 66, 777, 531, 933, 231},
        },
    }
    graph  = [][][][]int{
        {{{44}, {3, 5}}, {{55, 12, 3}, {22, 4}}},
        {{{22, 12, 9, 19}, {7, 9}}, {{43, 0, 44, 12}, {7}}},
    }
)
```

golang.fyi/ch07/sliceinit.go

As mentioned, the composite literal value of a slice is expressed using a similar form as the array. However, the number of elements provided in the literal is not bounded by a fixed size. This implies that the literal can be as large as needed. Under the cover though, Go creates and manages an array of appropriate size to store the values expressed in the literal.

Slice representation

Earlier it was mentioned that the slice value uses an underlying array to store data. The name *slice*, in fact, is a reference to a slice of data segment from the array. Internally, a slice is represented by a composite value with the followings three attributes:

Attribute	Description
a *pointer*	The pointer is the address of the first element of the slice stored in an underlying array. When the slice value is uninitialized, its pointer value is nil, indicating that it is not pointing to an array yet. Go uses the pointer as the zero value of the slice itself. An uninitialized slice will return nil as its zero value. However, the slice value is not treated as a reference value by the type system. This means certain functions can be applied to a nil slice while others will cause a panic. Once a slice is created, the pointer does not change. To point to a different starting point, a new slice must be created.
a *length*	The length indicates the number of contiguous elements that can be accessed starting with the first element. It is a dynamic value that can grow up to the capacity of the slice (see capacity next). The length of a slice is always less than or equal to its capacity. Attempts to access elements beyond the length of a slice, without resizing, will result in a panic. This is true even when the capacity is larger than the length.
a *capacity*	The capacity of a slice is the maximum number of elements that may be stored in the slice, starting from its first element. The capacity of a slice is bounded by the length of the underlying array.

So, when the following variable `halfyr` is initialized as shown:

```
halfyr := []string{"Jan","Feb","Mar","Apr","May","Jun"}
```

It will be stored in an array of type `[6]string` with a pointer to the first element, a length, and a capacity of 6, as represented graphically in the following figure:

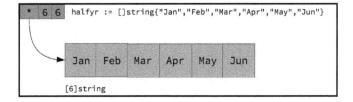

Slicing

Another way to create a slice value is by slicing an existing array or another slice value (or pointers to these values). Go provides an indexing format that makes it easy to express the slicing operation, as follows:

<slice or array value>[<low_index>:<high_index>]

The slicing expression uses the [:] operator to specify the low and high bound indices, separated by a colon, for the slice segment.

- The *low* value is the zero-based index where the slice segment starts
- The *high* value is the nth element offset where the segment stops

The following table shows examples of slice expressions by re-slicing the following value:
`halfyr := []string{"Jan","Feb","Mar","Apr","May","Jun"}.`

Expression	Description

`all :=`
`halfyr[:]`
	Omitting the low and high indices in the expression is equivalent to the following:
	`all := halfyr[0 : 6]`
	This produces a new slice segment equal to the original, which starts at index position 0 and stops at offset position 6:
	`["Jan","Feb","Mar","Apr","May","Jun"]`

`q1 :=` `halfyr[:3]`	Here the slice expression omits low index value and specifies a slice segment length of 3. It returns new slice, `["Jan","Feb","Mar"]`.
`q2 :=` `halfyr[3:]`	This creates a new slice segment with the last three elements by specifying the staring index position of 3 and omitting the high bound index value, which defaults to 6.
`mapr :=` `halfyr[2:4]`	To clear any confusion about slicing expressions, this example shows how to create a new slice with the months `"Mar"` and `"Apr"`. This returns a slice with the value `["Mar","Apr"]`.

Slicing a slice

Slicing an existing slice or array value does not create a new underlying array. The new slice creates new pointer location to the underlying array. For instance, the following code shows the slicing of the slice value `halfyr` into two additional slices:

```
var (
    halfyr = []string{
        "Jan", "Feb", "Mar",
        "Apr", "May", "Jun",
    }

    q1 = halfyr[:3]
    q2 = halfyr[3:]
)
```

golang.fyi/ch07/slice_reslice.go

The backing array may have many slices projecting a particular view of its data. The following figure illustrates how slicing in the previous code may be represented visually:

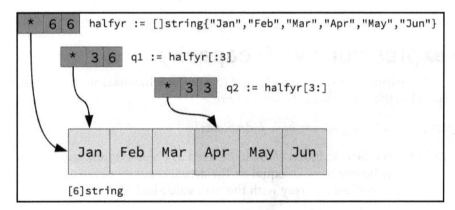

Notice that both slices q1 and q2 are pointing to different elements in the same underlying array. Slice q1 has an initial length of 3 with a capacity of 6. This implies q1 can be resized up to 6 elements in total. Slice q2, however, has a size of 3 and a capacity of 3 and cannot grow beyond its initial size (slice resizing is covered later).

Slicing an array

As mentioned, an array can also be sliced directly. When that is the case, the provided array value becomes the underlying array. The capacity and the length the slices will be calculated using the provided array. The following source snippet shows the slicing of an existing array value called months:

```go
var (
    months [12]string = [12]string{
        "Jan", "Feb", "Mar", "Apr", "May", "Jun",
        "Jul", "Aug", "Sep", "Oct", "Nov", "Dec",
    }

    halfyr = months[:6]
    q1 = halfyr[:3]
    q2 = halfyr[3:6]
    q3 = months[6:9]
    q4 = months[9:]
)
```

golang.fyi/ch07/slice_reslice_arr.go

Slice expressions with capacity

Lastly, Go's slice expression supports a longer form where the maximum capacity of the slice is included in the expression, as shown here:

<slice_or_array_value>[<low_index>:<high_index>:max]

The *max* attribute specifies the index value to be used as the maximum capacity of the new slice. That value may be less than, or equal to, the actual capacity of the underlying array. The following example slices an array with the max value included:

```go
var (
    months [12]string = [12]string{
        "Jan", "Feb", "Mar", "Apr", "May", "Jun",
        "Jul", "Aug", "Sep", "Oct", "Nov", "Dec",
    }
    summer1 = months[6:9:9]
)
```

golang.fyi/ch07/slice_reslice_arr.go

The previous code snippet creates a new slice value `summer1` with size 3 (starting at index position 6 to 9). The max index is set to position 9, which means the slice has a capacity of 3. If the max was not specified, the maximum capacity would automatically be set to the last position of the underlying array as before.

Making a slice

A slice can be initialized at runtime using the built-in function `make`. This function creates a new slice value and initializes its elements with the zero value of the element type. An uninitialized slice has a nil zero value an indication that it is not pointing an underlying array. Without an explicitly initialization, with a composite literal value or using the `make()` function, attempts to access elements of a slice will cause a panic. The following snippet reworks the previous example to use the `make()` function to initialize the slice:

```
func main() {
    months := make([]string, 6)
    ...
}
```

golang.fyi/ch07/slicemake.go

The `make()` function takes as an argument the type of the slice to be initialized and an initial size for the slice. Then it returns a slice value. In the previous snippet, `make()` does the followings:

- Creates an underlying array of type `[6]string`
- Creates the slice value with length and capacity of 6
- Returns a slice value (not a pointer)

After initialization with the `make()` function, access to a legal index position will return the zero value for the slice element instead of causing a program panic. The `make()` function can take an optional third parameter that specifies the maximum capacity of the slice, as shown in the following example:

```
func main() {
    months := make([]string, 6, 12)
    ...
}
```

golang.fyi/ch07/slicemake2.go

The preceding snippet will initialize the `months` variable with a slice value with an initial length of 6 and a maximum capacity of 12.

Using slices

The simplest operation to do with a slice value is to access its elements. As was mentioned, slices use index notation to access its elements similar to arrays. The following example accesses element at index position 0 and updates to 15:

```go
func main () {
    h := []float64{12.5, 18.4, 7.0}
    h[0] = 15
    fmt.Println(h[0])
    ...
}
```

golang.fyi/ch07/slice_use.go

When the program runs, it prints the updated value using index expression `h[0]` to retrieve the value of the item at position 0. Note that the slice expression with only the index number, `h[0]` for instance, returns the value of the item at that position. When, however, the expression includes a colon, say `h[2:]` or `h[:6]`, that expression returns a new slice.

Slice traversal can be done using the traditional `for` statement or with the, more idiomatic, `for...range` statement as shown in the following code snippets:

```go
func scale(factor float64, vector []float64) []float64 {
    for i := range vector {
        vector[i] *= factor
    }
    return vector
}

func contains(val float64, numbers []float64) bool {
    for _, num := range numbers {
        if num == val {
            return true
        }
    }
    return false
}
```

golang.fyi/ch07/slice_loop.go

In the previous code snippet, function `scale` uses index variable `i` to update the values in slice `factor` directly, while function `contains` uses the iteration-emitted value stored in `num` to access the slice element. If you need further detail on the `for...range` statement, see `Chapter 3`, *Go Control Flow*.

Slices as parameters

When a function receives a slice as its parameter, the internal pointer of that slice points to the underlying array of the slice. Therefore, all updates to the slice, within the function, will be seen by the function's caller. For instance, in the following code snippet, all changes to the `vector` parameter will be seen by the caller of function `scale`:

```go
func scale(factor float64, vector []float64) {
    for i := range vector {
        vector[i] *= factor
    }
}
```

golang.fyi/ch07/slice_loop.go

Length and capacity

Go provides two built-in functions to query the length and capacity attributes of a slice. Given a slice, its length and maximum capacity can be queried, using the `len` and `cap` functions respectively, as shown in the following example:

```go
func main() {
    var vector []float64
    fmt.Println(len(vector)) // prints 0, no panic
    h := make([]float64, 4, 10)
    fmt.Println(len(h), ",", cap(h))
}
```

Recall that a slice is a value (not a pointer) that has a nil as its zero-value. Therefore, the code is able to query the length (and capacity) of an uninitialized slice without causing a panic at runtime.

Appending to slices

The one indispensable feature of slice types is their ability to dynamically grow. By default, a slice has a static length and capacity. Any attempt to access an index beyond that limit will cause a panic. Go makes available the built-in variadic function `append` to dynamically add new values to a specified slice, growing its lengths and capacity, as necessary. The following code snippet shows how that is done:

```
func main() {
   months := make([]string, 3, 3)
   months = append(months, "Jan", "Feb", "March",
    "Apr", "May", "June")
   months = append(months, []string{"Jul", "Aug", "Sep"}...)
   months = append(months, "Oct", "Nov", "Dec")
   fmt.Println(len(months), cap(months), months)
}
```

golang.fyi/ch07/slice_append.go

The previous snippet starts with a slice with a size and capacity of 3. The `append` function is used to dynamically add new values to the slice beyond its initial size and capacity. Internally, `append` will attempt to fit the appended values within the target slice. If the slice has not been initialized or has an inadequate capacity, append will allocate a new underlying array, to store the values of the updated slice.

Copying slices

Recall that assigning or slicing an existing slice value simply creates a new slice value pointing to the same underlying array structure. Go offers the `copy` function, which returns a deep copy of the slice along with a new underlying array. The following snippet shows a `clone()` function, which makes a new copy of a slice of numbers:

```
func clone(v []float64) (result []float64) {
   result = make([]float64, len(v), cap(v))
   copy(result, v)
   return
}
```

golang.fyi/ch07/slice_use.go

In the previous snippet, the `copy` function copies the content of v slice into `result`. Both source and target slices must be the same size and of the same type or the copy operation will fail.

Strings as slices

Internally, the string type is implemented as a slice using a composite value that points to an underlying array of rune. This affords the string type the same idiomatic treatment given to slices. For instance, the following code snippet uses index expressions to extract slices of strings from a given string value:

```
func main() {
    msg := "Bobsayshelloworld!"
    fmt.Println(
            msg[:3], msg[3:7], msg[7:12],
            msg[12:17], msg[len(msg)-1:],
    )
}
```

golang.fyi/ch07/slice_string.go

The slice expression on a string will return a new string value pointing to its underlying array of runes. The string values can be converted to a slice of byte (or slice of rune) as shown in the following function snippet, which sorts the characters of a given string:

```
func sort(str string) string {
    bytes := []byte(str)
    var temp byte
    for i := range bytes {
            for j := i + 1; j < len(bytes); j++ {
                    if bytes[j] < bytes[i] {
                            temp = bytes[i]
                            bytes[i], bytes[j] = bytes[j], temp
                    }
            }
    }
    return string(bytes)
}
```

golang.fyi/ch07/slice_string.go

The previous code shows the explicit conversion of a slice of bytes to a string value. Note that each character may be accessed using the index expression.

The map type

The Go map is a composite type that is used as containers for storing unordered elements of the same type indexed by an arbitrary key value. The following code snippet shows a variety of map variables declarations with a variety of key types:

```
var (
    legends map[int]string
    histogram map[string]int
    calibration map[float64]bool
    matrix map[[2][2]int]bool      // map with array key type
    table map[string][]string      // map of string slices

    // map (with struct key) of map of string
    log map[struct{name string}]map[string]string
)
```

golang.fyi/ch07/maptypes.go

The previous code snippet shows several variables declared as maps of different types with a variety of key types. In general, map type is specified as follows:

map[<key_type>]<element_type>

The *key* specifies the type of a value that will be used to index the stored elements of the map. Unlike arrays and slices, map keys can be of any type, not just `int`. Map keys, however, must be of types that are comparable including numeric, string, Boolean, pointers, arrays, struct, and interface types (see `Chapter 4`, *Data Types*, for discussion on comparable types).

Map initialization

Similar to a slice, a map manages an underlying data structure, opaque to its user, to store its values. An uninitialized map has a nil zero-value as well. Attempts to insert into an uninitialized map will result in a program panic. Unlike a slice, however, it is possible to access elements from a nil map, which will return the zero value of the element.

Like other composite types, maps may be initialized using a composite literal value of the following form:

<map_type>{<comma-separated list of key:value pairs>}

The following snippet shows variable initialization with map composite literals:

```
var (
    histogram map[string]int = map[string]int{
        "Jan":100, "Feb":445, "Mar":514, "Apr":233,
        "May":321, "Jun":644, "Jul":113, "Aug":734,
        "Sep":553, "Oct":344, "Nov":831, "Dec":312,
    }

    table = map[string][]int {
        "Men":[]int{32, 55, 12, 55, 42, 53},
        "Women":[]int{44, 42, 23, 41, 65, 44},
    }
)
```

golang.fyi/ch07/mapinit.go

The literal mapped values are specified using a colon-separated pair of key and value as shown in the previous example. The type of each key and value pair must match that of the declared elements in the map.

Making Maps

Similar to a slice, a map value can also be initialized using the *make* function. Using the make function initializes the underlying storage allowing data to be inserted in the map as shown in the following short snippet:

```
func main() {
    hist := make(map[int]string)
    hist["Jan"] = 100
    hist["Feb"] = 445
    hist["Mar"] = 514
    ...
}
```

golang.fyi/ch07/maptypes.go

The make function takes as argument the type of the map and it returns an initialized map. In the previous example, the make function will initialize a map of type map[int]string. The make function can optionally take a second parameter to specify the capacity of the map. However, a map will continue to grow as needed ignoring the initial capacity specified.

Using maps

As is done with slice and arrays, index expressions are used to access and update the elements stored in maps. To set or update a `map` element, use the index expression, on the left side of an assignment, to specify the key of the element to update. The following snippet shows an element with the `"Jan"` key being updated with the value `100`:

```
hist := make(map[int]string)
hist["Jan"] = 100
```

Accessing an element with a given key is done with an index expression, placed on the right side of an assignment, as shown in the following example, where the value indexed with the `"Mar"` key is assigned the `val` variable:

```
val := hist["Mar"]
```

Earlier it was mentioned that accessing a non-existent key will return the zero-value for that element. For instance, the previous code would return 0 if the element with the key `"Mar"` does not exist in the map. As you can imagine, this can be a problem. How would you know whether you are getting an actual value or the zero-value? Fortunately, Go provides a way to explicitly test for the absence of an element by returning an optional Boolean value as part of the result of an index expression, as shown in the following snippet:

```
func save(store map[string]int, key string, value int) {
    val, ok := store[key]
    if !ok {
        store[key] = value
    }else{
        panic(fmt.Sprintf("Slot %d taken", val))
    }
}
```

golang.fyi/ch07/map_use.go

The function in the preceding snippet tests the existence of a key before updating its value. Called the *comma-ok* idiom, the Boolean value stored in the `ok` variable is set to false when the value is not actually found. This allows the code to distinguish between the absence of a key and the zero value of the element.

Map traversal

The `for...range` loop statement can be used to walk the content of a map value. The `range` expression emits values for both key and element values with each iteration. The following code snippet shows the traversal of map `hist`:

```
for key, val := range hist {
    adjVal := int(float64(val) * 0.100)
    fmt.Printf("%s (%d):", key, val)
    for i := 0; i < adjVal; i++ {
        fmt.Print(".")
    }
    fmt.Println()
}
```

golang.fyi/ch07/map_use.go

Each iteration returns a key and its associated element value. Iteration order, however, is not guaranteed. The internal map iterator may traverse the map in a different order with each run of the program. In order to maintain a predictable traversal order, keep (or generate) a copy of the keys in a separate structure, such as a slice for instance. During traversal, range over the slice of keys to traverse in a predictable manner.

You should be aware that update done to the emitted value during the iteration will be lost. Instead, use an index expression, such as `hist[key]` to update an element during iteration. For details on `for...range` loop, refer to `Chapter 3`, *Go Control Flow*, for a thorough explanation of Go `for` loops.

Map functions

Besides the `make` function, discussed earlier, map types support two additional functions discussed in the following table:

Function	Description

len(map)	As with other composite types, the built-in `len()` function returns the number of entries in a map. For instance, the following would print **3**:
	`h := map[int]bool{3:true, 7:false, 9:false}`
	`fmt.Println(len(h))`
	The `len` function will return zero for an uninitialized map.

delete(map, key)	The built-in `delete` function deletes an element from a given map associated with the provided key. The following code snippet would print **2**:
	`h := map[int]bool{3:true, 7:false, 9:false}`
	`delete(h,7)`
	`fmt.Println(len(h))`

Maps as parameters

Because a map maintains an internal pointer to its backing storage structure, all updates to map parameter within a called function will be seen by the caller once the function returns. The following sample shows a call to the `remove` function to change the content of a map. The passed variable, `hist`, will reflect the change once the `remove` function returns:

```
func main() {
    hist := make(map[string]int)
    hist["Jun"] = 644
    hist["Jul"] = 113
    remove(hit, "Jun")
    len(hist) // returns 1
}
func remove(store map[string]int, key string) error {
    _, ok := store[key]
    if !ok {
        return fmt.Errorf("Key not found")
    }
    delete(store, key)
    return nil
}
```

golang.fyi/ch07/map_use.go

The struct type

The last type discussed in this chapter is Go's `struct`. It is a composite type that serves as a container for other named types known as fields. The following code snippet shows several variables declared as structs:

```
var(
    empty struct{}
    car struct{make, model string}
    currency struct{name, country string; code int}
    node struct{
        edges []string
        weight int
    }
    person struct{
        name string
        address struct{
            street string
            city, state string
            postal string
        }
    }
)
```

golang.fyi/ch07/structtypes.go

Note that the struct type has the following general format:

struct{<field declaration set>}

The `struct` type is constructed by specifying the keyword `struct` followed by a set of field declarations enclosed within curly brackets. In its most common form, a field is a unique identifier with an assigned type which follows Go's variable declaration conventions as shown in the previous code snippet (`struct` also support anonymous fields, covered later).

It is crucial to understand that the type definition for a `struct` includes all of its declared fields. For instance, the type for the person variable (see earlier code snippet) is the entire set of fields in the declaration `struct { name string; address struct { street string; city string; state string; postal string }}`. Therefore, any variable or expression requiring that type must repeat that long declaration. We will see later how that is mitigated by using named types for `struct`.

Accessing struct fields

A struct uses a *selector expression* (or dot notation) to access the values stored in fields. For instance, the following would print the value of the `name` field of the person struct variable from the previous code snippet:

```
fmt.Pritnln(person.name)
```

Selectors can be chained to access fields that are nested inside a struct. The following snippet would print the street and city for the nested address value of a `person` variable:

```
fmt.Pritnln(person.address.street)
fmt.Pritnln(person.address.city)
```

Struct initialization

Similar to arrays, structs are pure values with no additional underlying storage structure. The fields for an uninitialized struct are assigned their respective zero values. This means an uninitialized struct requires no further allocation and is ready to be used.

Nevertheless, a struct variable can be explicitly initialized using a composite literal of the following form:

<struct_type>{<positional or named field values>}

The composite literal value for a struct can be initialized by a set of field values specified by their respective positions. Using this approach, all field values must be provided, to match their respective declared types, as shown in the following snippet:

```
var (
    currency = struct{
        name, country string
        code int
    }{
        "USD", "United States",
        840,
    }
    ...
)
```

golang.fyi/ch07/structinit.go

In the previous struct literal, all field values of the `struct` are provided, matching their declared field types. Alternatively, the composite literal value of a `struct` can be specified using a field indices and their associated value. As before, the index (the field name) and its value is separated by a colon, as shown in the following snippet:

```
var(
    car = struct{make, model string}{make:"Ford", model:"F150"}
    node = struct{
            edges []string
            weight int
    }{
            edges: []string{"north", "south", "west"},
    }
    ...
)
```

golang.fyi/ch07/structinit.go

As you can see, field values of the composite literal can be selectively specified when the index and its value are provided. For instance, in the initialization of the node variable, the edge field is initialized while `weight` is omitted.

Declaring named struct types

Attempting to reuse struct types can get unwieldy fast. For instance, having to write `struct { name string; address struct { street string; city string; state string; postal string }}` to express a struct type, every time it is needed, would not scale, would be error prone, and would make for grumpy Go developers. Luckily, the proper idiom to fix this is to use named types, as illustrated in the following source code snippet:

```
type person struct {
    name        string
    address address
}

type address struct {
    street          string
    city, state string
    postal          string
}

func makePerson() person {
    addr := address{
```

```
                city: "Goville",
                state: "Go",
                postal: "12345",
        }
        return person{
                name: "vladimir vivien",
                address: addr,
        }
}
```

The previous example binds struct type definitions to the identifiers person and address. This allows the struct types to be reused in different contexts without the need to carry around the long form of the type definitions. You can refer to Chapter 4, *Data Types*, to learn more about named types.

The anonymous field

Previous definitions of struct types involved the use of named fields. However, it is also possible to define a field with only its type, omitting the identifier. This is known as an anonymous field. It has the effect of embedding the type directly into the struct.

This concept is demonstrated in the following code snippet. Both types, diameter and the name, are embedded as anonymous fields in the planet type:

```
type diameter int

type name struct {
    long    string
    short   string
    symbol rune
}
type planet struct {
    diameter
    name
    desc string
}

func main() {
    earth := planet{
            diameter: 7926,
            name: name{
                    long:    "Earth",
                    short:   "E",
```

```
        symbol: '\u2641',
    },
    desc: "Third rock from the Sun",
}
...
}
```

golang.fyi/ch07/struct_embed.go

The `main` function in the previous snippet shows how the anonymous fields are accessed and updated, as is done in the `planet` struct. Notice the names of the embedded types become the field identifiers in the composite literal value for the struct.

To simplify field name resolution, Go follows the following rules when using anonymous fields:

- The name of the type becomes the name of the field
- The name of an anonymous field may not clash with other field names
- Use only the unqualified (omit package) type name of imported types

These rules also hold when accessing the fields of embedded structs directly using selector expressions, as is shown in the following code snippet. Notice the name of the embedded types are resolved as fields names:

```
func main(){
    jupiter := planet{}
    jupiter.diameter = 88846
    jupiter.name.long = "Jupiter"
    jupiter.name.short = "J"
    jupiter.name.symbol = '\u2643'
    jupiter.desc = "A ball of gas"
    ...
}
```

golang.fyi/ch07/struct_embed.go

Promoted fields

Fields of an embedded struct can be *promoted* to its enclosing type. Promoted fields appear in selector expressions without the qualified name of their types, as shown in the following example:

```
func main() {
    ...
```

```
saturn := planet{}
saturn.diameter = 120536
saturn.long = "Saturn"
saturn.short = "S"
saturn.symbol = '\u2644'
saturn.desc = "Slow mover"
...
}
```

golang.fyi/ch07/struct_embed.go

In the previous snippet, the highlighted fields are promoted from the embedded type `name` by omitting it from the selector expression. The values of the fields `long`, `short`, and `symbol` come from embedded type `name`. Again, this will only work if the promotion does not cause any identifier clashes. In case of ambiguity, the fully qualified selector expression can be used.

Structs as parameters

Recall that struct variables store actual values. This implies that a new copy of a struct value is created whenever a `struct` variable is reassigned or passed in as a function parameter. For instance, the following will not update the value of name after the call to `updateName()`:

```
type person struct {
    name      string
    title string
}
func updateName(p person, name string) {
    p.name = name
}

func main() {
    p := person{}
    p.name = "uknown"
    ...
    updateName(p, "Vladimir Vivien")
}
```

golang.fyi/ch07/struct_ptr.go

This can be remedied by passing a pointer to the `struct` value of the person type, as shown in the following snippet:

```
type person struct {
    name     string
    title string
}

func updateName(p *person, name string) {
    p.name = name
}

func main() {
    p := new(person)
    p.name = "uknown"
    ...
    updateName(p, "Vladimir Vivien")
}
```

golang.fyi/ch07/struct_ptr2.go

In this version, the p variable is declared as *person and is initialized using the built-in new() function. After updateName() returns, its changes are seen by the calling function.

Field tags

The last topic on structs has to do with field tags. During the definition of a `struct` type, optional `string` values may be added to each field declaration. The value of the string is arbitrary and it can serve as hints to tools or other APIs that use reflection to consume the tags.

The following shows a definition of the Person and Address structs that are tagged with JSON annotation which can be interpreted by Go's JSON encoder and decoder (found in the standard library):

```
type Person struct {
    Name     string `json:"person_name"`
    Title    string `json:"person_title"`
    Address `json:"person_address_obj"`
}

type Address struct {
    Street string `json:"person_addr_street"`
    City   string `json:"person_city"`
    State  string `json:"person_state"`
```

```
        Postal string `json:"person_postal_code"`
    }
func main() {
    p := Person{
            Name: "Vladimir Vivien",
            Title : "Author",
            ...
    }
    ...
    b, _ := json.Marshal(p)
    fmt.Println(string(b))
}
```

golang.fyi/ch07/struct_ptr2.go

Notice the tags are represented as raw string values (wrapped within a pair of ` `). The tags are ignored by normal code execution. However, they can be collected using Go's reflection API as is done by the JSON library. You will encounter more on this subject in `Chapter 10`, *Data IO in Go*, when the book discusses input and output streams.

Summary

This chapter covered a lot of ground as it walked through each of the composite types found in Go to provide insightful coverage of their characteristics. The chapter opened with a coverage of the array type, where readers learned how to declare, initialize, and use array values. Next, readers learned all about the slice type, specifically the declaration, initialization, and practical examples that uses slice index expressions to create new or re-slice existing slices. The chapter covered the map type, which included information on map initialization, access, update, and traversal. Lastly, the chapter provided information about the definition, initialization, and usage of the struct type.

Needless to say, this is probably one of the longest chapters of the book. However, the information covered here will prove to be invaluable as the book continues to explore new topics. The next chapter will introduce the idea of using Go to support object-like idioms using methods and interfaces.

8
Methods, Interfaces, and Objects

Using your skills at this point, you can write an effective Go program using the fundamental concepts covered so far. As you will see in this chapter, the Go type system can support idioms that go beyond simple functions. While the designers of Go did not intend to create an object-oriented language with deep class hierarchies, the language is perfectly capable of supporting type compositions with advanced features to express the creation of complex object-like structures, as covered in the following topics:

- Go methods
- Objects in Go
- The interface type
- Type assertion

Go methods

A Go function can be defined with a scope narrowed to that of a specific type. When a function is scoped to a type, or attached to the type, it is known as a *method*. A method is defined just like any other Go function. However, its definition includes a *method receiver*, which is an extra parameter placed before the method's name, used to specify the host type to which the method is attached.

To better illustrate this concept, the following figure highlights the different parts involved in defining a method. It shows the `quart` method attached to the `type gallon` based receiver via the `g gallon` receiver parameter:

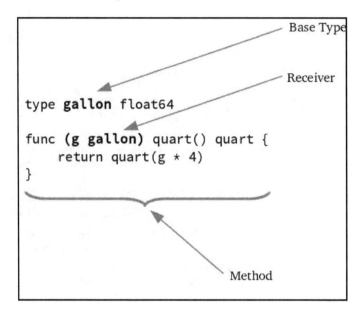

As mentioned, a method has the scope of a type. Therefore, it can only be accessed via a declared value (concrete or pointer) of the attached type using *dot notation*. The following program shows how the declared method `quart` is accessed using this notation:

```
package main
import "fmt"

type gallon float64

func (g gallon) quart() float64 {
    return float64(g * 4)
}
func main(){
    gal := gallon(5)
    fmt.Println(gal.quart())
}
```

golang.fyi/ch08/method_basic.go

In the previous example, the `gal` variable is initialized as the `gallon` type. Therefore, the `quart` method can be accessed using `gal.quart()`.

At runtime, the receiver parameter provides access to the value assigned to the base type of the method. In the example, the `quart` method receives the `g` parameter, which passes in a copy of the value for the declared type. So when the `gal` variable is initialized with a value of 5, a call to `gal.quart()` sets the receiver parameter `g` to 5. So the following would then print a value of 20:

```
func main(){
    gal := gallon(5)
    fmt.Println(gal.quart())
}
```

It is important to note that the base type for method receivers cannot be a pointer (nor an interface). For instance, the following will not compile:

```
type gallon *float64
func (g gallon) quart() float64 {
   return float64(g * 4)
}
```

The following shows a lengthier version of the source that implements a more general liquid volume conversion program. Each volumetric type receives its respective methods to expose behaviors attributed to that type:

```
package main
import "fmt"

type ounce float64
func (o ounce) cup() cup {
    return cup(o * 0.1250)
}

type cup float64
func (c cup) quart() quart {
    return quart(c * 0.25)
}
func (c cup) ounce() ounce {
    return ounce(c * 8.0)
}

type quart float64
func (q quart) gallon() gallon {
    return gallon(q * 0.25)
}
func (q quart) cup() cup {
```

```
        return cup(q * 4.0)
    }

    type gallon float64
    func (g gallon) quart() quart {
        return quart(g * 4)
    }

    func main() {
        gal := gallon(5)
        fmt.Printf("%.2f gallons = %.2f quarts\n", gal, gal.quart())
        ozs := gal.quart().cup().ounce()
        fmt.Printf("%.2f gallons = %.2f ounces\n", gal, ozs)
    }
```

github.com/vladimirvivien/learning-go/ch08/methods.go

For instance, converting 5 gallons to ounces can be done by invoking the proper conversion methods on a given value, as follows:

```
gal := gallon(5)
ozs := gal.quart().cup().ounce()
```

The entire implementation uses a simple, but effective, typical structure to represent both data type and behavior. Reading the code, it cleanly expresses its intended meaning without any reliance on heavy class structures.

Method set

The number of methods attached to a type, via the receiver parameter, is known as the type's *method set*. This includes both concrete and pointer value receivers. The concept of a method set is important in determining type equality, interface implementation, and support of the notion of the empty method set for the *empty interface* (all discussed in this chapter).

Value and pointer receivers

One aspect of methods that has escaped discussion so far is that receivers are normal function parameters. Therefore, they follow the pass-by-value mechanism of Go functions. This implies that the invoked method gets a copy of the original value from the declared type.

Receiver parameters can be passed as either values of or pointers of the base type. For instance, the following program shows two methods, `half` and `double`; both directly update the value of their respective method receiver parameters, g:

```
package main
import "fmt"
type gallon float64
func (g gallon) quart() float64 {
  return float64(g * 4)
}
func (g gallon) half() {
  g = gallon(g * 0.5)
}
func (g *gallon) double() {
  *g = gallon(*g * 2)
}
func main() {
  var gal gallon = 5
  gal.half()
  fmt.Println(gal)
  gal.double()
  fmt.Println(gal)
}
```

golang.fyi/ch08/receiver_ptr.go

In the `half` method, the code updates the receiver parameter with `g = gallon(g * 0.5)`. As you would expect, this will not update the original declared value, but rather the copy stored in the `g` parameter. So, when `gal.half()` is invoked in `main`, the original value remains unchanged and the following would print 5:

```
func main() {
  var gal gallon = 5
  gal.half()
  fmt.Println(gal)
}
```

Similar to regular function parameters, a receiver parameter that uses a pointer to refer to its base value allows the code to dereference the original value to update it. This is highlighted in the `double` method following snippet. It uses a method receiver of the `*gallon` type, which is updated using `*g = gallon(*g * 2)`. So when the following is invoked in `main`, it would print a value of **10**:

```
func main() {
    var gal gallon = 5
    gal.double()
    fmt.Println(gal)
}
```

Pointer receiver parameters are widely used in Go. This is because they make it possible to express object-like primitives that can carry both state and behaviors. As the next section shows, pointer receivers, along with other type features, are the basis for creating objects in Go.

Objects in Go

The lengthy introductory material from the previous sections was the setup to lead to the discussion of objects in Go. It has been mentioned that Go was not designed to function as traditional object-oriented language. There are no object or class keywords defined in Go. So then, why are we discussing objects in Go at all? Well, it turns out that Go perfectly supports object idioms and the practice of object-oriented programming without the heavy baggage of classical hierarchies and complex inheritance structures found in other object-oriented languages.

Let us review some of the primordial features usually attributed to an object-oriented language in the following table.

Object feature	Go	Comment
Object: A data type that stores states and exposes behavior	Yes	In Go all types can achieve this. There is no special type called a class or object to do this. Any type can receive a set of method to define its behavior, although the `struct` type comes the closest to what is commonly called an object in other languages.
Composition	Yes	Using a type such as a `struct` or an `interface` (discussed later), it is possible to create objects and express their polymorphic relationships through composition.

Subtype via interface	Yes	A type that defines a set of behaviors (methods) that other types may implement. Later you will see how it is used to implement object sub-typing.
Modularity and encapsulation	Yes	Go supports physical and logical modularity at its core with concepts such packages and an extensible type system, and code element visibility.
Type inheritance	No	Go does not support polymorphism through inheritance. A newly declared named type does not inherit all attributes of its underlying type and are treated differently by the type system. As a consequence, it is hard to implement inheritance via type lineage as found in other languages.
Classes	No	There is no notion of a class type that serves as the basis for objects in Go. Any data type in Go can be used as an object.

As the previous table suggests, Go supports the majority of concepts that are usually attributed to object-oriented programming. The remainder of this chapter covers topics and examples showing how to use Go as an object-oriented programming language.

The struct as object

Nearly all Go types can play the role of an object by storing states and exposing methods that are capable of accessing and modifying those states. The `struct` type, however, offers all of the features that are traditionally attributed to objects in other languages, such as:

- Ability to host methods
- Ability to be extended via composition
- Ability to be sub-typed (with help from the Go `interface` type)

The remainder of the chapter will base its discussion of objects on using the `struct` type.

Object composition

Let us start with the following simple example to demonstrate how the `struct` type may be used as an object that can achieve polymorphic composition. The following source code snippet implements a typical structure that models components of motorized transportation including `fuel,` `engine`, `vehicle`, `truck,` and `plane`:

```go
type fuel int
const (
    GASOLINE fuel = iota
    BIO
    ELECTRIC
    JET
)
type vehicle struct {
    make string
    model string
}

type engine struct {
    fuel fuel
    thrust int
}
func (e *engine) start() {
    fmt.Println ("Engine started.")
}

type truck struct {
    vehicle
    engine
    axels int
    wheels int
    class int
}
func (t *truck) drive() {
    fmt.Printf("Truck %s %s, on the go!\n", t.make, t.model)
}

type plane struct {
    vehicle
    engine
    engineCount int
    fixedWings bool
    maxAltitude int
}
func (p *plane) fly() {
    fmt.Printf(
```

```
        "Aircraft %s %s clear for takeoff!\n",
        p.make, p.model,
    )
}
```

golang.fyi/ch08/structobj.go

The components and their relationships declared in the previous code snippet are illustrated in the following figure to visualize the type mapping and their compositions:

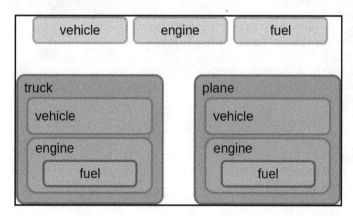

Go uses the *composition over inheritance* principle to achieve polymorphism using the type embedding mechanism supported by the `struct` type. In Go, there is no support for polymorphism via type inheritance. Recall that each type is independent and is considered to be different from all others. In fact, the semantics in the model above is slightly broken. Types `truck` and `plane` are shown to be composed of (or has-a) the `vehicle` type, which does not sound correct. Instead, the proper, or at least a more correct, representation would be to show that the types `truck` and `plane` *is a* `vehicle` via a subtype relationship. Later in the chapter, we will see how this can be achieved using the `interface` type.

Field and method promotion

Now that the objects have been established in the previous section, let us spend some time discussing the visibility of fields, methods, and embedded types inside the structs. The following source snippet shows a continuation of the previous example. It declares and initializes a variable t of type truck and p for plane. The former is initialized using a struct literal and the latter is updated using dot notation:

```
func main() {
    t := &truck {
            vehicle:vehicle{"Ford", "F750"},
            engine:engine{GASOLINE+BIO,700},
            axels:2,
            wheels:6,
            class:3,
    }
    t.start()
    t.drive()

    p := &plane{}
    p.make = "HondaJet"
    p.model = "HA-420"
    p.fuel = JET
    p.thrust = 2050
    p.engineCount = 2
    p.fixedWings = true
    p.maxAltitude = 43000
    p.start()
    p.fly()

}
```

golang.fyi/ch08/structobj.go

One of the more interesting details in the previous snippet is how the struct type embedding mechanism promotes fields and methods when accessed using dot notation. For instance, the following fields (make, mode, fuel, and thrust), are all declared in types that are embedded inside of the plane type:

```
p.make = "HondaJet"
p.model = "HA-420"
p.fuel = JET
p.thrust = 2050
```

The previous fields are promoted from their embedded types. They are accessed as if they are members of the `plane` type when, in fact, they are coming from the types `vehicle` and `engine` respectively. To avoid ambiguity, the name of the fields can be qualified as shown here:

```
p.vehicle.make = "HondaJet"
p.vehicle.model = "HA-420"
p.engine.fuel = JET
p.engine.thrust = 2050
```

Methods can also be promoted in a similar way. For instance, in the previous code we saw the methods `t.start()` and `p.start()` being invoked. However, neither type, `truck` nor `plane`, are receivers of a method named `start()`. As shown in the program from earlier, the `start()` method is defined for the `engine` type. Since the `engine` type is embedded in the types `truck` and `plane`, the `start()` method is promoted in scope to these enclosing types and is therefore accessible.

The constructor function

Since Go does not support classes, there is no such concept as a constructor. However, one conventional idiom you will encounter in Go is the use of a factory function to create and initialize values for a type. The following snippet shows a portion of the previous example that has been updated to use a constructor function for creating new values of the `plane` and `truck` types:

```
type truck struct {
    vehicle
    engine
    axels int
    wheels int
    class int
}
func newTruck(mk, mdl string) *truck {
    return &truck {vehicle:vehicle{mk, mdl}}
}

type plane struct {
    vehicle
    engine
    engineCount int
    fixedWings bool
    maxAltitude int
}
func newPlane(mk, mdl string) *plane {
```

```
    p := &plane{}
    p.make = mk
    p.model = mdl
    return p
}
```

golang.fyi/ch08/structobj2.go

While not required, providing a function to help with the initialization of composite values, such as a struct, increases the usability of the code. It provides a place to encapsulate repeatable initialization logic that can enforce validation requirements. In the previous example, both constructor functions, `newTruck` and `newPlane`, are passed the make and model information to create and initialize their respected values.

The interface type

When you talk to people who have been doing Go for a while, they almost always list the interface as one of their favorite features of the language. The concept of interfaces in Go, similar to other languages, such as Java, is a set of methods that serves as a template to describe behavior. A Go interface, however, is a type specified by the `interface{}` literal, which is used to list a set of methods that satisfies the interface. The following example shows the `shape` variable being declared as an interface:

```
var shape interface {
    area() float64
    perim() float64
}
```

In the previous snippet, the `shape` variable is declared and assigned an unnamed type, `interface{area()float64; perim()float64}`. Declaring variables with unnamed `interface` literal types is not really practical. Using idiomatic Go, an `interface` type is almost always declared as a named `type`. The previous snippet can be rewritten to use a named interface type, as shown in the following example:

```
type shape interface {
    area() float64
    perim() float64
}
var s shape
```

Implementing an interface

The interesting aspect of interfaces in Go is how they are implemented and ultimately used. Implementing a Go interface is done implicitly. There is no separate element or keyword required to indicate the intent of implementation. Any type that defines the method set of an `interface` type automatically satisfies its implementation.

The following source code shows the `rect` type as an implementation of the `interface` type `shape`. The `rect` type is defined as a `struct` with receiver methods `area` and `perim`. This fact automatically qualifies `rect` as an implementation of `shape`:

```
type shape interface {
    area() float64
    perim() float64
}

type rect struct {
    name string
    length, height float64
}

func (r *rect) area() float64 {
    return r.length * r.height
}

func (r *rect) perim() float64 {
    return 2*r.length + 2*r.height
}
```

golang.fyi/ch08/interface_impl.go

Subtyping with Go interfaces

Earlier, during the discussion on objects, it was mentioned that Go favors composition (*has-a*) relationships when building objects. While that is true, Go can also express "is-a" relationships among objects using subtyping via interfaces. In our previous example, it can be argued that the `rect` type (and any other type that implements the methods `area` and `perim`) can be treated as a subtype of `shape`, as shown in the following figure:

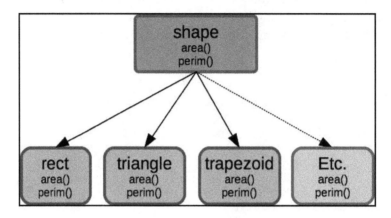

As you may expect, any subtype of `shape` can participate in expressions or be passed as functions (or methods) parameters where the `shape` type is expected. This is shown in the following code snippet where both types, `rect` (defined previously) and `triangle`, are able to be passed to the `shapeInfo(shape)` function to return a `string` value containing shape calculations:

```
type triangle struct {
    name string
    a, b, c float64
}

func (t *triangle) area() float64 {
    return 0.5*(t.a * t.b)
}

func (t *triangle) perim() float64 {
    return t.a + t.b + math.Sqrt((t.a*t.a) + (t.b*t.b))
}

func (t *triangle) String() string {
    return fmt.Sprintf(
        "%s[sides: a=%.2f b=%.2f c=%.2f]",
        t.name, t.a, t.b, t.c,
```

```
    )
}
func shapeInfo(s shape) string {
    return fmt.Sprintf(
        "Area = %.2f, Perim = %.2f",
        s.area(), s.perim(),
    )
}

func main() {
    r := &         rect{"Square", 4.0, 4.0}
    fmt.Println(r, "=>", shapeInfo(r))

    t := &         triangle{"Right Triangle", 1,2,3}
    fmt.Println(t, "=>", shapeInfo(t))
}
```

golang.fyi/ch08/interface_impl.go

Implementing multiple interfaces

The implicit mechanism of interfaces allows any named type to satisfy multiple interface types at once. This is achieved simply by having the method set of a given type intersect with the methods of each `interface` type to be implemented. Let us re-implement the previous code to show how this is done. Two new interfaces are introduced, `polygon` and `curved`, to better capture and categorize information and the behavior of shapes, as shown in the following code snippet:

```
type shape interface {
    area() float64
}

type polygon interface {
    perim()
}

type curved interface {
    circonf()
}
type rect struct {...}
func (r *rect) area() float64 {
    return r.length * r.height
}
func (r *rect) perim() float64 {
    return 2*r.length + 2*r.height
```

```
}

type triangle struct {...}
func (t *triangle) area() float64 {
    return 0.5*(t.a * t.b)
}
func (t *triangle) perim() float64 {
    return t.a + t.b + math.Sqrt((t.a*t.a) + (t.b*t.b))
}

type circle struct { ... }
func (c *circle) area() float64 {
    return math.Pi * (c.rad*c.rad)
}
func (c *circle) circonf() float64 {
    return 2 * math.Pi * c.rad
}
```

golang.fyi/ch08/interface_impl2.go

The previous source code snippet shows how types can automatically satisfy multiple interfaces by simply declaring methods that satisfy the interfaces' method sets. This is illustrated by the following figure:

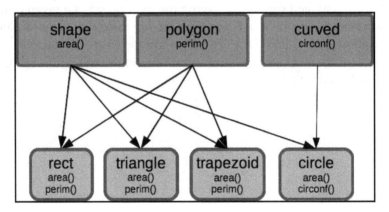

Interface embedding

Another interesting aspects of the `interface` type is its support for type embedding (similar to the `struct` type). This gives you the flexibility to structure your types in ways that maximize type reuse. Continuing with the shape example, the following code snippet reorganizes and reduces the previous interface count from three to two by embedding shape into the other two types:

```
type shape interface {
    area() float64
}

type polygon interface {
    shape
    perim()
}

type curved interface {
    shape
    circonf()
}
```

golang.fyi/ch08/interface_impl3.go

The following illustration shows how the interface types may be combined so the *is-a* relationship still satisfies the relationships between code components:

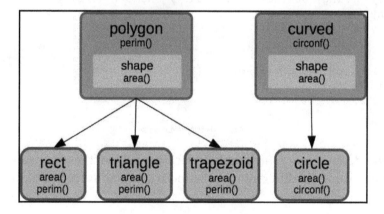

When embedding interface types, the enclosing type will inherit the method set of the embedded types. The compiler will complain if the embedded type causes method signatures to clash. Embedding becomes a crucial feature, especially when the code applies type validation using type checking. It allows a type to roll up type information, thus reducing unnecessary assertion steps (type assertion is discussed later).

The empty interface type

The `interface{}` type, or the empty `interface` type, is the literal representation of an `interface` type with an empty method set. According to our discussion so far, it can be deduced that *all types implement the empty interface* since all types can have a method set with zero or more members.

When a variable is assigned the `interface{}` type, the compiler relaxes its build-time type checks. The variable, however, still carries type information that can be queried at runtime. The following code illustrates how this works:

```go
func main() {
    var anyType interface{}
    anyType = 77.0
    anyType = "I am a string now"
    fmt.Println(anyType)

    printAnyType("The car is slow")
    m := map[string] string{"ID":"12345", "name":"Kerry"}
    printAnyType(m)
    printAnyType(1253443455)
}

func printAnyType(val interface{}) {
    fmt.Println(val)
}
```

golang.fyi/ch08/interface_empty.go

In the previous code, the `anyType` variable is declared to be of the type `interface{}`. It is able to be assigned values of different types without complaints from the compiler:

```go
anyType = 77.0
anyType = "I am a string now"
```

The `printAnyType()` function takes a parameter of the type `interface{}`. This means the function can be passed the values of any valid type, as shown here:

```
printAnyType("The car is slow")
m := map[string] string{"ID":"12345", "name":"Kerry"}
printAnyType(m)
printAnyType(1253443455)
```

The empty interface is crucially important for idiomatic Go. Delaying type-checking until runtime makes the language feels more dynamic without completely sacrificing strong typing. Go offers mechanisms such as type assertion (covered next) to query the type information carried by interfaces at runtime.

Type assertion

When an interface (empty or otherwise) is assigned to a variable, it carries type information that can be queried at runtime. Type assertion is a mechanism that is available in Go to idiomatically narrow a variable (of `interface` type) down to a concrete type and value that are stored in the variable. The following example uses type assertion in the `eat` function to select which `food` type to select in the `eat` function:

```
type food interface {
    eat()
}

type veggie string
func (v veggie) eat() {
    fmt.Println("Eating", v)
}

type meat string
func (m meat) eat() {
    fmt.Println("Eating tasty", m)
}

func eat(f food) {
    veg, ok := f.(veggie)
    if ok {
            if veg == "okra" {
                    fmt.Println("Yuk! not eating ", veg)
            }else{
                    veg.eat()
            }
```

```
            return
      }

      mt, ok := f.(meat)
      if ok {
            if mt == "beef" {
                  fmt.Println("Yuk! not eating ", mt)
            }else{
                  mt.eat()
            }
            return
      }

      fmt.Println("Not eating whatever that is: ", f)
}
```

golang.fyi/interface_assert.go

The eat function takes the food interface type as its parameter. The code shows how to use idiomatic Go to extract the static type and value stored in the f interface parameter using assertion. The general form for type assertion expression is given as follows:

<interface_variable>.(concrete type name)

The expression starts with the variable of the interface type. It is then followed by a dot and the concrete type being asserted enclosed in parentheses. The type assertion expression can return two values: one is the concrete value (extracted from the interface) and the second is a Boolean indicating the success of the assertion, as shown here:

value, boolean := <interface_variable>.(concrete type name)

This is the form of assertion that is shown in the following snippet (extracted from the earlier example) when narrowing the f parameter to a specific type of food. If the type is asserted to be meat, then the code continues to test the value of the mt variable:

```
mt, ok := f.(meat)
if ok {
   if mt == "beef" {
         fmt.Println("Yuk! not eating ", mt)
   }else{
         mt.eat()
   }
   return
}
```

A type assertion expression can also return just the value, as follows:

value := <interface_variable>.(concrete type name)

This form of assertion is risky to do as the runtime will cause a panic in the program if the value stored in the interface variable is not of the asserted type. Use this form only if you have other safeguards to either prevent or gracefully handle a panic.

Lastly, when your code requires multiple assertions to test many types at runtime, a much nicer idiom for assertions is the type `switch` statement. It uses the `switch` statement semantic to query static type information from an interface value using case clauses. The `eat` function from the previous food-related example can been updated to use a type `switch` instead of `if` statement, as shown in the following code snippet:

```
func eat(f food) {
    swtich morsel := f.(type){
    case veggie:
            if morsel == "okra" {
                    fmt.Println("Yuk! not eating ", mosel)
            }else{
                    mosel.eat()
            }
    case meat:
            if morsel == "beef" {
                    fmt.Println("Yuk! not eating ", mosel)
            }else{
                    mosel.eat()
            }
    default:
            fmt.Println("Not eating whatever that is: ", f)
    }
}
```

golang.fyi/interface_assert2.go

Notice the code is much nicer to read. It can support any number of cases and is clearly laid out with visual clues that makes it easy to reason about. The `switch` type also makes the panic issue go away by simply specifying a default case that can handle any types not specifically handled in the case clause.

Summary

This chapter attempted to give a broad and, at the same, somewhat comprehensive view of several important topics including methods, interfaces, and objects in Go. The chapter started with coverage of attaching methods to types using receiver parameters. Next the reader was introduced to objects and how to create idiomatic object-based programming in Go. Lastly, the chapter presented a comprehensive overview of the interface type and how it is used to support object semantics in Go. The next chapter takes the reader through one of the most fundamental concepts that has made Go such a sensation among developers: concurrency!

9
Concurrency

Concurrency is considered to be the one of the most attractive features of Go. Adopters of the language revel in the simplicity of its primitives to express correct concurrency implementations without the pitfalls that usually come with such endeavors. This chapter covers the necessary topics to understand and create concurrent Go programs, including the following:

- Goroutines
- Channels
- Writing concurrent programs
- The sync package
- Detecting race conditions
- Parallelism in Go

Goroutines

If you have worked in other languages, such as Java or C/C++, you are probably familiar with the notion of concurrency. It is the ability of a program to run two or more paths of execution independently. This is usually done by exposing a thread primitive directly to the programmer to create and manage concurrency.

Go has its own concurrency primitive called the *goroutine*, which allows a program to launch a function (routine) to execute independently from its calling function. Goroutines are lightweight execution contexts that are multiplexed among a small number of OS-backed threads and scheduled by Go's runtime scheduler. That makes them cheap to create without the overhead requirements of true kernel threads. As such, a Go program can initiate thousands (even hundreds of thousands) of goroutines with minimal impact on performance and resource degradation.

The go statement

Goroutines are launched using the go statement as follows:

go <function or expression>

A goroutine is created with the go keyword followed by the function to schedule for execution. The specified function can be an existing function, an anonymous function, or an expression that calls a function. The following code snippet shows an example of the use of goroutines:

```
func main() {
    go count(10, 50, 10)
    go count(60, 100, 10)
    go count(110, 200, 20)
}
func count(start, stop, delta int) {
    for i := start; i <= stop; i += delta {
        fmt.Println(i)
    }
}
```

golang.fyi/ch09/goroutine0.go

In the previous code sample, when the go count() statement is encountered in the main function, it launches the count function in an independent execution context. Both the main and count functions will be executing concurrently. As a side effect, main will complete before any of the count functions get a chance to print anything to the console.

Later in the chapter, we will see how to handle synchronization idiomatically between goroutines. For now, let us use fmt.Scanln() to block and wait for keyboard input, as shown in the following sample. In this version, the concurrent functions get a chance to complete while waiting for keyboard input:

```
func main() {
    go count(10, 30, 10)
    go count(40, 60, 10)
    go count(70, 120, 20)
    fmt.Scanln() // blocks for kb input
}
```

golang.fyi/ch09/goroutine1.go

Goroutines may also be defined as function literals directly in the go statement, as shown in this updated version of the example shown in the following code snippet:

```
func main() {
    go count(10, 30, 10)
    go func() {
            count(40, 60, 10)
    }()
    ...
}
```

The function literal provides a convenient idiom that allows programmers to assemble logic directly at the site of the go statement. When using the go statement with a function literal, it is treated as a regular closure with lexical access to non-local variables, as shown in the following example:

```
func main() {
    start := 0
    stop := 50
    step := 5
    go func() {
            count(start, stop, step)
    }()
}
```

In the previous code, the goroutine is able to access and use the variables start, stop, and step. This is safe as long as the variables captured in the closure are not expected to change after the goroutine starts. If these values are updated outside of the closure, it may create race conditions causing the goroutine to read unexpected values by the time it is scheduled to run.

The following snippet shows an example where the goroutine closure captures the variable `j` from the loop:

```
func main() {
    starts := []int{10,40,70,100}
    for _, j := range starts{
        go func() {
            count(j, j+20, 10)
        }()
    }
}
```

golang.fyi/ch09/goroutine4.go

Since `j` is updated with each iteration, it is impossible to determine what value will be read by the closure. In most cases, the goroutine closures will see the last updated value of `j` by the time they are executed. This can be easily fixed by passing the variable as a parameter in the function literal for the goroutine, as shown here:

```
func main() {
    starts := []int{10,40,70,100}
    for _, j := range starts{
        go func(s int) {
            count(s, s+20, 10)
        }(j)
    }
}
```

golang.fyi/ch09/goroutine5.go

The goroutine closures, invoked with each loop iteration, receive a copy of the `j` variable via the function parameter. This creates a local copy of the `j` value with the proper value to be used when the goroutine is scheduled to run.

Goroutine scheduling

In general, all goroutines run independently of each other, as depicted in the following illustration. A function that creates a goroutine does not wait for it to return, it continues with its own execution stream unless there is a blocking condition. Later, the chapter covers synchronization idioms to coordinate goroutines:

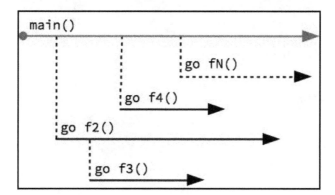

Go's runtime scheduler uses a form of cooperative scheduling to schedule goroutines. By default, the scheduler will allow a running goroutine to execute to completion. However, the scheduler will automatically yield to another goroutine for execution if one of the following events occurs:

- A go statement is encountered in the executing goroutine
- A channel operation is encountered (channels are covered later)
- A blocking system call (file or network IO for instance) is encountered
- After the completion of a garbage collection cycle

The scheduler will schedule a queued goroutines ready to enter execution when one of the previous events is encountered in a running goroutine. It is important to point out that the scheduler makes no guarantee of the order of execution of goroutines. When the following code snippet is executed, for instance, the output will be printed in an arbitrary order for each run:

```go
func main() {
    go count(10, 30, 10)
    go count(40, 60, 10)
    go count(70, 120, 20)
    fmt.Scanln() // blocks for kb input
}
func count(start, stop, delta int) {
    for i := start; i <= stop; i += delta {
        fmt.Println(i)
    }
}
```

golang.fyi/ch09/goroutine1.go

The following shows possible output for the previous program:

```
10
70
90
110
40
50
60
20
30
```

Channels

When talking about concurrency, one of the natural concerns that arises is that of data safety and synchronization among concurrently executing code. If you have done concurrent programming in languages such as Java or C/C++, you are likely familiar with the, sometimes brittle, choreography required to ensure running threads can safely access shared memory values to achieve communication and synchronization between threads.

This is one area where Go diverges from its C lineage. Instead of having concurrent code communicate by using shared memory locations, Go uses channels as a conduit between running goroutines to communicate and share data. The blog post *Effective Go* (https://go lang.org/doc/effective_go.html) has reduced this concept to the following slogan:

Do not communicate by sharing memory; instead, share memory by communicating.

 The concept of channel has its roots in **communicating sequential processes** (CSP), work done by renowned computer scientist C. A. Hoare, to model concurrency using communication primitives. As will be discussed in this section, channels provide the means to synchronize and safely communicate data between running goroutines.

This section discusses the Go channel type and provides insights into its characteristics. Later, you will learn how to use channels to craft concurrent programs.

The Channel type

The channel type declares a conduit within which only values of a given element type may be sent or received by the channel. The chan keyword is used to specify a channel type, as shown in the following declaration format:

chan <element type>

The following code snippet declares a bidirectional channel type, chan int, assigned to the variable ch, to communicate integer values:

```
func main() {
    var ch chan int
    ...
}
```

Later in the chapter, we will learn how to use the channel to send data between concurrent portions of a running program.

The send and receive operations

Go uses the <- (arrow) operator to indicate data movement within a channel. The following table summarizes how to send or receive data from a channel:

Example	Operation	Description
intCh <- 12	Send	When the arrow is placed to the left of the value, variable or expression, it indicates a send operation to the channel it points to. In this example, 12 is sent into channel intCh.
value := <- intCh	Receive	When the <- operator is place to the left of a channel, it indicates a receive operation from the channel. The value variable is assigned the value received from the intCh channel.

An uninitialized channel has a *nil* zero value and must be initialized using the built-in *make* function. As will be discussed in the following sections, a channel can be initialized as either unbuffered or buffered, depending on its specified capacity. Each of type of channel has different characteristics that are leveraged in different concurrency constructs.

Unbuffered channel

When the make function is invoked without the capacity argument, it returns a bidirectional *unbuffered* channel. The following snippet shows the creation of an unbuffered channel of type chan int:

```
func main() {
    ch := make(chan int) // unbuffered channel
    ...
}
```

The characteristics of an unbuffered channel are illustrated in the following figure:

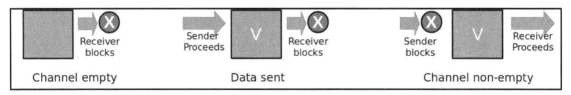

The sequence in the preceding figure (from left to right) shows how the unbuffered channel works:

- If the channel is empty, the receiver blocks until there is data
- The sender can send only to an empty channel and blocks until the next receive operation
- When the channel has data, the receiver can proceed to receive the data.

Sending to an unbuffered channel can easily cause a *deadlock* if the operation is not wrapped in a goroutine. The following code will block after sending 12 to the channel:

```
func main() {
    ch := make(chan int)
    ch <- 12 // blocks
    fmt.Println(<-ch)
}
```

golang.fyi/ch09/chan-unbuff0.go

When you run the previous program, you will get the following result:

```
$> go run chan-unbuff0.go
fatal error: all goroutines are asleep - deadlock!
```

Recall that the sender blocks immediately upon sending to an unbuffered channel. This means any subsequent statement, to receive from the channel for instance, becomes unreachable, causing a deadlock. The following code shows the proper way to send to an unbuffered channel:

```
func main() {
    ch := make(chan int)
    go func() { ch <- 12 }()
    fmt.Println(<-ch)
}
```

golang.fyi/ch09/chan-unbuff1.go

Notice that the send operation is wrapped in an anonymous function invoked as a separate goroutine. This allows the `main` function to reach the receive operation without blocking. As you will see later, this blocking property of unbuffered channels is used extensively as a synchronization and coordination idioms between goroutines.

Buffered channel

When the `make` function uses the capacity argument, it returns a bidirectional *buffered* channel, as shown in the following snippet:

```
func main
    ch := make(chan int, 3) // buffered channel
}
```

The previous code will create a buffered channel with a capacity of 3. The buffered channel operates as a first-in-first-out blocking queue, as illustrated in the following figure:

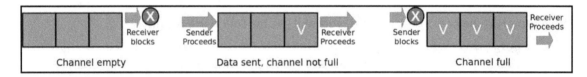

The buffered channel depicted in the preceding figure has the following characteristics:

- When the channel is empty, the receiver blocks until there is at least one element
- The sender always succeeds as long as the channel is not at capacity
- When the channel is at capacity, the sender blocks until at least one element is received

Using a buffered channel, it is possible to send and receive values within the same goroutine without causing a deadlock. The following shows an example of sending and receiving using a buffered channel with a capacity of 4 elements:

```
func main() {
    ch := make(chan int, 4)
    ch <- 2
    ch <- 4
    ch <- 6
    ch <- 8

    fmt.Println(<-ch)
    fmt.Println(<-ch)
    fmt.Println(<-ch)
```

```go
        fmt.Println(<-ch)
}
```

golang.fyi/ch09/chan0.go

The code in the previous example is able to send the values 2, 4, 6, and 8 to the ch channel without the risk of blocking. The four fmt.Println(<-ch) statements are used to receive the values buffered in the channel successively. However, if a fifth send operation is added, prior to the first receive, the code will deadlock as highlighted in the following snippet:

```go
func main() {
    ch := make(chan int, 4)
    ch <- 2
    ch <- 4
    ch <- 6
    ch <- 8
    ch <- 10
    fmt.Println(<-ch)
    ...
}
```

Later in the chapter, you will read more about idiomatic and safe ways to use channels for communications.

Unidirectional channels

At declaration, a channel type may also include a unidirectional operator (using the <- arrow again) to indicate whether a channel is send-only or receive-only, as listed in the following table:

Declaration	Operation
<- chan <element type>	Declares a receive-only channel as shown later. `var inCh chan<- int`
chan <-<element type>	Declares a send-only channel as shown later. `var outCh <-chan int`

The following code snippet shows function makeEvenNums with a send-only channel argument of type chan <- int:

```go
func main() {
    ch := make(chan int, 10)
```

```
    makeEvenNums(4, ch)

    fmt.Println(<-ch)
    fmt.Println(<-ch)
    fmt.Println(<-ch)
    fmt.Println(<-ch)
}

func makeEvenNums(count int, in chan<- int) {
    for i := 0; i < count; i++ {
        in <- 2 * i
    }
}
```

Since the directionality of the channel is baked in the type, access violations will be detected at compile time. So in the previous example, the in channel can only be used for receive operations.

A bidirectional channel can be converted to a unidirectional channel explicitly or automatically. For instance, when makeEvenNums() is called from main(), it receives the bidirectional channel ch as a parameter. The compiler automatically converts the channel to the appropriate type.

Channel length and capacity

The len and cap functions can be used to return a channel's length and capacity respectively. The len function returns the current number of elements queued in the channel prior to being read by a receiver. For instance, the following code snippet will print **2**:

```
func main() {
    ch := make(chan int, 4)
    ch <- 2
    ch <- 2
    fmt.Println(len(ch))
}
```

The cap function returns the declared capacity of the channel type which, unlike length, remains constant throughout the life of the channel.

An unbuffered channel has a length and a capacity of zero.

Closing a channel

Once a channel is initialized it is ready for send and receive operations. A channel will remain in that open state until it is forcibly closed using the built-in *close* function, as shown in the following example:

```
func main() {
    ch := make(chan int, 4)
    ch <- 2
    ch <- 4
    close(ch)
    // ch <- 6 // panic, send on closed channel

    fmt.Println(<-ch)
    fmt.Println(<-ch)
    fmt.Println(<-ch) // closed, returns zero value for element

}
```

golang.fyi/ch09/chan2.go

Once a channel is closed, it has the following properties:

- Subsequent send operations will cause a program to panic
- Receive operations never block (regardless of whether buffered or unbuffered)
- All receive operations return the zero value of the channel's element type

In the previous snippet, the ch channel is closed after two send operations. As indicated in the comment, a third send operation would cause a panic because the channel is closed. On the receiving side, the code gets the two elements in the channel before it is closed. A third receive operation returns 0, the zero value for the channel's elements.

Go offers a long form of the receive operation that returns the value read from the channel followed by a Boolean indicating the closed status of the channel. This can be used to properly handle the zero value from a closed channel, as shown in the following example:

```
func main() {
    ch := make(chan int, 4)
    ch <- 2
    ch <- 4
    close(ch)

    for i := 0; i < 4; i++ {
        if val, opened := <-ch; opened {
            fmt.Println(val)
        } else {
            fmt.Println("Channel closed!")
        }
    }
}
```

golang.fyi/ch09/chan3.go

Writing concurrent programs

Up to this point, the discussions about goroutines and channels remained deliberately separated to ensure that each topic is properly covered. However, the true power of channels and goroutines are realized when they are combined to create concurrent programs, as covered in this section.

Synchronization

One of the primary uses of channels is synchronization between running goroutines. To illustrate this use case, let us examine the following code, which implements a word histogram. The program reads the words from the `data` slice then, on a separate goroutine, collects the occurrence of each word:

```
func main() {
    data := []string{
        "The yellow fish swims slowly in the water",
        "The brown dog barks loudly after a drink ...",
        "The dark bird bird of prey lands on a small ...",
    }

    histogram := make(map[string]int)
```

```
    done := make(chan bool)

    // splits and count words
    go func() {
        for _, line := range data {
            words := strings.Split(line, " ")
            for _, word := range words {
                word = strings.ToLower(word)
                histogram[word]++
            }
        }
        done <- true
    }()

    if <-done {
        for k, v := range histogram {
            fmt.Printf("%s\t(%d)\n", k, v)
        }
    }
}
```

golang.fyi/ch09/pattern0.go

The code in the previous example uses `done := make(chan bool)` to create the channel that will be used to synchronize the two running goroutines in the program. The `main` function launches a secondary goroutine, which does the word counting, and then it continues execution until it blocks at the `<-done` expression, causing it to wait.

In the meantime, the secondary goroutine runs until it completes its loop. Then, it sends a value to the `done` channel with `done <- true`, causing the blocked `main` routine to become unblocked and continues with its execution.

 The previous code has a bug that may cause a race condition. A correction will be introduced later in the chapter.

In the previous example, the code allocates and actually sends a Boolean value that is used for the synchronization. Upon further inspection, it is clear that the value in the channel is irrelevant and we simply want it to signal. So, we can further distill the synchronization idiom into a colloquial form that is presented in the following code snippet:

```
func main() {
    ...
    histogram := make(map[string]int)
    done := make(chan struct{})
```

```
// splits and count
go func() {
        defer close(done) // closes channel upon fn return
        for _, line := range data {
                words := strings.Split(line, " ")
                for _, word := range words {
                        word = strings.ToLower(word)
                        histogram[word]++
                }
        }
}()

<-done // blocks until closed

for k, v := range histogram {
        fmt.Printf("%s\t(%d)\n", k, v)
}
}
```

golang.fyi/ch09/pattern1.go

This version of the code achieves goroutine synchronization using:

- The done channel, declared as type `chan struct{}`
- The main goroutine blocks at receive expression `<-done`
- When the done channel is closed, all receivers succeed without blocking

Although the signaling is done using different constructs, this version of the code is equivalent to the first version (`pattern0.go`). The emtpy `struct{}` type stores no value and it is used strictly for signaling. This version of the code closes the `done` channel (instead of sending a value). This has the effect of allowing the main goroutine to unblock and continue execution.

Streaming data

A natural use of channels is to stream data from one goroutine to another. This pattern is quite common in Go code and for it to work, the followings must be done:

- Continuously send data on a channel
- Continuously receive the incoming data from that channel
- Signal the end of the stream so the receiver may stop

As you will see, all of this can be done using a single channel. The following code snippet is a rewrite of the previous example. It shows how to use a single channel to stream data from one goroutine to another. The same channel is also used as a signaling device to indicate the end of the stream:

```go
func main(){
...
    histogram := make(map[string]int)
    wordsCh := make(chan string)

    // splits lines and sends words to channel
    go func() {
        defer close(wordsCh) // close channel when done
        for _, line := range data {
            words := strings.Split(line, " ")
            for _, word := range words {
                word = strings.ToLower(word)
                wordsCh <- word
            }
        }
    }()

    // process word stream and count words
    // loop until wordsCh is closed
    for {
        word, opened := <-wordsCh
        if !opened {
            break
        }
        histogram[word]++
    }

    for k, v := range histogram {
        fmt.Printf("%s\t(%d)\n", k, v)
    }
}
```

golang.fyi/ch09/pattern2.go

This version of the code produces the word histogram as before, but introduces a different approach. This is accomplished using the highlighted portion of the code shown in the following table:

Code	Description
`wordsCh := make(chan string)`	The channel used to stream data.
`wordsCh <- word`	The sender goroutine loops through the text line and sends a word at a time. It then blocks until the word is received by the receiving (main) goroutine.
`defer close(wordsCh)`	As the words are continuously received (see later), the sender goroutine closes the channel when it is done. This will be the signal to the receiver that it should also stop.

`for {`
`  word, opened := <- wordsCh`
`  if !opened {`
`    break`
`  }`
`  histogram[word]++`
`}`
	This is the receiver code. It is placed in a loop since it is does not know ahead of time how much data to expect. With each iteration of the loop, the code does the following:
	• Pulls the data from the channel
	• Checks the open status of the channel
	• If closed, break out of the loop
	• Otherwise record histogram

Using for...range to receive data

The previous pattern is so common in Go that the idiom is built into the language in the form of the following `for...range` statement:

for <elemem> := range <channel>{...}

With each iteration, this `for...range` statement will block until it receives incoming data from the indicated channel, as shown in the following snippet:

```
func main(){
...
    go func() {
        defer close(wordsCh)
        for _, line := range data {
            words := strings.Split(line, " ")
            for _, word := range words {
                word = strings.ToLower(word)
                wordsCh <- word
            }
        }
```

```
        }
    } ()

    for word := range wordsCh {
        histogram[word]++
    }
    ...
}
```

The previous code shows the an updated version of the code using a for-range statement, `for word := range wordsCh`. It successively emits the received value from the `wordsCh` channel. When the channel is closed (from the goroutine), the loop automatically breaks.

 Always remember to close the channel so receivers are signaled properly. Otherwise, the program may enter into a deadlock which could cause a panic.

Generator functions

Channels and goroutines provide a natural substrate for implementing a form of producer/producer pattern using generator functions. In this approach, a goroutine is wrapped in a function which generates values that are sent via a channel returned by the function. The consumer goroutine receives these values as they are generated.

The word histogram has been updated to use this pattern, as shown in the following code snippet:

```
func main() {
    data := []string{"The yellow fish swims...", ...}
    histogram := make(map[string]int)

    words := words(data) // returns handle to data channel
    for word := range words {
        histogram[word]++
    }
    ...
}

// generator function that produces data
func words(data []string) <-chan string {
    out := make(chan string)
    go func() {
```

```
        defer close(out) // closes channel upon fn return
        for _, line := range data {
                words := strings.Split(line, " ")
                for _, word := range words {
                        word = strings.ToLower(word)
                        out <- word
                }
        }
    }()
    return out
}
```

golang.fyi/ch09/pattern4.go

In this example, the generator function, declared as `func words(data []string) <-chan string`, returns a receive-only channel of string elements. The consumer function, in this instance `main()`, receives the data emitted by the generator function, which is processed using a `for...range` loop.

Selecting from multiple channels

Sometimes it is necessary for concurrent programs to handle send and receive operations for multiple channels at the same time. To facilitate such endeavor, the Go language supports the `select` statement that multiplexes selection among multiple send and receive operations:

select {

case <send_ or_receive_expression>:

default:

}

The `case` statement operates similarly to a `switch` statement with `case` clauses. The `select` statement, however, selects one of the send or receive cases which succeeded. If two or more communication cases happen to be ready at the same time, one will be selected at random. The default case is always selected when no other cases succeed.

The following snippet updates the histogram code to illustrate the use of the `select` statement. The generator function `words` select between two channels, `out` to send data as before and a new channel `stopCh`, passed as a parameter, which is used to detect an interruption signal to stop sending data:

```
func main() {
...
    histogram := make(map[string]int)
    stopCh := make(chan struct{}) // used to signal stop

    words := words(stopCh, data) // returns handle to channel
    for word := range words {
        if histogram["the"] == 3 {
            close(stopCh)
        }
        histogram[word]++
    }
...
}

func words(stopCh chan struct{}, data []string) <-chan string {
    out := make(chan string)
    go func() {
        defer close(out) // closes channel upon fn return
        for _, line := range data {
            words := strings.Split(line, " ")
            for _, word := range words {
                word = strings.ToLower(word)
                select {
                case out <- word:
                case <-stopCh: // succeeds first when close
                    return
                }
            }
        }
    }()
    return out
}
```

golang.fyi/ch09/pattern5.go

In the previous code snippet, the `words` generator function will select the first communication operation that succeeds: `out <- word` or `<-stopCh`. As long as the consumer code in `main()` continues to receive from the `out` channel, the send operation will succeed first. Notice, however, the code in `main()` closes the `stopCh` channel when it encounters the third instance of `"the"`. When that happens, it will cause the receive case, in the select statement, to proceed first causing the goroutine to return.

Channel timeout

One popular idiom that is commonly encountered with Go concurrency is the use of the select statement, introduced previously, to implement timeouts. This works by using the select statement to wait for a channel operation to succeed within a given time duration using the API from the `time` package (`https://golang.org/pkg/time/`).

The following code snippet shows a version of the word histogram example that times out if the program takes longer than 200 microseconds to count and print the words:

```go
func main() {
    data := []string{...}
    histogram := make(map[string]int)
    done := make(chan struct{})

    go func() {
        defer close(done)
        words := words(data) // returns handle to channel
        for word := range words {
            histogram[word]++
        }
        for k, v := range histogram {
            fmt.Printf("%s\t(%d)\n", k, v)
        }
    }()

    select {
    case <-done:
        fmt.Println("Done counting words!!!!")
    case <-time.After(200 * time.Microsecond):
        fmt.Println("Sorry, took too long to count.")
    }
}
func words(data []string) <-chan string {...}
```

golang.fyi/ch09/pattern6.go

This version of the histogram example introduces the done channel, which is used to signal when processing is done. In the select statement, the receive operation case<-done: blocks until the goroutine closes the done channel. Also in the select statement, the time.After() function returns a channel which will close after the indicated duration. If the 200 microseconds elapse before done is closed, the channel from time.After() will close first, causing the timeout case to succeed first.

The sync package

There are instances when accessing shared values using traditional methods are simpler and more appropriate then the use of channels. The *sync* package (https://golang.org/pkg/sync/) provides several synchronization primitives including mutual exclusion (mutex) locks and synchronization barriers for safe access to shared values, as discussed in this section.

Synchronizing with mutex locks

Mutex locks allow serial access of shared resources by causing goroutines to block and wait until locks are released. The following sample illustrates a typical code scenario with the Service type, which must be started before it is ready to be used. After the service has started, the code updates an internal bool variable, started, to store its current state:

```go
type Service struct {
    started bool
    stpCh   chan struct{}
    mutex   sync.Mutex
}
func (s *Service) Start() {
    s.stpCh = make(chan struct{})
    go func() {
        s.mutex.Lock()
        s.started = true
        s.mutex.Unlock()
        <-s.stpCh // wait to be closed.
    }()
}
func (s *Service) Stop() {
    s.mutex.Lock()
    defer s.mutex.Unlock()
    if s.started {
        s.started = false
        close(s.stpCh)
```

```
    }
}
func main() {
    s := &Service{}
    s.Start()
    time.Sleep(time.Second) // do some work
    s.Stop()
}
```

golang.fyi/ch09/sync2.go

The previous code snippet uses variable `mutex`, of type `sync.Mutex`, to synchronize access to the shared variable `started`. For this to work effectively, all contentious areas where the `started` variable is updated must use the same lock with successive calls to `mutex.Lock()` and `mutex.Unlock()`, as shown in the code.

One idiom you will often encounter is to embed the `sync.Mutex` type directly inside a struct, as shown in the next code snippet. This has the effect of promoting the `Lock()` and `Unlock()` methods as part of the struct itself:

```
type Service struct {
    ...
    sync.Mutex
}

func (s *Service) Start() {
    s.stpCh = make(chan struct{})
    go func() {
        s.Lock()
        s.started = true
        s.Unlock()
        <-s.stpCh // wait to be closed.
    }()
}

func (s *Service) Stop() {
    s.Lock()
    defer s.Unlock()
    ...
}
```

golang.fyi/ch09/sync3.go

The `sync` package also offers the RWMutex (read-write mutex), which can be used in cases where there is one writer that updates the shared resource, while there may be multiple readers. The writer would update the resource using a full lock, as before. However, readers use the `RLock()`/`RUnlock()` method pair (for read-lock/read-unlock respectively) to apply a read-only lock when reading the shared resource. The RWMutex type is used in the next section, *Synchronizing Access to Composite Values*.

Synchronizing access to composite values

The previous section discussed concurrency safety when sharing access to simple values. The same level of care must be applied when sharing access to composite type values such as maps and slices, since Go does not offer concurrency-safe version of these types, as illustrated in the following example:

```
type Service struct {
    started bool
    stpCh    chan struct{}
    mutex    sync.RWMutex
    cache    map[int]string
}

func (s *Service) Start() {
    ...
    go func() {
        s.mutex.Lock()
        s.started = true
        s.cache[1] = "Hello World"
        ...
        s.mutex.Unlock()
        <-s.stpCh // wait to be closed.
    }()
}
...
func (s *Service) Serve(id int) {
    s.mutex.RLock()
    msg := s.cache[id]
    s.mutex.RUnlock()
    if msg != "" {
        fmt.Println(msg)
    } else {
        fmt.Println("Hello, goodbye!")
    }
}
```

golang.fyi/ch09/sync4.go

The preceding code uses a `sync.RWMutex` variable (see preceding section, *Synchronizing with Mutex Locks*) to manage the locks when accessing the map variable `cache`. The code wraps the update operation to the `cache` variable within a pair of method calls, `mutex.Lock()` and `mutex.Unlock()`. However, when reading values from the `cache` variable, the `mutex.RLock()` and `mutex.RUnlock()` methods are used to provide concurrency safety.

Concurrency barriers with sync.WaitGroup

Sometimes when working with goroutines, you may need to create a synchronization barrier where you wish to wait for all running goroutines to finish before proceeding. The `sync.WaitGroup` type is designed for such a scenario, allowing multiple goroutines to rendezvous at specific point in the code. Using WaitGroup requires three things:

- The number of participants in the group via the Add method
- Each goroutine calls the Done method to signal completion
- Use the Wait method to block until all goroutines are done

WaitGroup is often used as a way to implement work distribution patterns. The following code snippet illustrates work distribution to calculate the sum of multiples of 3 and 5 up to MAX. The code uses the `WaitGroup` variable, `wg`, to create a concurrency barrier that waits for two goroutines to calculate the partial sums of the numbers, then gathers the result after all goroutines are done:

```go
const MAX = 1000

func main() {
    values := make(chan int, MAX)
    result := make(chan int, 2)
    var wg sync.WaitGroup
    wg.Add(2)
    go func() { // gen multiple of 3 & 5 values
        for i := 1; i < MAX; i++ {
            if (i%3) == 0 || (i%5) == 0 {
                values <- i // push downstream
            }
        }
        close(values)
    }()

    work := func() { // work unit, calc partial result
        defer wg.Done()
        r := 0
```

```
        for i := range values {
                r += i
        }
        result <- r
    }

    // distribute work to two goroutines
    go work()
    go work()

    wg.Wait()                       // wait for both groutines
    total := <-result + <-result // gather partial results
    fmt.Println("Total:", total)
}
```

golang.fyi/ch09/sync5.go

In the previous code, the method call, wg.Add(2), configures the WaitGroup variable wg because the work is distributed between two goroutines. The work function calls defer wg.Done() to decrement the WaitGroup counter by one every time it is completed.

Lastly, the wg.Wait() method call blocks until its internal counter reaches zero. As explained previously, this will happen when both goroutines' work running function complete successfully. When that happens, the program unblocks and gathers the partial results. It is important to remember that wg.Wait() will block indefinitely if its internal counter never reaches zero.

Detecting race conditions

Debugging concurrent code with a race condition can be time consuming and frustrating. When a race condition occurs, it is usually inconsistent and displays little to no discernible pattern. Fortunately, since Version 1.1, Go has included a race detector as part of its command-line tool chain. When building, testing, installing, or running Go source code, simply add the -race command flag to enable the race detector instrumentation of your code.

For instance, when the source file `golang.fyi/ch09/sync1.go` (a code with a race condition) is executed with the `-race` flag, the compiler's output shows the offending goroutine locations that caused the race condition, as shown in the following output:

```
$> go run -race sync1.go
==================
WARNING: DATA RACE
Read by main goroutine:
  main.main()
/github.com/vladimirvivien/learning-go/ch09/sync1.go:28 +0x8c

Previous write by goroutine 5:
  main.(*Service).Start.func1()
/github.com/vladimirvivien/learning-go/ch09/sync1.go:13 +0x2e

Goroutine 5 (running) created at:
  main.(*Service).Start()
/github.com/vladimirvivien/learning-go/ch09/sync1.go:15 +0x99
  main.main()
/github.com/vladimirvivien/learning-go/ch09/sync1.go:26 +0x6c
==================
Found 1 data race(s)
exit status 66
```

The race detector lists the line numbers where there is concurrent access to shared values. It lists the *read* operations followed by the locations where *write* operations may happen concurrently. Racy conditions in code can go unnoticed, even in well-tested code, until it manifests itself randomly. If you are writing concurrent code, it is highly recommended that you integrate the race detector as part of your testing suite.

Parallelism in Go

So far, the discussion in this chapter has focused on synchronizing concurrent programs. As was mentioned earlier in the chapter, the Go runtime scheduler automatically multiplexes and schedules goroutines across available OS-managed threads. This means concurrent programs that can be parallelized have the ability to take advantage of the underlying processor cores with little to no configuration. For instance, the following code cleanly segregates its work unit (to calculate sums of multiples of 3 and 5) to be calculated by launching `workers` number of goroutines:

```
const MAX = 1000
const workers = 2

func main() {
```

```
values := make(chan int)
result := make(chan int, workers)
var wg sync.WaitGroup

go func() { // gen multiple of 3 & 5 values
    for i := 1; i < MAX; i++ {
        if (i%3) == 0 || (i%5) == 0 {
            values <- i // push downstream
        }
    }
    close(values)
}()

work := func() { // work unit, calc partial result
    defer wg.Done()
    r := 0
    for i := range values {
        r += i
    }
    result <- r
}

//launch workers
wg.Add(workers)
for i := 0; i < workers; i++ {
    go work()
}

wg.Wait() // wait for all groutines
close(result)
total := 0
// gather partial results
for pr := range result {
    total += pr
}
fmt.Println("Total:", total)
}
```

golang.fyi/ch09/sync6.go

The previous code will automatically launch each goroutine, with `go work()`, in parallel when executed on a multi-core machine. The Go runtime scheduler, by default, will create a number of OS-backed threads for scheduling that is equal to the number of CPU cores. That quantity is identified by runtime value called *GOMAXPROCS*.

The GOMAXPROCS value can be explicitly changed to influence the number threads that are made available to the scheduler. That value can be changed using a command-line environment variable with the same name. GOMAXPROCS can also be updated in the using function `GOMAXPROCS()` from the *runtime* package (`https://golang.org/pkg/runtime`). Either approach allows programmers to fine-tune the number of threads that will participate in scheduling goroutines.

Summary

Concurrency can be a complex topic in any language. This chapter covered the major topics to guide readers around the use of concurrency primitives in the Go language. The first section of the chapter outlined the crucial properties of goroutines, including the creation and usage of the *go* statement. Next, the chapter covered the mechanism of Go's runtime scheduler and the notion of channels used for communication between running goroutines. Lastly, users were introduced to several concurrency patterns used to create concurrent programs using goroutines, channels, and the synchronization primitives from the sync package.

Next, you will be introduced to the standard APIs to do data input and output in Go.

10
Data IO in Go

Previous chapters of this book focused mainly on fundamentals. In this and future chapters, readers are introduced to some of the powerful APIs provided by Go's standard library. This chapter discusses in detail how to input, process, transform, and output data using APIs from the standard library and their respective packages with the following topics:

- IO with readers and writers
- The io.Reader interface
- The io.Writer interface
- Working with the io package
- Working with files
- Formatted IO with fmt
- Buffered IO
- In-memory IO
- Encoding and decoding data

IO with readers and writers

Similar to other languages, such as Java, Go models data input and output as a stream that flows from sources to targets. Data resources, such as files, networked connections, or even some in-memory objects, can be modeled as streams of bytes from which data can be *read* or *written* to, as illustrated in the following figure:

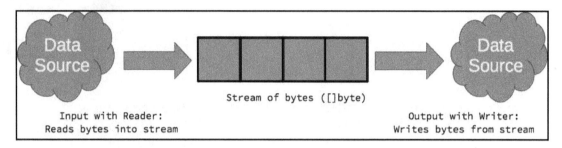

The stream of data is represented as a **slice of bytes ([]byte)** that can be accessed for reading or writing. As we will explore in this chapter, the `io` package makes available the `io.Reader` interface to implement code that *reads* and transfers data from a source into a stream of bytes. Conversely, the `io.Writer` interface lets implementers create code that reads data from a provided stream of bytes and *writes* it as output to a target resource. Both interfaces are used extensively in Go as a standard idiom to express IO operations. This makes it possible to interchange readers and writers of different implementations and contexts with predictable results.

The io.Reader interface

The `io.Reader` interface, as shown in the following listing, is simple. It consists of a single method, `Read([]byte)(int, error)`, intended to let programmers implement code that *reads* data, from an arbitrary source, and transfers it into the provided slice of bytes.

```
type Reader interface {
        Read(p []byte) (n int, err error)
}
```

The Read method returns the total number of bytes transferred into the provided slice and an error value (if necessary). As a guideline, implementations of the io.Reader should return an error value of io.EOF when the reader has no more data to transfer into stream p. The following shows the type alphaReader, a trivial implementation of the io.Reader that filters out non-alpha characters from its string source:

```go
type alphaReader string

func (a alphaReader) Read(p []byte) (int, error) {
    count := 0
    for i := 0; i < len(a); i++ {
        if (a[i] >= 'A' && a[i] <= 'Z') ||
                (a[i] >= 'a' && a[i] <= 'z') {
            p[i] = a[i]
        }
        count++
    }
    return count, io.EOF
}

func main() {
    str := alphaReader("Hello! Where is the sun?")
    io.Copy(os.Stdout, &str)
    fmt.Println()
}
```

golang.fyi/ch10/reader0.go

Since values of the alphaReader type implement the io.Reader interface, they can participate anywhere a reader is expected as shown in the call to io.Copy(os.Stdout, &str). This copies the stream of bytes emitted by the alphaReader variable into a writer interface, os.Stdout (covered later).

Chaining readers

Chances are the standard library already has a reader that you can reuse – so it is common to wrap an existing reader and use its stream as the source for the new implementation. The following snippet shows an updated version of alphaReader. This time, it takes an io.Reader as its source as shown in the following code:

```go
type alphaReader struct {
    src io.Reader
}
```

```
func NewAlphaReader(source io.Reader) *alphaReader {
    return &alphaReader{source}
}

func (a *alphaReader) Read(p []byte) (int, error) {
    if len(p) == 0 {
        return 0, nil
    }
    count, err := a.src.Read(p) // p has now source data
    if err != nil {
        return count, err
    }
    for i := 0; i < len(p); i++ {
        if (p[i] >= 'A' && p[i] <= 'Z') ||
            (p[i] >= 'a' && p[i] <= 'z') {
            continue
        } else {
            p[i] = 0
        }
    }
    return count, io.EOF
}

func main() {
    str := strings.NewReader("Hello! Where is the sun?")
    alpha := NewAlphaReader(str)
    io.Copy(os.Stdout, alpha)
    fmt.Println()
}
```

golang.fyi/ch10/reader1.go

The main change to note in this version of the code is that the `alphaReader` type is now a struct which embeds an `io.Reader` value. When `alphaReader.Read()` is invoked, it calls the wrapped reader as `a.src.Read(p)`, which will inject the source data into byte slice `p`. Then the method loops through `p` and applies the filter to the data. Now, to use the `alphaReader`, it must first be provided with an existing reader which is facilitated by the `NewAlphaReader()` constructor function.

The advantages of this approach may not be obvious at first. However, by using an io.Reader as the underlying data source the alphaReader type is capable of reading from any reader implementation. For instance, the following code snippet shows how the alphaReader type can now be combined with an os.File to filter out non-alphabetic characters from a file (the Go source code itself):

```
...
func main() {
    file, _ := os.Open("./reader2.go")
    alpha := NewAlphaReader(file)
    io.Copy(os.Stdout, alpha)
    fmt.Println()
}
```

golang.fyi/ch10/reader2.go

The io.Writer interface

The io.Writer interface, as shown in the following code, is just as simple as its reader counterpart:

```
type Writer interface {
    Write(p []byte) (n int, err error)
}
```

The interface requires the implementation of a single method, Write(p []byte)(c int, e error), that copies data from the provided stream p and *writes* that data to a sink resource such as an in-memory structure, standard output, a file, a network connection, or any number of io.Writer implementations that come with the Go standard library. The Write method returns the number of bytes copied from p followed by an error value if any was encountered.

The following code snippet shows the implementation of the channelWriter type, a writer that decomposes and serializes its stream that is sent over a Go channel as consecutive bytes:

```
type channelWriter struct {
    Channel chan byte
}

func NewChannelWriter() *channelWriter {
    return &channelWriter{
        Channel: make(chan byte, 1024),
```

```
    }
}

func (c *channelWriter) Write(p []byte) (int, error) {
    if len(p) == 0 {
            return 0, nil
    }

    go func() {
            defer close(c.Channel) // when done
            for _, b := range p {
                c.Channel <- b
            }
    }()

    return len(p), nil
}
```

golang.fyi/ch10/writer1.go

The `Write` method uses a goroutine to copy each byte, from `p`, and sends it across the `c.Channel`. Upon completion, the goroutine closes the channel so that consumers are notified when to stop consuming from the channel. As an implementation convention, writers should not modify slice `p` or hang on to it. When an error occurs, the writer should return the current number of bytes processed and an error.

Using the `channelWriter` type is simple. You can invoke the `Write()` method directly or, as is more common, use `channelWriter` with other IO primitives in the API. For instance, the following snippet uses the `fmt.Fprint` function to serialize the `"Stream me!"` string as a sequence of bytes over a channel using `channelWriter`:

```
func main() {
    cw := NewChannelWriter()
    go func() {
            fmt.Fprint(cw, "Stream me!")
    }()

    for c := range cw.Channel {
            fmt.Printf("%c\n", c)
    }
}
```

golang.fyi/ch10/writer1.go

In the previous snippet, the serialized bytes, queued in the channel, are consumed using a `for...range` statement as they are successively printed. The following snippet shows another example where the content of a file is serialized over a channel using the same `channelWriter`. In this implementation, an `io.File` value and `io.Copy` function are used to source the data instead of the `fmt.Fprint` function:

```
func main() {
    cw := NewChannelWriter()
    file, err := os.Open("./writer2.go")
    if err != nil {
        fmt.Println("Error reading file:", err)
        os.Exit(1)
    }
    _, err = io.Copy(cw, file)
    if err != nil {
        fmt.Println("Error copying:", err)
        os.Exit(1)
    }

    // consume channel
    for c := range cw.Channel {
        fmt.Printf("%c\n", c)
    }
}
```

golang.fyi/ch10/writer2.go.

Working with the io package

The obvious place to start with IO is, well, the io package (https://golang.org/pkg/io). As we have already seen, the io package defines input and output primitives as the io.Reader and io.Writer interfaces. The following table summarizes additional functions and types, available in the io package, that facilitate streaming IO operations.

Function	Description
io.Copy()	The io.Copy function (and its variants io.CopyBuffer and io.CopyN) make it easy to copy data from an arbitrary io.Reader source into an equally arbitrary io.Writer sink as shown in the following snippet: ```data := strings.NewReader("Write me down.")\nfile, _ := os.Create("./iocopy.data")\nio.Copy(file, data)``` golang.fyi/ch10/iocopy.go
PipeReader PipeWriter	The io package includes the *PipeReader* and *PipeWriter* types that model IO operations as an in-memory pipe. Data is written to the pipe's io.Writer and can independently be read at the pipe's io.Reader. The following abbreviated snippet illustrates a simple pipe that writes a string to the writer pw. The data is then consumed with the pr reader and copied to a file: ```file, _ := os.Create("./iopipe.data")\npr, pw := io.Pipe()\ngo func() {\n fmt.Fprint(pw, "Pipe streaming")\n pw.Close()\n}()\nwait := make(chan struct{})\ngo func() {\n io.Copy(file, pr)\n pr.Close()\n close(wait)\n}()\n<-wait //wait for pr to finish``` golang.fyi/ch10/iopipe.go Note that the pipe writer will block until the reader completely consumes the pipe content or an error is encountered. Therefore, both the reader and writer should be wrapped in a goroutine to avoid deadlocks.

| `io.TeeReader()` | Similar to the `io.Copy` function, `io.TeeReader` transfers content from a reader to a writer. However, the function also emits the copied bytes (unaltered) via a returned `io.Reader`. The TeeReader works well for composing multi-step IO stream processing. The following abbreviated snippet first calculates the SHA-1 hash of a file content using the `TeeReader`. The resulting reader, `data`, is then streamed to a gzip writer `zip`:<br><br>```go
fin, _ := os.Open("./ioteerdr.go")
defer fin.Close()
fout, _ := os.Create("./teereader.gz")
defer fout.Close()
zip := gzip.NewWriter(fout)
defer zip.Close()
sha := sha1.New()
data := io.TeeReader(fin, sha)
io.Copy(zip, data)
fmt.Printf("SHA1 hash %x\n",    sha.Sum(nil))
```<br>golang.fyi/ch10/ioteerdr0.go<br><br>If we wanted to calculate both SHA-1 and MD5, we can update the code to nest the two `TeeReader` values as shown in the following snippet:<br><br>```go
sha := sha1.New()
md := md5.New()
data := io.TeeReader(
   io.TeeReader(fin, md), sha,
)
io.Copy(zip, data)
```<br>golang.fyi/ch10/ioteerdr1.go |
| `io.WriteString()` | The `io.WriteString` function writes the content of string into a specified writer. The following writes the content of a string to a file:<br><br>```go
fout, err := os.Create("./iowritestr.data")
if err != nil {
    fmt.Println(err)
    os.Exit(1)
}
defer fout.Close()
io.WriteString(fout, "Hello    there!\n")
```<br>golang.fyi/ch10/iowritestr.go |
```

| io.LimitedReader | As its name suggests, the io.LimitedReader struct is a reader that reads only *N* number of bytes from the specified io.Reader. The following snippet will print the first 19 bytes from the string:<br><br>```go
str := strings.NewReader("The    quick brown " +
    "fox jumps over the lazy    dog")
limited :=    &io.LimitedReader{R: str, N: 19}
io.Copy(os.Stdout, limited)
```<br>golang.fyi/ch10/iolimitedrdr.go<br>```
$> go run iolimitedrd.go
The quick brown fox
``` |
|---|---|
| io.SectionReader | The io.SectionReader type implements seek and skip primitives by specifying an index (zero-based) where to start reading and an offset value indicating the number of bytes to read as shown in the following snippet:<br><br>```go
str := strings.NewReader("The    quick brown"+
    "fox jumps over the lazy    dog")
section := io.NewSectionReader(str,    19, 23)
io.Copy(os.Stdout, section)
```<br>golang.fyi/ch10/iosectionrdr.go<br>This example will print jumps over the lazy dog. |
| Package io/ioutil | The io/ioutil sub-package implements a small number of functions that provide utilitarian shortcuts to IO primitives such as file read, directory listing, temp directory creation, and file write. |

Working with files

The os package (https://golang.org/pkg/os/) exposes the os.File type which represents a file handle on the system. The os.File type implementsseveral IO primitives, including the io.Reader and io.Writer interfaces, which allows file content to be processed using the standard streaming IO API.

Creating and opening files

The os.Create function creates a new file with the specified path. If the file already exists, os.Create will overwrite it. The os.Open function, on the other hand, opens an existing file for reading.
```

The following source snippet opens an existing file and creates a copy of its content using the `io.Copy` function. One common, and recommended practice to notice is the deferred call to the method `Close` on the file. This ensures a graceful release of OS resources when the function exits:

```go
func main() {
    f1, err := os.Open("./file0.go")
    if err != nil {
        fmt.Println("Unable to open file:", err)
        os.Exit(1)
    }
    defer f1.Close()

    f2, err := os.Create("./file0.bkp")
    if err != nil {
        fmt.Println("Unable to create file:", err)
        os.Exit(1)
    }
    defer f2.Close()

    n, err := io.Copy(f2, f1)
    if err != nil {
        fmt.Println("Failed to copy:", err)
        os.Exit(1)
    }

    fmt.Printf("Copied %d bytes from %s to %s\n",
        n, f1.Name(), f2.Name())
}
```

golang.fyi/ch10/file0.go

Function os.OpenFile

The `os.OpenFile` function provides generic low-level functionalities to create a new file or open an existing file with fine-grained control over the file's behavior and its permission. Nevertheless, the `os.Open` and `os.Create` functions are usually used instead as they provide a simpler abstraction then the `os.OpenFile` function.

The os.OpenFile function take three parameters. The first one is the path of the file, the second parameter is a masked bit-field value to indicate the behavior of the operation (for example, read-only, read-write, truncate, and so on) and the last parameter is a posix-compliant permission value for the file.

The following abbreviated source snippet re-implements the file copy code, from earlier. This time, however, it uses the os.FileOpen function to demonstrate how it works:

```go
func main() {
    f1, err := os.OpenFile("./file0.go", os.O_RDONLY, 0666)
    if err != nil {...}
    defer f1.Close()

    f2, err := os.OpenFile("./file0.bkp", os.O_WRONLY, 0666)
    if err != nil {...}
    defer f2.Close()

    n, err := io.Copy(f2, f1)
    if err != nil {...}

    fmt.Printf("Copied %d bytes from %s to %s\n",
        n, f1.Name(), f2.Name())
}
```

golang.fyi/ch10/file1.go

> If you already have a reference to an OS file descriptor, you can also use the os.NewFile function to create a file handle in your program. The os.NewFile function is rarely used, as files are usually initialized using the file functions discussed previously.

Files writing and reading

We have already seen how to use the os.Copy function to move data into or out of a file. Sometimes, however, it will be necessary to have complete control over the logic that writes or reads file data. The following code snippet, for instance, uses the WriteString method from the os.File variable, fout, to create a text file:

```go
func main() {
    rows := []string{
            "The quick brown fox",
            "jumps over the lazy dog",
    }
```

```
fout, err := os.Create("./filewrite.data")
if err != nil {
        fmt.Println(err)
        os.Exit(1)
}
defer fout.Close()

for _, row := range rows {
        fout.WriteString(row)
}
}
```

If, however, the source of your data is not text, you can write raw bytes directly to the file as shown in the following source snippet:

```
func main() {
    data := [][]byte{
            []byte("The quick brown fox\n"),
            []byte("jumps over the lazy dog\n"),
    }
    fout, err := os.Create("./filewrite.data")
    if err != nil { ... }
    defer fout.Close()

    for _, out := range data {
            fout.Write(out)
    }
}
```

As an `io.Reader`, reading from of the `io.File` type directly can be done using the *Read* method. This gives access to the content of the file as a raw stream of byte slices. The following code snippet reads the content of file `../ch0r/dict.txt` as raw bytes assigned to slice p up to 1024-byte chunks at a time:

```
func main() {
    fin, err := os.Open("../ch05/dict.txt")
    if err != nil {
            fmt.Println(err)
            os.Exit(1)
    }
    defer fin.Close()
    p := make([]byte, 1024)
    for {
```

```
        n, err := fin.Read(p)
        if err == io.EOF {
            break
        }
        fmt.Print(string(p[:n]))
    }
}
```

Standard input, output, and error

The os package includes three pre-declared variables, os.Stdin, os.Stdout, and os.Stderr, that represent file handles for standard input, output, and error of the OS respectively. The following snippet reads the file f1 and writes its content to io.Stdout, standard output, using the os.Copy function (standard input is covered later):

```
func main() {
    f1, err := os.Open("./file0.go")
    if err != nil {
        fmt.Println("Unable to open file:", err)
        os.Exit(1)
    }
    defer f1.Close()

    n, err := io.Copy(os.Stdout, f1)
    if err != nil {
        fmt.Println("Failed to copy:", err)
        os.Exit(1)
    }

    fmt.Printf("Copied %d bytes from %s \n", n, f1.Name())
}
```

Formatted IO with fmt

One of the most widely used packages for IO is fmt (https://golang.org/pkg/fmt). It comes with an amalgam of functions designed for formatted input and output. The most common usage of the fmt package is for writing to standard output and reading from standard input. This section also highlights other functions that make fmt a great tool for IO.

Printing to io.Writer interfaces

The fmt package offers several functions designed to write text data to arbitrary implementations of io.Writer. The fmt.Fprint and fmt.Fprintln functions write text with the default format while fmt.Fprintf supports format specifiers. The following code snippet writes a columnar formatted list of metalloid data to a specified text file using the fmt.Fprintf function:

```go
type metalloid struct {
    name    string
    number  int32
    weight  float64
}

func main() {
    var metalloids = []metalloid{
        {"Boron", 5, 10.81},
        ...
        {"Polonium", 84, 209.0},
    }
    file, _ := os.Create("./metalloids.txt")
    defer file.Close()

    for _, m := range metalloids {
        fmt.Fprintf(
            file,
            "%-10s %-10d %-10.3f\n",
            m.name, m.number, m.weight,
        )
    }
}
```

golang.fyi/ch10/fmtfprint0.go

In the previous example, the `fmt.Fprintf` function uses format specifiers to write formatted text to the io.File `file` variable. The `fmt.Fprintf` function supports a large number of format specifiers whose proper treatment is beyond the scope of this text. Refer to the online documentation for complete coverage of these specifiers.

Printing to standard output

The `fmt.Print`, `fmt.Printf`, and `fmt.Println` have the exact same characteristics as the previous `Fprint`-series of functions seen earlier. Instead of an arbitrary `io.Writer` however, they write text to the standard output file handle `os.Stdout` (see the section *Standard output, input, and error* covered earlier).

The following abbreviated code snippet shows an updated version of the previous example that writes the list of metalloids to a standard output instead of a regular file. Note that it is the same code except for the use of the `fmt.Printf` instead of the `fmt.Fprintf` function:

```
type metalloid struct { ... }
func main() {
    var metalloids = []metalloid{
        {"Boron", 5, 10.81},
        ...
        {"Polonium", 84, 209.0},
    }

    for _, m := range metalloids {
        fmt.Printf(
            "%-10s %-10d %-10.3f\n",
            m.name, m.number, m.weight,
        )
    }
}
```

golang.fyi/ch10/fmtprint0.go

Reading from io.Reader

The `fmt` package also supports formatted reading of textual data from `io.Reader` interfaces. The `fmt.Fscan` and `fmt.Fscanln` functions can be used to read multiple values, separated by spaces, into specified parameters. The `fmt.Fscanf` function supports format specifiers for a richer and flexible parsing of data input from `io.Reader` implementations.

The following abbreviated code snippet uses the function `fmt.Fscanf` for the formatted input of a space-delimited file (`planets.txt`) containing planetary data:

```
func main() {
    var name, hasRing string
    var diam, moons int

    // read data
    data, err := os.Open("./planets.txt")
    if err != nil {
        fmt.Println("Unable to open planet data:", err)
        return
    }
    defer data.Close()

    for {
        _, err := fmt.Fscanf(
            data,
            "%s %d %d %s\n",
            &name, &diam, &moons, &hasRing,
        )
        if err != nil {
            if err == io.EOF {
                break
            } else {
                fmt.Println("Scan error:", err)
                return
            }
        }
        fmt.Printf(
            "%-10s %-10d %-6d %-6s\n",
            name, diam, moons, hasRing,
        )
    }
}
```

The code reads from the `io.File` variable `data`, until it encounters an `io.EOF` error indicating the end of the file. Each line of text it reads is parsed using format specifiers `"%s %d %d %s\n"` which matches the space-delimited layout of the records stored in the file. Each parsed token is then assigned to its respective variable `name`, `diam`, `moons`, and `hasRing`, which are printed to the standard output using the `fm.Printf` function.

Reading from standard input

Instead of reading from an arbitrary io.Reader, the fmt.Scan, fmt.Scanf, and fmt.Scanln are used to read data from standard input file handle, os.Stdin. The following code snippet shows a simple program that reads text input from the console:

```
func main() {
    var choice int
    fmt.Println("A square is what?")
    fmt.Print("Enter 1=quadrilateral 2=rectagonal:")

    n, err := fmt.Scanf("%d", &choice)
    if n != 1 || err != nil {
        fmt.Println("Follow directions!")
        return
    }
    if choice == 1 {
        fmt.Println("You are correct!")
    } else {
        fmt.Println("Wrong, Google it.")
    }
}
```

golang.fyi/ch10/fmtscan1.go

In the previous program, the fmt.Scanf function parses the input using the format specifier "%d" to read an integer value from the standard input. The function will throw an error if the value read does not match exactly the specified format. For instance, the following shows what happens when character D is read instead of an integer:

```
$> go run fmtscan1.go
A square is what?
Enter 1=quadrilateral 2=rectagonal: D
Follow directions!
```

Buffered IO

Most IO operations covered so far have been unbuffered. This implies that each read and write operation could be negatively impacted by the latency of the underlying OS to handle IO requests. Buffered operations, on the other hand, reduces latency by buffering data in internal memory during IO operations. The bufio package (https://golang.org/pkg/bufio/) offers functions for buffered read and write IO operations.

Buffered writers and readers

The `bufio` package offers several functions to do buffered writing of IO streams using an `io.Writer` interface. The following snippet creates a text file and writes to it using buffered IO:

```go
func main() {
    rows := []string{
        "The quick brown fox",
        "jumps over the lazy dog",
    }

    fout, err := os.Create("./filewrite.data")
    writer := bufio.NewWriter(fout)
    if err != nil {
        fmt.Println(err)
        os.Exit(1)
    }
    defer fout.Close()

    for _, row := range rows {
        writer.WriteString(row)
    }
    writer.Flush()
}
```

golang.fyi/ch10/bufwrite0.go

In general, the constructor functions in the `bufio` package create a buffered writer by wrapping an existing `io.Writer` as its underlying source. For instance, the previous code creates a buffered writer using the `bufio.NewWriter` function by wrapping the io.File variable, `fout`.

To influence the size of the internal buffer, use the constructor function `bufio.NewWriterSize(w io.Writer, n int)` to specify the internal buffer size. The `bufio.Writer` type also offers the methods `Write` and `WriteByte` for writing raw bytes and `WriteRune` for writing Unicode-encoded characters.

Reading buffered streams can be done simply by calling the constructor function *bufio.NewReader* to wrap an existing `io.Reader`. The following code snippet creates a `bufio.Reader` variable `reader` by wrapping the `file` variable as its underlying source:

```go
func main() {
    file, err := os.Open("./bufread0.go")
    if err != nil {
        fmt.Println("Unable to open file:", err)
```

[253]

```
            return
    }
    defer file.Close()

    reader := bufio.NewReader(file)
    for {
            line, err := reader.ReadString('\n')
            if err != nil {
                    if err == io.EOF {
                            break
                    } else {
                            fmt.Println("Error reading:, err")
                            return
                    }
            }
            fmt.Print(line)
    }
}
```

golang.`fyi/ch10/bufread0.go`

The previous code uses the `reader.ReadString` method to read a text file using the `'\n'` character as the content delimiter. To influence the size of the internal buffer, use the constructor function `bufio.NewReaderSize(w io.Reader, n int)` to specify the internal buffer size. The `bufio.Reader` type also offers the *Read, ReadByte,* and *ReadBytes* methods for reading raw bytes from a stream and the *ReadRune* method for reading Unicode-encoded characters.

Scanning the buffer

The `bufio` package also makes available primitives that are used to scan and tokenize buffered input data from an `io.Reader` source. The `bufio.Scanner` type scans input data using the *Split* method to define tokenization strategies. The following code snippet shows a reimplementation of the planetary example (from earlier). This time, the code uses `bufio.Scanner` (instead of the `fmt.Fscan` function) to scan the content of the text file using the `bufio.ScanLines` function:

```
func main() {
    file, err := os.Open("./planets.txt")
    if err != nil {
            fmt.Println("Unable to open file:", err)
            return
    }
    defer file.Close()
```

```
fmt.Printf(
        "%-10s %-10s %-6s %-6s\n",
        "Planet", "Diameter", "Moons", "Ring?",
    )
    scanner := bufio.NewScanner(file)
    scanner.Split(bufio.ScanLines)
    for scanner.Scan() {
        fields := strings.Split(scanner.Text(), " ")
        fmt.Printf(
                "%-10s %-10s %-6s %-6s\n",
                fields[0], fields[1], fields[2], fields[3],
            )
    }
}
```

golang.fyi/ch10/bufscan0.go

Using bufio.Scanner is done in four steps as shown in the previous example:

- First, use bufio.NewScanner(io.Reader) to create a scanner
- Call the scanner.Split method to configure how the content is tokenized
- Traverse the generated tokens with the scanner.Scan method
- Read the tokenized data with the scanner.Text method

The code uses the pre-defined function bufio.ScanLines to parse the buffered content using a line-delimiter. The bufio package comes with several pre-defined splitter functions including *ScanBytes* to scan each byte as a token, *ScanRunes* to scan UTF-8 encoded tokens, and *ScanWords* which scan each space-separated words as tokens.

In-memory IO

The bytes package offers common primitives to achieve streaming IO on blocks of bytes, stored in memory, represented by the bytes.Buffer type. Since the bytes.Buffer type implements both io.Reader and io.Writer interfaces it is a great option to stream data into or out of memory using streaming IO primitives.

The following snippet stores several string values in the byte.Buffer variable, book. Then the buffer is streamed to os.Stdout:

```
func main() {
    var books bytes.Buffer
    books.WriteString("The Great Gatsby")
    books.WriteString("1984")
```

```
      books.WriteString("A Tale of Two Cities")
      books.WriteString("Les Miserables")
      books.WriteString("The Call of the Wild")

      books.WriteTo(os.Stdout)
}
```

The same example can easily be updated to stream the content to a regular file as shown in the following abbreviate code snippet:

```
func main() {
    var books bytes.Buffer
    books.WriteString("The Great Gatsby\n")
    books.WriteString("1984\n")
    books.WriteString("A Take of Two Cities\n")
    books.WriteString("Les Miserables\n")
    books.WriteString("The Call of the Wild\n")

    file, err := os.Create("./books.txt")
    if err != nil {
          fmt.Println("Unable to create file:", err)
          return
    }
    defer file.Close()
    books.WriteTo(file)
}
```

Encoding and decoding data

Another common aspect of IO in Go is the encoding of data, from one representation to another, as it is being streamed. The encoders and decoders of the standard library, found in the *encoding* package (`https://golang.org/pkg/encoding/`), use the `io.Reader` and `io.Writer` interfaces to leverage IO primitives as a way of streaming data during encoding and decoding.

Go supports several encoding formats for a variety of purposes including data conversion, data compaction, and data encryption. This chapter will focus on encoding and decoding data using the *Gob* and *JSON* format for data conversion. In `Chapter 11`, *Writing Networked Programs*, we will explore using encoders to convert data for client and server communication using **remote procedure calls** (**RPC**).

Binary encoding with gob

The gob package (*https://golang.org/pkg/encoding/gob*) provides an encoding format that can be used to convert complex Go data types into binary. Gob is self-describing, meaning each encoded data item is accompanied by a type description. The encoding process involves streaming the gob-encoded data to an io.Writer so it can be written to a resource for future consumption.

The following snippet shows an example code that encodes variable books, a slice of the Book type with nested values, into the gob format. The encoder writes its generated binary data to an os.Writer instance, in this case the file variable of the *os.File type:

```
type Name struct {
    First, Last string
}

type Book struct {
    Title       string
    PageCount   int
    ISBN        string
    Authors     []Name
    Publisher   string
    PublishDate time.Time
}

func main() {
    books := []Book{
        Book{
            Title:       "Leaning Go",
            PageCount:   375,
            ISBN:        "9781784395438",
            Authors:     []Name{{"Vladimir", "Vivien"}},
            Publisher:   "Packt",
            PublishDate: time.Date(
                2016, time.July,
                0, 0, 0, 0, 0, time.UTC,
            ),
        },
        Book{
            Title:       "The Go Programming Language",
            PageCount:   380,
            ISBN:        "9780134190440",
            Authors:     []Name{
                {"Alan", "Donavan"},
                {"Brian", "Kernighan"},
            },
            Publisher:   "Addison-Wesley",
```

```
                    PublishDate: time.Date(
                        2015, time.October,
                        26, 0, 0, 0, 0, time.UTC,
                    ),
                },
                ...
            }

            // serialize data structure to file
            file, err := os.Create("book.dat")
            if err != nil {
                    fmt.Println(err)
                    return
            }
            enc := gob.NewEncoder(file)
            if err := enc.Encode(books); err != nil {
                    fmt.Println(err)
            }
    }
```

golang.fyi/ch10/gob0.go

Although the previous example is lengthy, it is mostly made of the definition of the nested data structure assigned to variable `books`. The last half-dozen or more lines are where the encoding takes place. The gob encoder is created with `enc := gob.NewEncoder(file)`. Encoding the data is done by simply calling `enc.Encode(books)` which streams the encoded data to the provide file.

The decoding process does the reverse by streaming the gob-encoded binary data using an `io.Reader` and automatically reconstructing it as a strongly-typed Go value. The following code snippet decodes the gob data that was encoded and stored in the `books.data` file in the previous example. The decoder reads the data from an `io.Reader`, in this instance the variable `file` of the `*os.File` type:

```
type Name struct {
    First, Last string
}

type Book struct {
    Title       string
    PageCount   int
    ISBN        string
    Authors     []Name
    Publisher   string
    PublishDate time.Time
}
```

```
func main() {
    file, err := os.Open("book.dat")
    if err != nil {
            fmt.Println(err)
            return
    }

    var books []Book
    dec := gob.NewDecoder(file)
    if err := dec.Decode(&books); err != nil {
            fmt.Println(err)
            return
    }
}
```

golang.fyi/ch10/gob1.go

Decoding a previously encoded gob data is done by creating a decoder using `dec :=` `gob.NewDecoder(file)`. The next step is to declare the variable that will store the decoded data. In our example, the `books` variable, of the `[]Book` type, is declared as the destination of the decoded data. The actual decoding is done by invoking `dec.Decode(&books)`. Notice the `Decode()` method takes the address of its target variable as an argument. Once decoded, the `books` variable will contain the reconstituted data structure streamed from the file.

 As of this writing, gob encoder and decoder APIs are only available in the Go programming language. This means that data encoded as gob can only be consumed by Go programs.

Encoding data as JSON

The encoding package also comes with a *json* encoder sub-package (https://golang.org/pkg/encoding/json/) to support JSON-formatted data. This greatly broadens the number of languages with which Go programs can exchange complex data structures. JSON encoding works similarly as the encoder and decoder from the gob package. The difference is that the generated data takes the form of a clear text JSON-encoded format instead of a binary. The following code updates the previous example to encode the data as JSON:

```
type Name struct {
    First, Last string
}

type Book struct {
```

```go
        Title       string
        PageCount   int
        ISBN        string
        Authors     []Name
        Publisher   string
        PublishDate time.Time
    }

    func main() {
        books := []Book{
            Book{
                Title:       "Leaning Go",
                PageCount:   375,
                ISBN:        "9781784395438",
                Authors:     []Name{{"Vladimir", "Vivien"}},
                Publisher:   "Packt",
                PublishDate: time.Date(
                    2016, time.July,
                    0, 0, 0, 0, 0, time.UTC),
            },
            ...
        }

        file, err := os.Create("book.dat")
        if err != nil {
            fmt.Println(err)
            return
        }
        enc := json.NewEncoder(file)
        if err := enc.Encode(books); err != nil {
            fmt.Println(err)
        }
    }
```

golang.fyi/ch10/json0.go

The code is exactly the same as before. It uses the same slice of nested structs assigned to the books variable. The only difference is the encoder is created with enc := json.NewEncoder(file) which creates a JSON encoder that will use the file variable as its io.Writer destination. When enc.Encode(books) is executed, the content of the variable books is serialized as JSON to the local file books.dat, shown in the following code (formatted for readability):

```json
[
    {
        "Title":"Leaning Go",
        "PageCount":375,
```

```
                "ISBN":"9781784395438",
                "Authors":[{"First":"Vladimir","Last":"Vivien"}],
                "Publisher":"Packt",
                "PublishDate":"2016-06-30T00:00:00Z"
        },
        {

                "Title":"The Go Programming Language",
                "PageCount":380,
                "ISBN":"9780134190440",
                "Authors":[
                        {"First":"Alan","Last":"Donavan"},
                        {"First":"Brian","Last":"Kernighan"}
                ],
                "Publisher":"Addison-Wesley",
                "PublishDate":"2015-10-26T00:00:00Z"
        },
        . . .

    ]
```

File books.dat (formatted)

The generated JSON-encoded content uses the name of the struct fields as the name for the JSON object keys by default. This behavior can be controlled using struct tags (see the section, *Controlling JSON mapping with struct tags*).

Consuming the JSON-encoded data in Go is done using a JSON decoder that streams its source from an `io.Reader`. The following snippet decodes the JSON-encoded data, generated in the previous example, stored in the file `book.dat`. Note that the data structure (not shown in the following code) is the same as before:

```go
func main() {
    file, err := os.Open("book.dat")
    if err != nil {
        fmt.Println(err)
        return
    }

    var books []Book
    dec := json.NewDecoder(file)
    if err := dec.Decode(&books); err != nil {
        fmt.Println(err)
        return
    }
}
```

golang.fyi/ch10/json1.go

The data in the books.dat file is stored as an array of JSON objects. Therefore, the code must declare a variable capable of storing an indexed collection of nested struct values. In the previous example, the `books` variable, of the type `[]Book` is declared as the destination of the decoded data. The actual decoding is done by invoking `dec.Decode(&books)`. Notice the `Decode()` method takes the address of its target variable as an argument. Once decoded, the `books` variable will contain the reconstituted data structure streamed from the file.

Controlling JSON mapping with struct tags

By default, the name of a struct field is used as the key for the generated JSON object. This can be controlled using `struct` type tags to specify how JSON object key names are mapped during encoding and decoding of the data. For instance, the following code snippet declares struct fields with the `json:` tag prefix to specify how object keys are to be encoded and decoded:

```
type Book struct {
    Title       string    `json:"book_title"`
    PageCount   int       `json:"pages,string"`
    ISBN        string    `json:"-"`
    Authors     []Name    `json:"auths,omniempty"`
    Publisher   string    `json:",omniempty"`
    PublishDate time.Time `json:"pub_date"`
}
```

golang.fyi/ch10/json2.go

The tags and their meaning are summarized in the following table:

Tags	Description
`Title string `json:"book_title"``	Maps the `Title` struct field to the JSON object key, `"book_title"`.
`PageCount int `json:"pages,string"``	Maps the `PageCount` struct field to the JSON object key, `"pages"`, and outputs the value as a string instead of a number.
`ISBN string `json:"-"``	The dash causes the `ISBN` field to be skipped during encoding and decoding.

`Authors []Name` `` `json:"auths,omniempty"` ``	Maps the `Authors` field to the JSON object key, `"auths"`. The annotation, `omniempty`, causes the field to be omitted if its value is nil.
`Publisher string` `` `json:",omniempty"` ``	Maps the struct field name, `Publisher`, as the JSON object key name. The annotation, `omniempty`, causes the field to be omitted when empty.
`PublishDate time.Time` `` `json:"pub_date"` ``	Maps the field name, `PublishDate`, to the JSON object key, `"pub_date"`.

When the previous struct is encoded, it produces the following JSON output in the `books.dat` file (formatted for readability):

```
...
{
    "book_title":"The Go Programming Language",
    "pages":"380",
    "auths":[
            {"First":"Alan","Last":"Donavan"},
            {"First":"Brian","Last":"Kernighan"}
    ],
    "Publisher":"Addison-Wesley",
    "pub_date":"2015-10-26T00:00:00Z"
}
...
```

Notice the JSON object keys are titled as specified in the `struct` tags. The object key `"pages"` (mapped to the struct field, `PageCount`) is encoded as a string. Finally, the struct field, `ISBN`, is omitted, as annotated in the `struct` tag.

Custom encoding and decoding

The JSON package uses two interfaces, *Marshaler* and *Unmarshaler*, to hook into encoding and decoding events respectively. When the encoder encounters a value whose type implements `json.Marshaler`, it delegates serialization of the value to the method `MarshalJSON` defined in the Marshaller interface. This is exemplified in the following abbreviated code snippet where the type `Name` is updated to implement `json.Marshaller` as shown:

```
type Name struct {
    First, Last string
}
```

```
func (n *Name) MarshalJSON() ([]byte, error) {
    return []byte(
        fmt.Sprintf(""%s, %s"", n.Last, n.First)
    ), nil
}

type Book struct {
    Title        string
    PageCount    int
    ISBN         string
    Authors      []Name
    Publisher    string
    PublishDate  time.Time
}
func main(){
    books := []Book{
        Book{
                Title:        "Leaning Go",
                PageCount:    375,
                ISBN:         "9781784395438",
                Authors:      []Name{{"Vladimir", "Vivien"}},
                Publisher:    "Packt",
                PublishDate:  time.Date(
                    2016, time.July,
                    0, 0, 0, 0, 0, time.UTC),
        },
        ...
    }
    ...
    enc := json.NewEncoder(file)
    if err := enc.Encode(books); err != nil {
        fmt.Println(err)
    }
}
```

golang.fyi/ch10/json3.go

In the previous example, values of the Name type are serialized as a JSON string (instead of an object as earlier). The serialization is handled by the method Name.MarshallJSON which returns an array of bytes that contains the last and first name separated by a comma. The preceding code generates the following JSON output:

```
[
    ...
    {
        "Title":"Leaning Go",
        "PageCount":375,
```

```
        "ISBN":"9781784395438",
        "Authors":["Vivien, Vladimir"],
        "Publisher":"Packt",
        "PublishDate":"2016-06-30T00:00:00Z"
    },
    ...
]
```

For the inverse, when a decoder encounters a piece of JSON text that maps to a type that implements `json.Unmarshaler`, it delegates the decoding to the type's `UnmarshalJSON` method. For instance, the following shows the abbreviated code snippet that implements `json.Unmarshaler` to handle the JSON output for the `Name` type:

```go
type Name struct {
    First, Last string
}

func (n *Name) UnmarshalJSON(data []byte) error {
    var name string
    err := json.Unmarshal(data, &name)
    if err != nil {
        fmt.Println(err)
        return err
    }
    parts := strings.Split(name, ", ")
    n.Last, n.First = parts[0], parts[1]
    return nil
}
```

golang.fyi/ch10/json4.go

The `Name` type is an implementation of `json.Unmarshaler`. When the decoder encounters a JSON object with the key `"Authors"`, it uses the method `Name.Unmarshaler` to reconstitute the Go struct `Name` type from the JSON string.

 The Go standard libraries offer additional encoders (not covered here) including `base32`, `bas364`, `binary`, `csv`, `hex`, `xml`, `gzip`, and numerous encryption format encoders.

Summary

This chapter provides a high-level view of Go's data input and output idioms and the packages involved in implementing IO primitives. The chapter starts by covering the fundamentals of a stream-based IO in Go with the io.Reader and io.Writer interfaces. Readers are walked through the implementation strategies and examples for both an io.Reader and an io.Writer.

The chapter goes on to cover packages, types, and functions that that support the streaming IO mechanism including working with files, formatted IO, buffered, and in-memory IO. The last portion of the chapter covers encoders and decoders that convert data as it is being streamed. In the next chapter, the IO theme is carried further when the discussion turns to creating programs that use IO to communicate via networking.

11
Writing Networked Services

One of the many reasons for Go's popularity, as a system language, is its inherent support for creating networked programs. The standard library exposes APIs ranging from low-level socket primitives to higher-level service abstractions such as HTTP and RPC. This chapter explores fundamental topics about creating connected applications including the following:

- The net package
- A TCP API server
- The HTTP package
- A JSON API server

The net package

The starting point for all networked programs in Go is the *net* package (https://golang.org/pkg/net). It provides a rich API to handle low-level networking primitives as well as application-level protocols such as HTTP. Each logical component of a network is represented by a Go type including hardware interfaces, networks, packets, addresses, protocols, and connections. Furthermore, each type exposes a multitude of methods giving Go one of the most complete standard libraries for network programming supporting both IPv4 and IPv6.

Whether creating a client or a server program, Go programmers will need, at a minimum, the network primitives covered in the following sections. These primitives are offered as functions and types to facilitate clients connecting to remote services and servers to handle incoming requests.

Addressing

One of the basic primitives, when doing network programming, is the *address*. The types and functions of the `net` package use a string literal to represent an address such as `"127.0.0.1"`. The address can also include a service port separated by a colon such as `"74.125.21.113:80"`. Functions and methods in the `net` package also support string literal representation for IPv6 addresses such as `"::1"` or `"[2607:f8b0:4002:c06::65]:80"` for an address with a service port of 80.

The net.Conn Type

The `net.Conn` interface represents a generic connection established between two nodes on the network. It implements `io.Reader` and `io.Writer` interfaces which allow connected nodes to exchange data using streaming IO primitives. The `net` package offers network protocol-specific implementations of the `net.Conn` interface such as *IPConn, UDPConn,* and *TCPConn*. Each implementation exposes additional methods specific to its respective network and protocol. However, as we will see in this chapter, the default method set defined in net.Conn is adequate for most uses.

Dialing a connection

Client programs use the `net.Dial` function, which has the following signature, to connect to a host service over the network:

```
func Dial(network, address string) (Conn, error)
```

The function takes two parameters where the first parameter, *network,* specifies the network protocol for the connection which can be:

- `tcp, tcp4, tcp6` : tcp defaults to `tcp4`
- `udp, udp4, udp6`: udp defaults to `udp4`
- `ip, ip4, ip6`: ip defaults to `ip4`
- `unix, unixgram, unixpacket`: for Unix domain sockets

The latter parameter of the `net.Dial` function specifies a string value for the host address to which to connect. The address can be provided as IPv4 or IPv6 addresses as discussed earlier. The `net.Dial` function returns an implementation of the `net.Conn` interface that matches the specified network parameter.

For instance, the following code snippet dials a "tcp" network at the host address, www.gutenberg.org:80, which returns a TCP connection of the *net.TCPConn type. The abbreviated code uses the TCP connection to issue an "HTTP GET" request to retrieve the full text of the literary classic Beowulf from the Project Gutenberg's website (http://gutenb erg.org/). The raw and unparsed HTTP response is subsequently written to a local file, beowulf.txt:

```
func main() {
    host, port := "www.gutenberg.org", "80"
    addr := net.JoinHostPort(host, port)
    httpRequest:="GET  /cache/epub/16328/pg16328.txt HTTP/1.1\n" +
            "Host: " + host + "\n\n"

    conn, err := net.Dial("tcp", addr)
    if err != nil {
            fmt.Println(err)
            return
    }
    defer conn.Close()

    if _, err = conn.Write([]byte(httpRequest)); err != nil {
            fmt.Println(err)
            return
    }

    file, err := os.Create("beowulf.txt")
    if err != nil {
            fmt.Println(err)
            return
    }
    defer file.Close()

    io.Copy(file, conn)
    fmt.Println("Text copied to file", file.Name())
}
```

golang.fyi/ch11/dial0.go

Because the net.Conn type implements the io.Reader and io.Writer, it can be used to both send data and receive data using streaming IO semantics. In the preceding example, conn.Write([]byte(httpRequest)) sends the HTTP request to the server. The response returned by the host is copied from the conn variable to the file variable using io.Copy(file, conn).

Note that the previous is an illustration that shows how to connect to an HTTP server using raw TCP. The Go standard library provides a separate package designed specifically for HTTP programming which abstracts away the low-level protocol details (covered later in the chapter).

The `net` package also makes available network specific dialing functions such as `DialUDP`, `DiapTCP`, or `DialIP`, each returning its respective connection implementation. In most cases, the `net.Dial` function and the `net.Conn` interface provide adequate capabilities to connect and manage connections to a remote host.

Listening for incoming connections

When creating a service program, one the first steps is to announce the port which the service will use to listen for incoming requests from the network. This is done by invoking the `net.Listen` function which has the following signature:

```
func Listen(network, laddr string) (net.Listener, error)
```

It takes two parameters where the first parameter specifies a protocol with valid values of `"tcp"`, `"tcp4"`, `"tcp6"`, `"unix"`, or `"unixpacket"`.

The second parameter is the local host address for the service. The local address can be specified without an IP address such as `":4040"`. Omitting the IP address of the host means that the service is bound to all network card interfaces installed on the host. As an alternative, the service can be bound to a specific network hardware interface on the host by specifying its IP address on the network, that is, `"10.20.130.240:4040"`.

A successful call to the `net.Listen` function returns a value of the `net.Listener` type (or a non-nil error if it fails). The `net.Listener` interface exposes methods used to manage the life cycle of incoming client connections. Depending on the value of the `network` parameter (`"tcp"`, `"tcp4"`, `"tcp6"`, and so on.), `net.Listen` will return either a `net.TCPListener` or `net.UnixListener`, both of which are concrete implementations of the `net.Listener` interface.

Accepting client connections

The `net.Listener` interface uses the *Accept* method to block indefinitely until a new connection arrives from a client. The following abbreviated code snippet shows a simple server that returns the string "Nice to meet you!" to each client connection and then disconnects immediately:

```
func main() {
    listener, err := net.Listen("tcp", ":4040")
    if err != nil {
        fmt.Println(err)
        return
    }
    defer listener.Close()

    for {
        conn, err := listener.Accept()
        if err != nil {
            fmt.Println(err)
            return
        }
        conn.Write([]byte("Nice to meet you!"))
        conn.Close()
    }
}
```

golang.fyi/ch11/listen0.go

In the code, the `listener.Accept` method returns a value of the `net.Conn` type to handle data exchange between the server and the client (or it returns a non-nil `error` if it fails). The `conn.Write([]byte("Nice to meet you!"))` method call is used to write the response to the client. When the server program is running, it can be tested using a *telnet* client as shown in the following output:

```
$> go run listen0.go &
[1] 83884

$> telnet 127.0.0.1 4040
Trying 127.0.0.1...
Connected to localhost.
Escape character is '^]'.
Nice to meet you! Connection closed by foreign host.
```

To ensure that the server program continues to run and handle subsequent client connections, the call to the `Accept` method is wrapped within an infinite for-loop. As soon as a connection is closed, the loop restarts the cycle to wait for the next client connection. Also notice that it is a good practice to close the listener when the server process is shutting down with a call to `Listener.Close()`.

 The observant reader may notice that this simple server will not scale as it cannot handle more than one client request at once. In the next section, we will see the techniques for creating a scalable server.

A TCP API server

At this point, the chapter has covered the minimum networking components necessary to create client and service programs. The remainder of the chapter will discuss different versions of a server that implement a *monetary currency information* service. The service returns ISO 4217 monetary currency information with each request. The intent is to show the implications of creating networked services, along with their clients, using different application-level protocols.

Earlier we introduced a very simple server to demonstrate the necessary steps required to set up a networked service. This section dives deeper into network programming by creating a TCP server that scales to handle many concurrent connections. The server code presented in this section has the following design goals:

- Use raw TCP to communicate between client and server
- Develop a simple text-based protocol, over TCP, for communication
- Clients can query the server for global currency information with text commands
- Use a goroutine per connection to handle connection concurrency
- Maintain connection until the client disconnects

The following lists an abbreviated version of the server code. The program uses the `curr` package (found at `https://github.com/vladimirvivien/learning-go/ch11/curr0`), not discussed here, to load monetary currency data from a local CSV file into slice `currencies`.

Upon successful connection to a client, the server parses the incoming client commands specified with a simple text protocol with the format *GET <currency-filter-value>* where *<currency-filter-value>* specifies a string value used to search for currency information:

```
import (
    "net"
    ...
    curr "https://github.com/vladimirvivien/learning-go/ch11/curr0"
)

var currencies = curr.Load("./data.csv")

func main() {
    ln, _ := net.Listen("tcp", ":4040")
    defer ln.Close()
    // connection loop
    for {
        conn, err := ln.Accept()
        if err != nil {
            fmt.Println(err)
            conn.Close()
            continue
        }
        go handleConnection(conn)
    }
}

// handle client connection
func handleConnection(conn net.Conn) {
    defer conn.Close()

    // loop to stay connected with client
    for {
        cmdLine := make([]byte, (1024 * 4))
        n, err := conn.Read(cmdLine)
        if n == 0 || err != nil {
            return
        }
        cmd, param := parseCommand(string(cmdLine[0:n]))
        if cmd == "" {
            continue
        }

        // execute command
        switch strings.ToUpper(cmd) {
        case "GET":
            result := curr.Find(currencies, param)
            // stream result to client
```

```
                    for _, cur := range result {
                        _, err := fmt.Fprintf(
                            conn,
                            "%s %s %s %s\n",
                            cur.Name, cur.Code,
                            cur.Number, cur.Country,
                        )
                        if err != nil {
                            return
                        }
                        // reset deadline while writing,
                        // closes conn if client is gone
                        conn.SetWriteDeadline(
                            time.Now().Add(time.Second * 5))
                    }
                    // reset read deadline for next read
                    conn.SetReadDeadline(
                        time.Now().Add(time.Second * 300))

            default:
                conn.Write([]byte("Invalid command\n"))
            }
        }
    }

func parseCommand(cmdLine string) (cmd, param string) {
    parts := strings.Split(cmdLine, " ")
    if len(parts) != 2 {
        return "", ""
    }
    cmd = strings.TrimSpace(parts[0])
    param = strings.TrimSpace(parts[1])
    return
}
```

golang.fyi/ch11/tcpserv0.go

Unlike the simple server introduced in the last section, this server is able to service multiple client connections at the same time. Upon accepting a new connection, with `ln.Accept()`, it delegates the handling of new client connections to a goroutine with `go handleConnection(conn)`. The connection loop then continues immediately and waits for the next client connection.

The `handleConnection` function manages the server communication with the connected client. It first reads and parses a slice of bytes, from the client, into a command string using `cmd, param := parseCommand(string(cmdLine[0:n]))`. Next, the code tests the command with a `switch` statement. If the `cmd` is equal to `"GET"`, the code searches slice `currencies` for values that matches `param` with a call to `curr.Find(currencies, param)`. Finally, it streams the search result to the client's connection using `fmt.Fprintf(conn, "%s %s %s %s\n", cur.Name, cur.Code, cur.Number, cur.Country)`.

The simple text protocol supported by the server does not include any sort of session control or control messages. Therefore, the code uses the `conn.SetWriteDeadline` method to ensure the connection to the client does not linger unnecessarily for long periods of time. The method is called during the loop that streams out a response to the client. It is set for a deadline of 5 seconds to ensure the client is always ready to receive the next chunk of bytes within that time, otherwise it times the connection out.

Connecting to the TCP server with telnet

Because the currency server presented earlier uses a simple text-based protocol, it can be tested using a telnet client, assuming the server code has been compiled and running (and listening on port `4040`). The following shows the output of a telnet session querying the server for currency information:

```
$> telnet localhost 4040
Trying ::1...
Connected to localhost.
Escape character is '^]'.
GET Gourde
Gourde HTG 332 HAITI
GET USD
US Dollar USD 840 AMERICAN SAMOA
US Dollar USD 840 BONAIRE, SINT EUSTATIUS AND SABA
US Dollar USD 840 GUAM
US Dollar USD 840 HAITI
US Dollar USD 840 MARSHALL ISLANDS (THE)
US Dollar USD 840 UNITED STATES OF AMERICA (THE)
...
```

```
get india
Indian Rupee INR 356 BHUTAN
US Dollar USD 840 BRITISH INDIAN OCEAN TERRITORY (THE)
Indian Rupee INR 356 INDIA
```

As you can see, you can query the server by using the get command followed by a filter parameter as explained earlier. The telnet client sends the raw text to the server which parses it and sends back raw text as the response. You can open multiple telnet sessions against the server and all request are served concurrently in their respective goroutine.

Connecting to the TCP server with Go

A simple TCP client can also be written in Go to connect to the TCP server. The client captures the command from the console's standard input and sends it to the server as is shown in the following code snippet:

```go
var host, port = "127.0.0.1", "4040"
var addr = net.JoinHostPort(host, port)
const prompt = "curr"
const buffLen = 1024

func main() {
    conn, err := net.Dial("tcp", addr)
    if err != nil {
        fmt.Println(err)
        return
    }
    defer conn.Close()
    var cmd, param string
    // repl - interactive shell for client
    for {
        fmt.Print(prompt, "> ")
        _, err = fmt.Scanf("%s %s", &cmd, &param)
        if err != nil {
            fmt.Println("Usage: GET <search string or *>")
            continue
        }
        // send command line
        cmdLine := fmt.Sprintf("%s %s", cmd, param)
        if n, err := conn.Write([]byte(cmdLine));
        n == 0 || err != nil {
            fmt.Println(err)
            return
        }

        // stream and display response
```

```
            conn.SetReadDeadline(
                    time.Now().Add(time.Second * 5))
            for {
                    buff := make([]byte, buffLen)
                    n, err := conn.Read(buff)
                    if err != nil { break }
                    fmt.Print(string(buff[0:n]))
                    conn.SetReadDeadline(
                            time.Now().Add(time.Millisecond * 700))
            }
    }
}
```

golang.fyi/ch11/tcpclient0.go

The source code for the Go client follows the same pattern as we have seen in the earlier client example. The first portion of the code dials out to the server using net.Dial(). Once a connection is obtained, the code sets up an event loop to capture text commands from the standard input, parses it, and sends it as a request to the server.

There is a nested loop that is set up to handle incoming responses from the server (see code comment). It continuously streams incoming bytes into variables buff with conn.Read(buff). This continues until the Read method encounters an error. The following lists the sample output produced by the client when it is executed:

```
$> Connected to Global Currency Service
curr> get pound
Egyptian Pound EGP 818 EGYPT
Gibraltar Pound GIP 292 GIBRALTAR
Sudanese Pound SDG 938 SUDAN (THE)
...
Syrian Pound SYP 760 SYRIAN ARAB REPUBLIC
Pound Sterling GBP 826 UNITED KINGDOM OF GREAT BRITAIN (THE)
curr>
```

An even better way of streaming the incoming bytes from the server is to use buffered IO as done in the following snippet of code. In the updated code, the conbuf variable, of the bufio.Buffer type, is used to read and split incoming streams from the server using the conbuf.ReadString method:

```
            conbuf := bufio.NewReaderSize(conn, 1024)
            for {
                    str, err := conbuf.ReadString('\n')
                    if err != nil {
                            break
                    }
```

```
        fmt.Print(str)
        conn.SetReadDeadline(
                time.Now().Add(time.Millisecond * 700))
}
```

golang.fyi/ch11/tcpclient1.go

As you can see, writing networked services directly on top of raw TCP has some costs. While raw TCP gives the programmer complete control of the application-level protocol, it also requires the programmer to carefully handle all data processing which can be error-prone. Unless it is absolutely necessary to implement your own custom protocol, a better approach is to leverage an existing and proven protocols to implement your server programs. The remainder of this chapter continues to explore this topic using services that are based on HTTP as an application-level protocol.

The HTTP package

Due to its importance and ubiquity, HTTP is one of a handful of protocols directly implemented in Go. The `net/http` package (`https://golang.org/pkg/net/http/`) provides code to implement both HTTP clients and HTTP servers. This section explores the fundamentals of creating HTTP clients and servers using the `net/http` package. Later, we will return our attention back to building versions of our currency service using HTTP.

The http.Client type

The `http.Client` struct represents an HTTP client and is used to create HTTP requests and retrieve responses from a server. The following illustrates how to retrieve the text content of Beowulf from Project Gutenberg's website located at `http://gutenberg.org/cache/epub/16328/pg16328.txt`, using the `client` variable of the `http.Client` type and prints its content to a standard output:

```
func main() {
    client := http.Client{}
    resp, err := client.Get(
            " http://gutenberg.org/cache/epub/16328/pg16328.txt")
    if err != nil {
            fmt.Println(err)
            return
    }
    defer resp.Body.Close()
    io.Copy(os.Stdout, resp.Body)
```

```
}
```

golang.fyi/ch11/httpclient1.go

The previous example uses the `client.Get` method to retrieve content from the remote server using the HTTP protocol method `GET` internally. The `GET` method is part of several convenience methods offered, by the Client type, to interact with HTTP servers as summarized in the following table. Notice that all of these methods return a value of the `*http.Response` type (discussed later) to handle responses returned by the HTTP server.

Method	Description

Client.Get	As discussed earlier, `Get` is a convenience method that issues an HTTP `GET` method to retrieve the resource specified by the `url` parameter from the server:
	`Get(url string,`
	`) (resp *http.Response, err    error)`

Client.Post	The `Post` method is a convenience method that issues an HTTP `POST` method to send the content specified by the `body` parameter to the server specified by the `url` parameter:
	`Post(`
	`   url string,`
	`   bodyType string,`
	`   body io.Reader,`
	`) (resp *http.Response, err error)`

Client.PostForm	The `PostForm` method is a convenience method that uses the HTTP `POST` method to send form `data`, specified as mapped key/value pairs, to the server:
	`PostForm(`
	`   url string,`
	`   data url.Values,`
	`) (resp *http.Response, err error)`

Client.Head	The `Head` method is a convenience method that issues an HTTP method, `HEAD`, to the remote server specified by the `url` parameter:
	`Head(url string,`
	`)(resp *http.Response, err error)`

Client.Do	This method generalizes the request and response interaction with a remote HTTP server. It is wrapped internally by the methods listed in this table. Section *Handling client requests and responses* discusses how to use this method to talk to the server.

It should be noted that the HTTP package uses an internal `http.Client` variable designed to mirror the preceding methods as package functions for further convenience. They include `http.Get`, *http.Post*, `http.PostForm`, and `http.Head`. The following snippet shows the previous example using `http.Get` instead of the method from the `http.Client`:

```go
func main() {
    resp, err := http.Get(
        "http://gutenberg.org/cache/epub/16328/pg16328.txt")
    if err != nil {
        fmt.Println(err)
        return
    }
    defer resp.Body.Close()
    io.Copy(os.Stdout, resp.Body)
}
```

golang.fyi/ch11/httpclient1a.go

Configuring the client

Besides the methods to communicate with the remote server, the `http.Client` type exposes additional attributes that can be used to modify and control the behavior of the client. For instance, the following source snippet sets the timeout to handle a client request to complete within 21 seconds using the `Timeout` attribute of the `Client` type:

```go
func main() {
    client := &http.Client{
        Timeout: 21 * time.Second
    }
    resp, err := client.Get(
        "http://tools.ietf.org/rfc/rfc7540.txt")
    if err != nil {
        fmt.Println(err)
        return
    }
    defer resp.Body.Close()
    io.Copy(os.Stdout, resp.Body)
}
```

golang.fyi/ch11/httpclient2.go

The `Transport` field of the `Client` type provides further means of controlling the settings of a client. For instance, the following snippet creates a client that disables the connection reuse between successive HTTP requests with the `DisableKeepAlive` field. The code also uses the `Dial` function to specify further granular control over the HTTP connection used by the underlying client, setting its timeout value to 30 seconds:

```
func main() {
    client := &http.Client{
        Transport: &http.Transport{
            DisableKeepAlives: true,
            Dial: (&net.Dialer{
                Timeout:   30 * time.Second,
            }).Dial,
        },
    }
    ...
}
```

Handling client requests and responses

An `http.Request` value can be explicitly created using the `http.NewRequest` function. A request value can be used to configure HTTP settings, add headers, and specify the content body of the request. The following source snippet uses the `http.Request` type to create a new request which is used to specify the headers sent to the server:

```
func main() {
    client := &http.Client{}
    req, err := http.NewRequest(
        "GET", "http://tools.ietf.org/rfc/rfc7540.txt", nil,
    )
    req.Header.Add("Accept", "text/plain")
    req.Header.Add("User-Agent", "SampleClient/1.0")

    resp, err := client.Do(req)
    if err != nil {
        fmt.Println(err)
        return
    }
    defer resp.Body.Close()
    io.Copy(os.Stdout, resp.Body)
}
```

golang.fyi/ch11/httpclient3.go

The `http.NewRequest` function has the following signature:

```
func NewRequest(method, uStr string, body io.Reader) (*http.Request, error)
```

It takes a string that specifies the HTTP method as its first argument. The next argument specifies the destination URL. The last argument is an `io.Reader` that can be used to specify the content of the request (or set to nil if the request has no content). The function returns a pointer to a `http.Request` struct value (or a non-nil `error` if one occurs). Once the request value is created, the code uses the `Header` field to add HTTP headers to the request to be sent to the server.

Once a request is prepared (as shown in the previous source snippet), it is sent to the server using the *Do* method of the `http.Client` type and has the following signature:

```
Do(req *http.Request) (*http.Response, error)
```

The method accepts a pointer to an `http.Request` value, as discussed in the previous section. It then returns a pointer to an `http.Response` value or an error if the request fails. In the previous source code, `resp, err := client.Do(req)` is used to send the request to the server and assigns the response to the `resp` variable.

The response from the server is encapsulated in struct `http.Response` which contains several fields to describe the response including the HTTP response status, content length, headers, and the response body. The response body, exposed as the `http.Response.Body` field, implements the `io.Reader` which affords the use streaming IO primitives to consume the response content.

The `Body` field also implements *io.Closer* which allows the closing of IO resources. The previous source uses `defer resp.Body.Close()` to close the IO resource associated with the response body. This is a recommended idiom when the server is expected to return a non-nil body.

A simple HTTP server

The HTTP package provides two main components to accept HTTP requests and serve responses:

- The `http.Handler` interface
- The `http.Server` type

The `http.Server` type uses the `http.Handler` interface type, defined in the following listing, to receive requests and server responses:

```
type Handler interface {
        ServeHTTP(ResponseWriter, *Request)
}
```

Any type that implements `http.Handler` can be registered (explained next) as a valid handler. The Go `http.Server` type is used to create a new server. It is a struct whose values can be configured, at a minimum, with the TCP address of the service and a handler that will respond to incoming requests. The following code snippet shows a simple HTTP server that defines the `msg` type as handler registered to handle incoming client requests:

```
type msg string

func (m msg) ServeHTTP(
    resp http.ResponseWriter, req *http.Request) {
    resp.Header().Add("Content-Type", "text/html")
    resp.WriteHeader(http.StatusOK)
    fmt.Fprint(resp, m)
}

func main() {
    msgHandler := msg("Hello from high above!")
    server := http.Server{Addr: ":4040", Handler: msgHandler}
    server.ListenAndServe()
}
```

golang.fyi/ch11/httpserv0.go

In the previous code, the `msg` type, which uses a string as its underlying type, implements the `ServeHTTP()` method making it a valid HTTP handler. Its `ServeHTTP` method uses the response parameter, `resp`, to print response headers "`200 OK`" and "`Content-Type: text/html`". The method also writes the string value `m` to the response variable using `fmt.Fprint(resp, m)` which is sent back to the client.

In the code, the variable `server` is initialized as `http.Server{Addr: ":4040", Handler: msgHandler}`. This means the server will listen on all network interfaces at port `4040` and will use variable `msgHandler` as its `http.Handler` implementation. Once initialized, the server is started with the `server.ListenAndServe()` method call that is used to block and listen for incoming requests.

Besides the `Addr` and `Handler`, the `http.Server` struct exposes several additional fields that can be used to control different aspects of the HTTP service such as connection, timeout values, header sizes, and TLS configuration. For instance, the following snippet shows an updated example which specifies the server's read and write timeouts:

```
type msg string
func (m msg) ServeHTTP(
    resp http.ResponseWriter, req *http.Request) {
    resp.Header().Add("Content-Type", "text/html")
    resp.WriteHeader(http.StatusOK)
    fmt.Fprint(resp, m)
}
func main() {
    msgHandler := msg("Hello from high above!")
    server := http.Server{
        Addr:         ":4040",
        Handler:      msgHandler,
        ReadTimeout:  time.Second * 5,
        WriteTimeout: time.Second * 3,
    }
    server.ListenAndServe()
}
```

golang.fyi/ch11/httpserv1.go

The default server

It should be noted that the HTTP package includes a default server that can be used in simpler cases when there is no need for configuration of the server. The following abbreviated code snippet starts a simple server without explicitly creating a server variable:

```
type msg string

func (m msg) ServeHTTP(
    resp http.ResponseWriter, req *http.Request) {
    resp.Header().Add("Content-Type", "text/html")
    resp.WriteHeader(http.StatusOK)
    fmt.Fprint(resp, m)
}
    func main() {
    msgHandler := msg("Hello from high above!")
    http.ListenAndServe(":4040", msgHandler)
}
```

golang.fyi/ch11/httpserv2.go

In the code, the `http.ListenAndServe(":4040", msgHandler)` function is used to start a server which is declared as a variable in the HTTP package. The server is configured with the local address `":4040"` and the handler `msgHandler` (as was done earlier) to handle all incoming requests.

Routing requests with http.ServeMux

The `http.Handler` implementation introduced in the previous section is not sophisticated. No matter what URL path is sent with the request, it sends the same response back to the client. That is not very useful. In most cases, you want to map each path of a request URL to a different response.

Fortunately, the HTTP package comes with the `http.ServeMux` type which can multiplex incoming requests based on URL patterns. When an `http.ServeMux` handler receives a request, associated with a URL path, it dispatches a function that is mapped to that URL. The following abbreviated code snippet shows `http.ServeMux` variable `mux` configured to handle two URL paths `"/hello"` and `"/goodbye"`:

```
func main() {
    mux := http.NewServeMux()
    hello := func(resp http.ResponseWriter, req *http.Request) {
        resp.Header().Add("Content-Type", "text/html")
        resp.WriteHeader(http.StatusOK)
        fmt.Fprint(resp, "Hello from Above!")
    }

    goodbye := func(resp http.ResponseWriter, req *http.Request) {
        resp.Header().Add("Content-Type", "text/html")
        resp.WriteHeader(http.StatusOK)
        fmt.Fprint(resp, "Goodbye, it's been real!")
    }

    mux.HandleFunc("/hello", hello)
    mux.HandleFunc("/goodbye", goodbye)

    http.ListenAndServe(":4040", mux)
}
```

golang.fyi/ch11/httpserv3.go

The code declares two functions assigned to variables `hello` and `goodbye`. Each function is mapped to a path `"/hello"` and `"/goodbye"` respectively using the `mux.HandleFunc("/hello", hello)` and `mux.HandleFunc("/goodbye", goodbye)` method calls. When the server is launched, with `http.ListenAndServe(":4040", mux)`, its handler will route the request `"http://localhost:4040/hello"` to the `hello` function and requests with the path `"http://localhost:4040/goodbye"` to the `goodbye` function.

The default ServeMux

It is worth pointing out that the HTTP package makes available a default ServeMux internally. When used, it is not necessary to explicitly declare a ServeMux variable. Instead the code uses the package function, `http.HandleFunc`, to map a path to a handler function as illustrated in the following code snippet:

```
func main() {
    hello := func(resp http.ResponseWriter, req *http.Request) {
    ...
    }

    goodbye := func(resp http.ResponseWriter, req *http.Request) {
    ...
    }

    http.HandleFunc("/hello", hello)
    http.HandleFunc("/goodbye", goodbye)

    http.ListenAndServe(":4040", nil)
}
```

golang.fyi/ch11/httpserv4.go

To launch the server, the code calls `http.ListenAndServe(":4040", nil)` where the ServerMux parameter is set to `nil`. This implies that the server will default to the per-declared package instance of http.ServeMux to handle incoming requests.

A JSON API server

Armed with the information from the last section, it is possible to use the HTTP package to create services over HTTP. Earlier we discussed the perils of creating services using raw TCP directly when we created a server for our global monetary currency service. In this section, we explore how to create an API server for the same service using HTTP as the underlying protocol. The new HTTP-based service has the following design goals:

- Use HTTP as the transport protocol
- Use JSON for structured communication between client and server
- Clients query the server for currency information using JSON-formatted requests
- The server respond using JSON-formatted responses

The following shows the code involved in the implementation of the new service. This time, the server will use the `curr1` package (see `github.com/vladimirvivien/learning-go /ch11/curr1`) to load and query ISO 4217 currency data from a local CSV file.

The code in the curr1 package defines two types, `CurrencyRequest` and `Currency`, intended to represent the client request and currency data returned by the server, respectively as listed here:

```go
type Currency struct {
    Code    string `json:"currency_code"`
    Name    string `json:"currency_name"`
    Number  string `json:"currency_number"`
    Country string `json:"currency_country"`
}

type CurrencyRequest struct {
    Get    string `json:"get"`
    Limit int     `json:limit`
}
```

golang.fyi/ch11/curr1/currency.go

Note that the preceding struct types shown are annotated with tags that describe the JSON properties for each field. This information is used by the JSON encoder to encode the key name of JSON objects (see `Chapter 10`, *Data IO in Go*, for detail on encoding). The remainder of the code, listed in the following snippet, defines the functions that set up the server and the handler function for incoming requests:

```go
import (
    "encoding/json"
    "fmt"
```

```
    "net/http"

    " github.com/vladimirvivien/learning-go/ch11/curr1"
)
var currencies = curr1.Load("./data.csv")

func currs(resp http.ResponseWriter, req *http.Request) {
    var currRequest curr1.CurrencyRequest
    dec := json.NewDecoder(req.Body)
    if err := dec.Decode(&currRequest); err != nil {
        resp.WriteHeader(http.StatusBadRequest)
        fmt.Println(err)
        return
    }

    result := curr1.Find(currencies, currRequest.Get)
    enc := json.NewEncoder(resp)
    if err := enc.Encode(&result); err != nil {
        fmt.Println(err)
        resp.WriteHeader(http.StatusInternalServerError)
        return
    }
}

func main() {
    mux := http.NewServeMux()
    mux.HandleFunc("/currency", get)

    if err := http.ListenAndServe(":4040", mux); err != nil {
        fmt.Println(err)
    }
}
```

golang.fyi/ch11/jsonserv0.go

Since we are leveraging HTTP as the transport protocol for the service, you can see the code is now much smaller than the prior implementation which used pure TCP. The `currs` function implements the handler responsible for incoming requests. It sets up a decoder to decode the incoming JSON-encoded request to a value of the `curr1.CurrencyRequest` type as highlighted in the following snippet:

```
var currRequest curr1.CurrencyRequest
dec := json.NewDecoder(req.Body)
if err := dec.Decode(&currRequest); err != nil { ... }
```

Next, the function executes the currency search by calling `curr1.Find(currencies, currRequest.Get)` which returns the slice `[]Currency` assigned to the `result` variable. The code then creates an encoder to encode the `result` as a JSON payload, highlighted in the following snippet:

```
result := curr1.Find(currencies, currRequest.Get)
enc := json.NewEncoder(resp)
if err := enc.Encode(&result); err != nil { ... }
```

Lastly, the handler function is mapped to the `"/currency"` path in the `main` function with the call to `mux.HandleFunc("/currency", currs)`. When the server receives a request for that path, it automatically executes the `currs` function.

Testing the API server with cURL

Because the server is implemented over HTTP, it can easily be tested with any client-side tools that support HTTP. For instance, the following shows how to use thecURL command line tool (`http://curl.haxx.se/`) to connect to the API end-point and retrieve currency information about the `Euro`:

```
$> curl -X POST -d '{"get":"Euro"}' http://localhost:4040/currency
[
...
  {
    "currency_code": "EUR",
    "currency_name": "Euro",
    "currency_number": "978",
    "currency_country": "BELGIUM"
  },
  {
    "currency_code": "EUR",
    "currency_name": "Euro",
    "currency_number": "978",
    "currency_country": "FINLAND"
  },
  {
    "currency_code": "EUR",
    "currency_name": "Euro",
    "currency_number": "978",
    "currency_country": "FRANCE"
  },
...
]
```

The cURL command posts a JSON-formatted request object to the server using the -X POST -d '{"get":"Euro"}' parameters. The output (formatted for readability) from the server is comprised of a JSON array of the preceding currency items.

An API server client in Go

An HTTP client can also be built in Go to consume the service with minimal efforts. As is shown in the following code snippet, the client code uses the http.Client type to communicate with the server. It also uses the encoding/json sub-package to decode incoming data (note that the client also makes use of the curr1 package, shown earlier, which contains the types needed to communicate with the server):

```go
import (
    "bytes"
    "encoding/json"
    "fmt"
    "net/http"

    " github.com/vladimirvivien/learning-go/ch11/curr1"
)

func main() {
    var param string
    fmt.Print("Currency> ")
    _, err := fmt.Scanf("%s", &param)

    buf := new(bytes.Buffer)
    currRequest := &curr1.CurrencyRequest{Get: param}
    err = json.NewEncoder(buf).Encode(currRequest)
    if err != nil {
        fmt.Println(err)
        return
    }

    // send request
    client := &http.Client{}
    req, err := http.NewRequest(
        "POST", "http://127.0.0.1:4040/currency", buf)
    if err != nil {
        fmt.Println(err)
        return
    }

    resp, err := client.Do(req)
    if err != nil {
```

```
            fmt.Println(err)
            return
    }
    defer resp.Body.Close()

    // decode response
    var currencies []curr1.Currency
    err = json.NewDecoder(resp.Body).Decode(&currencies)
    if err != nil {
            fmt.Println(err)
            return
    }
    fmt.Println(currencies)
}
```

golang.fyi/ch11/jsonclient0.go

In the previous code, an HTTP client is created to send JSON-encoded request values as
`currRequest := &curr1.CurrencyRequest{Get: param}` where `param` is the
currency string to retrieve. The response from the server is a payload that represents an
array of JSON-encoded objects (see the JSON array in the section, *Testing the API Server with
cURL*). The code then uses a JSON decoder,
`json.NewDecoder(resp.Body).Decode(&currencies)`, to decode the payload from the
response body into the slice, `[]curr1.Currency`.

A JavaScript API server client

So far, we have seen how to use the API service using the `cURL` command-line tool and a
native Go client. This section shows the versatility of using HTTP to implement networked
services by showcasing a web-based JavaScript client. In this approach, the client is a web-
based GUI that uses modern HTML, CSS, and JavaScript to create an interface that interacts
with the API server.

First, the server code is updated with an additional handler to serve the static HTML file
that renders the GUI on the browser. This is illustrated in the following code:

```
// serves HTML gui
func gui(resp http.ResponseWriter, req *http.Request) {
    file, err := os.Open("./currency.html")
    if err != nil {
            resp.WriteHeader(http.StatusInternalServerError)
            fmt.Println(err)
            return
    }
```

```
    io.Copy(resp, file)
}

func main() {
    mux := http.NewServeMux()
    mux.HandleFunc("/", gui)
    mux.HandleFunc("/currency", currs)

    if err := http.ListenAndServe(":4040", mux); err != nil {
        fmt.Println(err)
    }
}
```

golang.fyi/ch11/jsonserv1.go

The preceding code snippet shows the declaration of the `gui` handler function responsible for serving a static HTML file that renders the GUI for the client. The root URL path is then mapped to the function with `mux.HandleFunc("/", gui)`. So, in addition to the `"/currency"` path, which hosts the API end-point the `"/"` path will return the web page shown in the following screenshot:

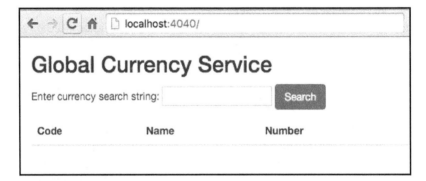

The next HTML page (`golang.fyi/ch11/currency.html`) is responsible for displaying the result of a currency search. It uses JavaScritpt functions along with the `jQuery.js` library (not covered here) to post JSON-encoded requests to the backend Go service as shown in the following abbreviated HTML and JavaScript snippets:

```
<body>
<div class="container">
   <h2>Global Currency Service</h2>
   <p>Enter currency search string: <input id="in">
      <button type="button" class="btn btn-primary"
onclick="doRequest()">Search</button>
   </p>
```

```html
<table id="tbl" class="table table-striped">
  <thead>
    <tr>
        <th>Code</th>
        <th>Name</th>
        <th>Number</th>
        <th>Country</th>
    </tr>
  </thead>
  <tbody/>
</table>
</div>

<script>
 var tbl = document.getElementById("tbl");
    function addRow(code, name, number, country) {
        var rowCount = tbl.rows.length;
        var row = tbl.insertRow(rowCount);
        row.insertCell(0).innerHTML = code;
        row.insertCell(1).innerHTML = name;
        row.insertCell(2).innerHTML = number;
        row.insertCell(3).innerHTML = country;
    }

    function doRequest() {
    param = document.getElementById("in").value
        $.ajax('/currency', {
            method: 'PUT',
                contentType: 'application/json',
                processData: false,
                data: JSON.stringify({get:param})
        }).then(
        function success(currencies) {
                currs = JSON.parse(currencies)
                for (i=0; i < currs.length; i++) {
                    addRow(
                            currs[i].currency_code,
                            currs[i].currency_name,
                            currs[i].currency_number,
                            currs[i].currency_country
                    );
                }

        });
    }
</script>
```

A line-by-line analysis of the HTML and JavaScript code in this example is beyond the scope of the book; however, it is worth pointing out that the JavaScript `doRequest` function is where the interaction between the client and the server happens. It uses the jQuery's `$.ajax` function to build an HTTP request with a `PUT` method and to specify a JSON-encoded currency request object, `JSON.stringify({get:param})`, to send to the server. The `then` method accepts the callback function, `success(currencies)`, which handles the response from the server that parses displays in an HTML table.

When a search value is provided in the text box on the GUI, the page displays its results in the table dynamically as shown in the following screenshot:

Global Currency Service

Enter currency search string: Franc　　　　　　　　　　 [Search]

Code	Name	Number	Country
XOF	CFA Franc BCEAO	952	BENIN
XOF	CFA Franc BCEAO	952	BURKINA FASO
BIF	Burundi Franc	108	BURUNDI
XAF	CFA Franc BEAC	950	CAMEROON
XAF	CFA Franc BEAC	950	CENTRAL AFRICAN REPUBLIC (THE)
XAF	CFA Franc BEAC	950	CHAD
KMF	Comoro Franc	174	COMOROS (THE)

Summary

This chapter condenses several important notions about creating networked services in Go. It starts with a walkthrough of Go's net package including the net.Conn type to create a connection between network nodes, the net.Dial function to connect to a remote service, and the net.Listen function to handle incoming connections from a client. The chapter continues to cover different implementations of clients and server programs and shows the implications of creating custom protocols directly over raw TCP versus using an existing protocol such as HTTP with JSON data format.

The next chapter takes a different direction. It explores the packages, types, functions, and tools that are available in Go to facilitate source code testing.

12
Code Testing

Testing is a critical ritual of modern software development practices. Go brings testing directly into the development cycle by offering an API and command-line tool to seamlessly create and integrate automated test code. Here we will cover the Go testing suite, including the following:

- The Go test tool
- Writing Go tests
- HTTP testing
- Test coverage
- Code benchmark

The Go test tool

Prior to writing any test code, let's take a detour to discuss the tooling for automated testing in Go. Similar to the `go build` command, the `go test` command is designed to compile and exercise test source files in specified packages, as illustrated in the following command:

```
$> go test .
```

The previous command will exercise all test functions in the current package. Although it appears to be simple, the previous command accomplishes several complex steps, including:

- The compilation of all test files found in the current package
- Generating an instrumented binary from the test file
- Executing the test functions in the code

When the `go test` command targets multiple packages, the test tool generates multiple test binaries that are executed and tested independently, as shown in the following:

```
$> go test ./...
```

Test file names

The test command uses the import path standard (see `Chapter 6`, *Go Packages and Programs*) to specify which packages to test. Within a specified package, the test tool will compile all files with the `*_test.go` name pattern. For instance, assuming that we have a project that has a simple implementation of a mathematical vector type in a file called `vec.go`, a sensible name for its test file would be `vec_test.go`.

Test organization

Traditionally, test files are kept in the same package (directory) as the code being tested. This is because there is no need to separate tests files, as they are excluded from the compiled program binary. The following shows the directory layout for a typical Go package, in this instance the `fmt` package from the standard library. It shows all of the test files for the package in the same directory as the regular source code:

```
$>tree go/src/fmt/
├── doc.go
├── export_test.go
├── fmt_test.go
├── format.go
├── norace_test.go
├── print.go
├── race_test.go
├── scan.go
├── scan_test.go
└── stringer_test.go
```

Besides having a simpler project structure, keeping the files together gives test functions full visibility of the package being tested. This facilitates access to and verification of package elements that would otherwise be opaque to testing code. When your functions are placed in a separate package from the code to be tested, they lose access to non-exported elements of the code.

Writing Go tests

A Go test file is simply a set of functions with the following signature:

*func Test<Name>(*testing.T)*

Here, *<Name>* is an arbitrary name that reflects the purpose of the test. The test functions are intended to exercise a specific functional unit (or unit test) of the source code.

Before we write the test functions, let us review the code that will be tested. The following source snippet shows a simple implementation of a mathematical vector with Add, Sub, and Scale methods (see the full source code listed at `https://github.com/vladimirvivien/learning-go/ch12/vector/vec.go`). Notice that each method implements a specific behavior as a unit of functionality, which will make it easy to test:

```
type Vector interface {
    Add(other Vector) Vector
    Sub(other Vector) Vector
    Scale(factor float64)
    ...
}

func New(elems ...float64) SimpleVector {
    return SimpleVector(elems)
}

type SimpleVector []float64

func (v SimpleVector) Add(other Vector) Vector {
    v.assertLenMatch(other)
    otherVec := other.(SimpleVector)
    result := make([]float64, len(v))
    for i, val := range v {
        result[i] = val + otherVec[i]
    }
    return SimpleVector(result)
}
```

```
func (v SimpleVector) Sub(other Vector) Vector {
    v.assertLenMatch(other)
    otherVec := other.(SimpleVector)
    result := make([]float64, len(v))
    for i, val := range v {
        result[i] = val - otherVec[i]
    }
    return SimpleVector(result)
}

func (v SimpleVector) Scale(scale float64) {
    for i := range v {
        v[i] = v[i] * scale
    }
}
...
```

golang.fyi/ch12/vector/vec.go

The test functions

The test source code in file `vec_test.go` defines a series of functions that exercise the behavior of type `SimpleVector` (see the preceding section) by testing each of its methods independently:

```
import "testing"

func TestVectorAdd(t *testing.T) {
    v1 := New(8.218, -9.341)
    v2 := New(-1.129, 2.111)
    v3 := v1.Add(v2)
    expect := New(
        v1[0]+v2[0],
        v1[1]+v2[1],
    )

    if !v3.Eq(expect) {
        t.Logf("Addition failed, expecting %s, got %s",
            expect, v3)
        t.Fail()
    }
    t.Log(v1, "+", v2, v3)
}

func TestVectorSub(t *testing.T) {
    v1 := New(7.119, 8.215)
```

```
    v2 := New(-8.223, 0.878)
    v3 := v1.Sub(v2)
    expect := New(
        v1[0]-v2[0],
        v1[1]-v2[1],
    )
    if !v3.Eq(expect) {
        t.Log("Subtraction failed, expecting %s, got %s",
            expect, v3)
            t.Fail()
    }
    t.Log(v1, "-", v2, "=", v3)
}

func TestVectorScale(t *testing.T) {
    v := New(1.671, -1.012, -0.318)
    v.Scale(7.41)
    expect := New(
        7.41*1.671,
        7.41*-1.012,
        7.41*-0.318,
    )
    if !v.Eq(expect) {
        t.Logf("Scalar mul failed, expecting %s, got %s",
            expect, v)
        t.Fail()
    }
    t.Log("1.671,-1.012, -0.318 Scale", 7.41, "=", v)
}
```

golang.fyi/ch12/vector/vec_test.go

As shown in the previous code, all test source code must import the "testing" package. This is because each test function receives an argument of type *testing.T as its parameter. As is discussed further in the chapter, this allows the test function to interact with the Go test runtime.

It is crucial to realize that each test function should be idempotent, with no reliance on any previously saved or shared states. In the previous source code snippet, each test function is executed as a standalone piece of code. Your test functions should not make any assumption about the order of execution as the Go test runtime makes no such guarantee.

The source code of a test function usually sets up an expected value, which is pre-determined based on knowledge of the tested code. That value is then compared to the calculated value returned by the code being tested. For instance, when adding two vectors, we can calculate the expected result using the rules of vector additions, as shown in the following snippet:

```
v1 := New(8.218, -9.341)
v2 := New(-1.129, 2.111)
v3 := v1.Add(v2)
expect := New(
    v1[0]+v2[0],
    v1[1]+v2[1],
)
```

In the preceding source snippet, the expected value is calculated using two simple vector values, v1 and v2, and stored in the variable expect. Variable v3, on the other hand, stores the actual value of the vector, as calculated by the tested code. This allows us to test the actual versus the expected, as shown in the following:

```
if !v3.Eq(expect) {
    t.Log("Addition failed, expecting %s, got %s", expect, v3)
    t.Fail()
}
```

In the preceding source snippet, if the tested condition is false, then the test has failed. The code uses t.Fail() to signal the failure of the test function. Signaling failure is discussed in more detail in the Reporting failure section.

Running the tests

As mentioned in the introductory section of this chapter, test functions are executed using the go test command-line tool. For instance, if we run the following command from within the package vector, it will automatically run all of the test functions of that package:

```
$> cd vector
$> go test .
ok      github.com/vladimirvivien/learning-go/ch12/vector      0.001s
```

The test can also be executed by specifying a sub-package (or all packages with package wildcard ./...) relative to where the command is issued, as shown in the following:

```
$> cd $GOPATH/src/github.com/vladimirvivien/learning-go/ch12/
$> go test ./vector
ok      github.com/vladimirvivien/learning-go/ch12/vector       0.005s
```

Filtering executed tests

During the development of a large set of test functions, it is often desirable to focus on a function (or set of functions) during debugging phases. The Go test command-line tool supports the -run flag, which specifies a regular expression that executes only functions whose names match the specified expression. The following command will only execute test function TestVectorAdd:

```
$> go test -run=VectorAdd -v
=== RUN    TestVectorAdd
--- PASS: TestVectorAdd (0.00s)
PASS
ok      github.com/vladimirvivien/learning-go/ch12/vector       0.025s
```

The use of the -v flag confirms that only one test function, TestVectorAdd, has been executed. As another example, the following executes all test functions that end with VectorA.*$ or match function name TestVectorMag, while ignoring everything else:

```
> go test -run="VectorA.*$|TestVectorMag" -v
=== RUN    TestVectorAdd
--- PASS: TestVectorAdd (0.00s)
=== RUN    TestVectorMag
--- PASS: TestVectorMag (0.00s)
=== RUN    TestVectorAngle
--- PASS: TestVectorAngle (0.00s)
PASS
ok      github.com/vladimirvivien/learning-go/ch12/vector       0.043s
```

Test logging

When writing new or debugging existing test functions, it is often helpful to print information to a standard output. Type `testing.T` offers two logging methods: `Log`, which uses a default formatter, and `Logf`, which formats its output using formatting verbs (as defined in package to `fmt`). For instance, the following test function snippet from the vector example shows the code logging information with `t.Logf("Vector = %v; Unit vector = %v\n", v, expect)`:

```
func TestVectorUnit(t *testing.T) {
    v := New(5.581, -2.136)
    mag := v.Mag()
    expect := New((1/mag)*v[0], (1/mag)*v[1])
    if !v.Unit().Eq(expect) {
        t.Logf("Vector Unit failed, expecting %s, got %s",
            expect, v.Unit())
        t.Fail()
    }
    t.Logf("Vector = %v; Unit vector = %v\n", v, expect)
}
```

golang.fyi/ch12/vector/vec_test.go

As seen previously, the Go test tool runs tests with minimal output unless there is a test failure. However, the tool will output test logs when the verbose flag −v is provided. For instance, running the following in package vector will mute all logging statements:

```
> go test -run=VectorUnit
PASS
ok      github.com/vladimirvivien/learning-go/ch12/vector        0.005s
```

When the verbose flag −v is provided, as shown in the following command, the test runtime prints the output of the logs as shown:

```
$> go test -run=VectorUnit -v
=== RUN   TestVectorUnit
--- PASS: TestVectorUnit (0.00s)
vec_test.go:100: Vector = [5.581,-2.136]; Unit vector =
[0.9339352140866403,-0.35744232526233]
PASS
ok      github.com/vladimirvivien/learning-go/ch12/vector        0.001s
```

Reporting failure

By default, the Go test runtime considers a test a success if the test function runs and returns normally without a panic. For example, the following test function is broken, since its expected value is not properly calculated. The test runtime, however, will always report it as passing because it does not include any code to report the failure:

```
func TestVectorDotProd(t *testing.T) {
    v1 := New(7.887, 4.138).(SimpleVector)
    v2 := New(-8.802, 6.776).(SimpleVector)
    actual := v1.DotProd(v2)
    expect := v1[0]*v2[0] - v1[1]*v2[1]
    if actual != expect {
        t.Logf("DotPoduct failed, expecting %d, got %d",
            expect, actual)
    }
}
```

golang.fyi/ch12/vec_test.go

This false positive condition may go unnoticed, especially if the verbose flag is turned off, minimizing any visual clues that it is broken:

```
$> go test -run=VectorDot
PASS
ok      github.com/vladimirvivien/learning-go/ch12/vector      0.001s
```

One way the previous test can be fixed is by using the `Fail` method from type `testing.T` to signal failure, as shown in the following snippet:

```
func TestVectorDotProd(t *testing.T) {
...
    if actual != expect {
        t.Logf("DotPoduct failed, expecting %d, got %d",
            expect, actual)
        t.Fail()
    }
}
```

So now, when the test is executed, it correctly reports that it is broken, as shown in the following output:

```
$> go test -run=VectorDot
--- FAIL: TestVectorDotProd (0.00s)
vec_test.go:109: DotPoduct failed, expecting -97.460462, got -41.382286
FAIL
exit status 1
FAIL  github.com/vladimirvivien/learning-go/ch12/vector      0.002s
```

It is important to understand that method `Fail` only reports failure and does not halt the execution of a test function. On the other hand, when it makes sense to actually exit the function upon a failed condition, the test API offers the method `FailNow`, which signals failure and exits the currently executing test function.

Type `testing.T` provides the convenience methods `Logf` and `Errorf`, which combine both logging and failure reporting. For instance, the following snippet uses the `Errorf` method, which is equivalent to calling the `Logf` and `Fail` methods:

```
func TestVectorMag(t *testing.T) {
    v  := New(-0.221, 7.437)
    expected := math.Sqrt(v[0]*v[0] + v[1]*v[1])
    if v.Mag() != expected {
    t.Errorf("Magnitude failed, execpted %d, got %d",
        expected, v.Mag())
    }
}
```

golang.fyi/ch12/vector/vec.go

Type `testing.T` also offers `Fatal` and `Formatf` methods as a way of combining the logging of a message and the immediate termination of a test function.

Skipping tests

It is sometimes necessary to skip test functions due to a number of factors such as environment constraints, resource availability, or inappropriate environment settings. The testing API makes it possible to skip a test function using the `SkipNow` method from type `testing.T`. The following source code snippet will only run the test function when the arbitrary operating system environment variable named RUN_ANGLE is set. Otherwise, it will skip the test:

```
func TestVectorAngle(t *testing.T) {
    if os.Getenv("RUN_ANGLE") == "" {
```

```
        t.Skipf("Env variable RUN_ANGLE not set, skipping:")
    }
    v1 := New(3.183, -7.627)
    v2 := New(-2.668, 5.319)
    actual := v1.Angle(v2)
    expect := math.Acos(v1.DotProd(v2) / (v1.Mag() * v2.Mag()))
    if actual != expect {
        t.Logf("Vector angle failed, expecting %d, got %d",
            expect, actual)
        t.Fail()
    }
    t.Log("Angle between", v1, "and", v2, "=", actual)
}
```

Notice the code is using the `Skipf` method, which is a combination of the methods `SkipNow` and `Logf` from type `testing.T`. When the test is executed without the environment variable, it outputs the following:

```
$> go test -run=Angle -v
=== RUN   TestVectorAngle
--- SKIP: TestVectorAngle (0.00s)
        vec_test.go:128: Env variable RUN_ANGLE not set, skipping:
PASS
ok      github.com/vladimirvivien/learning-go/ch12/vector      0.006s
```

When the environment variable is provided, as is done with the following Linux/Unix command, the test executes as expected (consult your OS on how to set environment variables):

```
> RUN_ANGLE=1 go test -run=Angle -v
=== RUN   TestVectorAngle
--- PASS: TestVectorAngle (0.00s)
        vec_test.go:138: Angle between [3.183,-7.627] and [-2.668,5.319]
= 3.0720263098372476
PASS
ok      github.com/vladimirvivien/learning-go/ch12/vector      0.005s
```

Table-driven tests

One technique you often encounter in Go is the use of table-driven tests. This is where a set of input and expected output is stored in a data structure, which is then used to cycle through different test scenarios. For instance, in the following test function, the `cases` variable, of type `[]struct{vec SimpleVector; expected float64}`, to store several vector values and their expected magnitude values used to test the vector method `Mag`:

```
func TestVectorMag(t *testing.T) {
    cases := []struct{
        vec SimpleVector
        expected float64

    }{
        {New(1.2, 3.4), math.Sqrt(1.2*1.2 + 3.4*3.4)},
        {New(-0.21, 7.47), math.Sqrt(-0.21*-0.21 + 7.47*7.47)},
        {New(1.43, -5.40), math.Sqrt(1.43*1.43 + -5.40*-5.40)},
        {New(-2.07, -9.0), math.Sqrt(-2.07*-2.07 + -9.0*-9.0)},
    }
    for _, c := range cases {
        mag := c.vec.Mag()
        if mag != c.expected {
          t.Errorf("Magnitude failed, execpted %d, got %d",
              c.expected, mag)
        }
    }
}
```

golang.fyi/ch12/vector/vec.go

With each iteration of the loop, the code tests the value calculated by the `Mag` method against an expected value. Using this approach, we can test several combinations of input and their respective output, as is done in the preceding code. This technique can be expanded as necessary to include more parameters. For instance, a name field can be used to name each case, which is useful when the number of test cases is large. Or, to be even more fancy, one can include a function field in the test case struct to specify custom logic to use for each respective case.

HTTP testing

In Chapter 11, *Writing Networked Services*, we saw that Go offers first-class APIs to build client and server programs using HTTP. The net/http/httptest sub-package, part of the Go standard library, facilitates the testing automation of both HTTP server and client code, as discussed in this section.

To explore this space, we will implement a simple API service that exposes the vector operations (covered in earlier sections) as HTTP endpoints. For instance, the following source snippet partially shows the methods that make up the server (for a complete listing, see https://github.com/vladimirvivien/learning-go/ch12/service/serv.go):

```go
package main

import (
    "encoding/json"
    "fmt"
    "net/http"

    "github.com/vladimirvivien/learning-go/ch12/vector"
)
func add(resp http.ResponseWriter, req *http.Request) {
    var params []vector.SimpleVector
    if err := json.NewDecoder(req.Body).Decode(&params);
        err != nil {
        resp.WriteHeader(http.StatusBadRequest)
        fmt.Fprintf(resp, "Unable to parse request: %s\n", err)
        return
    }
    if len(params) != 2 {
        resp.WriteHeader(http.StatusBadRequest)
        fmt.Fprintf(resp, "Expected 2 or more vectors")
        return
    }
    result := params[0].Add(params[1])
    if err := json.NewEncoder(resp).Encode(&result); err != nil {
        resp.WriteHeader(http.StatusInternalServerError)
        fmt.Fprintf(resp, err.Error())
        return
    }
}
...
func main() {
    mux := http.NewServeMux()
    mux.HandleFunc("/vec/add", add)
    mux.HandleFunc("/vec/sub", sub)
```

```
    mux.HandleFunc("/vec/dotprod", dotProd)
    mux.HandleFunc("/vec/mag", mag)
    mux.HandleFunc("/vec/unit", unit)

    if err := http.ListenAndServe(":4040", mux); err != nil {
        fmt.Println(err)
    }
}
```

golang.fyi/ch12/service/serv.go

Each function (add, sub, dotprod, mag, and unit) implements the http.Handler interface. The functions are used to handle HTTP requests from the client to calculate the respective operations from the vector package. Both requests and responses are formatted using JSON for simplicity.

Testing HTTP server code

When writing HTTP server code, you will undoubtedly run into the need to test your code, in a robust and repeatable manner, without having to set up some fragile code harness to simulate end-to-end testing. Type httptest.ResponseRecorder is designed specifically to provide unit testing capabilities for exercising the HTTP handler methods by inspecting state changes to the http.ResponseWriter in the tested function. For instance, the following snippet uses httptest.ResponseRecorder to test the server's add method:

```
import (
    "net/http"
    "net/http/httptest"
    "strconv"
    "strings"
    "testing"

    "github.com/vladimirvivien/learning-go/ch12/vector"
)

func TestVectorAdd(t *testing.T) {
    reqBody := "[[1,2],[3,4]]"
    req, err := http.NewRequest(
        "POST", "http://0.0.0.0/", strings.NewReader(reqBody))
    if err != nil {
        t.Fatal(err)
    }
    actual := vector.New(1, 2).Add(vector.New(3, 4))
    w := httptest.NewRecorder()
    add(w, req)
```

```
        if actual.String() != strings.TrimSpace(w.Body.String()) {
            t.Fatalf("Expecting actual %s, got %s",
                actual.String(), w.Body.String(),
            )
        }
    }
}
```

The code uses `reg, err := http.NewRequest("POST", "http://0.0.0.0/",` `strings.NewReader(reqBody))` to create a new `*http.Request` value with a `"POST"` method, a fake URL, and a request body, variable `reqBody`, encoded as a JSON array. Later in the code, `w := httptest.NewRecorder()` is used to create an `httputil.ResponseRecorder` value, which is used to invoke the `add(w, req)` function along with the created request. The value recorded in `w`, during the execution of function `add`, is compared with expected value stored in `atual` with `if actual.String() !=` `strings.TrimSpace(w.Body.String()){...}`.

Testing HTTP client code

Creating test code for an HTTP client is more involved, since you actually need a server running for proper testing. Luckily, package `httptest` provides type `httptest.Server` to programmatically create servers to test client requests and send back mock responses to the client.

To illustrate, let us consider the following code, which partially shows the implementation of an HTTP client to the vector server presented earlier (see the full code listing at `https://github.com/vladimirvivien/learning-go/ch12/client/client.go`). The `add` method encodes the parameters `vec0` and `vec2` of type `vector.SimpleVector` as JSON objects, which are sent to the server using `c.client.Do(req)`. The response is decoded from the JSON array into type `vector.SimpleVector` assigned to variable `result`:

```
type vecClient struct {
    svcAddr string
    client *http.Client
}
func (c *vecClient) add(
    vec0, vec1 vector.SimpleVector) (vector.SimpleVector, error) {
    uri := c.svcAddr + "/vec/add"

    // encode params
    var body bytes.Buffer
     params := []vector.SimpleVector{vec0, vec1}
    if err := json.NewEncoder(&body).Encode(&params); err != nil {
```

```
            return []float64{}, err
    }
    req, err := http.NewRequest("POST", uri, &body)
    if err != nil {
            return []float64{}, err
    }

    // send request
    resp, err := c.client.Do(req)
    if err != nil {
            return []float64{}, err
    }
    defer resp.Body.Close()

    // handle response
    var result vector.SimpleVector
    if err := json.NewDecoder(resp.Body).
            Decode(&result); err != nil {
            return []float64{}, err
    }
    return result, nil
}
```

We can use type `httptest.Server` to create code to test the requests sent by a client and to return data to the client code for further inspection. Function `httptest.NewServer` takes a value of type `http.Handler`, where the test logic for the server is encapsulated. The function then returns a new running HTTP server ready to serve on a system-selected port.

The following test function shows how to use `httptest.Server` to exercise the `add` method from the client code presented earlier. Notice that when creating the server, the code uses type `http.HandlerFunc`, which is an adapter that takes a function value to produce an `http.Handler`. This convenience allows us to skip the creation of a separate type to implement a new `http.Handler`:

```
import(
    "net/http"
    "net/http/httptest"
    ...
)
func TestClientAdd(t *testing.T) {
    server := httptest.NewServer(http.HandlerFunc(
            func(resp http.ResponseWriter, req *http.Request) {
                // test incoming request path
                if req.URL.Path != "/vec/add" {
```

```
                        t.Errorf("unexpected request path %s",
                            req.URL.Path)
                        return
                }
                // test incoming params
                body, _ := ioutil.ReadAll(req.Body)
                params := strings.TrimSpace(string(body))
                if params != "[[1,2],[3,4]]" {
                        t.Errorf("unexpected params '%v'", params)
                        return
                }
                // send result
                result := vector.New(1, 2).Add(vector.New(3, 4))
                err := json.NewEncoder(resp).Encode(&result)
                if err != nil {
                        t.Fatal(err)
                        return
                }
        },
    ))
    defer server.Close()
    client := newVecClient(server.URL)
    expected := vector.New(1, 2).Add(vector.New(3, 4))
    result, err := client.add(vector.New(1, 2), vector.New(3, 4))
    if err != nil {
        t.Fatal(err)
    }
    if !result.Eq(expected) {
        t.Errorf("Expecting %s, got %s", expected, result)
    }
}
```

The test function first sets up the `server` along with its handler function. Inside the function of `http.HandlerFunc`, the code first ensures that the client requests the proper path of `"/vec/add"`. Next, the code inspects the request body from the client, ensuring proper JSON format and valid parameters for the add operation. Finally, the handler function encodes the expected result as JSON and sends it as a response to the client.

The code uses the system-generated `server` address to create a new `client` with `newVecClient(server.URL)`. Method call `client.add(vector.New(1, 2), vector.New(3, 4))` sends a request to the test server to calculate the vector addition of the two values in its parameter list. As shown earlier, the test server merely simulates the real server code and returns the calculated vector value. The `result` is inspected against the `expected` value to ensure proper working of the `add` method.

Test coverage

When writing tests, it is often important to know how much of the actual code is getting exercised (or covered) by the tests. That number is an indication of the penetration of the test logic against the source code. Whether you agree or not, in many software development practices, test coverage is a critical metric as it is a measure of how well the code is tested.

Fortunately, the Go test tool comes with a built-in coverage tool. Running the Go test command with the -cover flag instruments the original source code with coverage logic. It then runs the generated test binary, providing a summary of the overall coverage profile of the package, as shown in the following:

```
$> go test -cover
PASS
coverage: 87.8% of statements
ok      github.com/vladimirvivien/learning-go/ch12/vector      0.028s
```

The result shows a well-tested code with a coverage number of 87.8%. We can use the test tool to extract more details about the section of the code that is tested. To do this, we use the -coverprofile flag to record coverage metrics to a file, as shown:

```
$> go test -coverprofile=cover.out
```

The cover tool

Once the coverage data is saved, it can be presented in a textual tab-formatted table using the go tool cover command. The following shows a partial output of the breakdown of the coverage metrics for each tested function in the coverage file generated previously:

```
$> go tool cover -func=cover.out
. . .
learning-go/ch12/vector/vec.go:52:    Eq          100.0%
learning-go/ch12/vector/vec.go:57:    Eq2          83.3%
learning-go/ch12/vector/vec.go:74:    Add         100.0%
learning-go/ch12/vector/vec.go:85:    Sub         100.0%
learning-go/ch12/vector/vec.go:96:    Scale       100.0%
. . .
```

The cover tool can overlay the coverage metrics over the actual code, providing a visual aid to show the covered (and uncovered) portion of the code. Use the -html flag to generate an HTML page using the coverage data gathered previously:

```
$> go tool cover -html=cover.out
```

The command opens the installed default web browser and displays the coverage data, as shown in the following screenshot:

```
github.com/vladimirvivien/learning-go/ch12/vector/vec.go (87.8%)    not tracked   not covered   covered

// Eq compares vector magnitude and directions
func (v SimpleVector) Eq(other Vector) bool {
        return v.Mag() == other.Mag() && (v.Angle(other) <= zero || math.I
}

// Eq compares each vector components for equality
func (v SimpleVector) Eq2(other Vector) bool {
        v.assertLenMatch(other)
        otherVec := other.(SimpleVector)
        for i, val := range v {
                if val != otherVec[i] {
                        return false
                }
        }
        return true
}

// Test for the zero vector
func (v SimpleVector) IsZero() bool {
        return v.Mag() <= zero
}

// Add returns the sum of two vectors
func (v SimpleVector) Add(other Vector) Vector {
        v.assertLenMatch(other)
        otherVec := other.(SimpleVector)
        result := make([]float64, len(v))
        for i, val := range v {
                result[i] = val + otherVec[i]
        }
        return SimpleVector(result)
}
```

The preceding screenshot shows only a portion of the generated HTML page. It shows covered code in green and code that is not covered in red. Anything else is displayed in gray.

Code benchmark

The purpose of benchmarking is to measure a code's performance. The Go test command-line tool comes with support for the automated generation and measurement of benchmark metrics. Similar to unit tests, the test tool uses benchmark functions to specify what portion of the code to measure. The benchmark function uses the following function naming pattern and signature:

*func Benchmark<Name>(*testing.B)*

Benchmark functions are expected to have names that start with *benchmark* and accept a pointer value of type `*testing.B`. The following shows a function that benchmarks the `Add` method for type `SimpleVector` (introduced earlier):

```
import (
    "math/rand"
    "testing"
    "time"
)
. . .
func BenchmarkVectorAdd(b *testing.B) {
    r := rand.New(rand.NewSource(time.Now().UnixNano()))
    for i := 0; i < b.N; i++ {
        v1 := New(r.Float64(), r.Float64())
        v2 := New(r.Float64(), r.Float64())
        v1.Add(v2)
    }
}
```

golang.fyi/ch12/vector/vec_bench_test.go

Go's test runtime invokes the benchmark functions by injecting pointer `*testing.B` as a parameter. That value defines methods for interacting with the benchmark framework such as logging, failure-signaling, and other functionalities similar to type `testing.T`. Type `testing.B` also offers additional benchmark-specific elements, including an integer field N. It is intended to be the number of iterations that the benchmark function should use for effective measurements.

The code being benchmarked should be placed within a `for` loop bounded by N, as illustrated in the previous example. For the benchmark to be effective, there should be no variances in the size of the input for each iteration of the loop. For instance, in the preceding benchmark, each iteration always uses a vector of size 2 (while the actual values of the vectors are randomized).

Running the benchmark

Benchmark functions are not executed unless the test command-line tool receives the flag –bench. The following command runs all the benchmarks functions in the current package:

```
$> go test -bench=.
PASS
BenchmarkVectorAdd-2          2000000             761 ns/op
BenchmarkVectorSub-2          2000000             788 ns/op
BenchmarkVectorScale-2        5000000             269 ns/op
BenchmarkVectorMag-2          5000000             243 ns/op
BenchmarkVectorUnit-2         3000000             507 ns/op
BenchmarkVectorDotProd-2      3000000             549 ns/op
BenchmarkVectorAngle-2        2000000             659 ns/op
ok     github.com/vladimirvivien/learning-go/ch12/vector     14.123s
```

Before dissecting the benchmark result, let us understand the previously issued command. The go test -bench=. command first executes all the test functions in the package followed by all the benchmark functions (you can verify this by adding the verbose flag –v to the command).

Similar to the –run flag, the –bench flag specifies a regular expression used to select the benchmark functions that get executed. The –bench=. flag matches the name of all benchmark functions, as shown in the previous example. The following, however, only runs benchmark functions that contain the pattern "VectorA" in their names. This includes the BenchmarkVectroAngle() and BenchmarkVectorAngle() functions:

```
$> go test -bench="VectorA"
PASS
BenchmarkVectorAdd-2     2000000             764 ns/op
BenchmarkVectorAngle-2   2000000             665 ns/op
ok     github.com/vladimirvivien/learning-go/ch12/vector     4.396s
```

Skipping test functions

As mentioned previously, when benchmarks are executed, the test tool will also run all test functions. This may be undesirable, especially if you have a large number of tests in your package. A simple way to skip the test functions during benchmark execution is to set the –run flag to a value that matches no test functions, as shown in the following:

```
> go test -bench=. -run=NONE -v
PASS
BenchmarkVectorAdd-2          2000000             791 ns/op
BenchmarkVectorSub-2          2000000             777 ns/op
```

```
. . .
BenchmarkVectorAngle-2          2000000               653 ns/op
ok      github.com/vladimirvivien/learning-go/ch12/vector       14.069s
```

The previous command only executes benchmark functions, as shown by the partial verbose output. The value of the -run flag is completely arbitrary and can be set to any value that will cause it to skip the execution of test functions.

The benchmark report

Unlike tests, a benchmark report is always verbose and displays several columns of metrics, as shown in the following:

```
$> go test -run=NONE -bench="Add|Sub|Scale"
PASS
BenchmarkVectorAdd-2      2000000               800 ns/op
BenchmarkVectorSub-2      2000000               798 ns/op
BenchmarkVectorScale-2    5000000               266 ns/op
ok      github.com/vladimirvivien/learning-go/ch12/vector       6.473s
```

The first column contains the names of the benchmark functions, with each name suffixed with a number that reflects the value of *GOMAXPROCS*, which can be set at test time using the -cpu flag (relevant for running benchmarks in parallel).

The next column displays the number of iterations for each benchmark loop. For instance, in the previous report, the first two benchmark functions looped 2 million times, while the final benchmark function iterated 5 million times. The last column of the report shows the average time it takes to execute the tested function. For instance, the 5 million calls to the Scale method executed in benchmark function BenchmarkVectorScale took on average 266 nanoseconds to complete.

Adjusting N

By default, the test framework gradually adjusts N to be large enough to arrive at stable and meaningful metrics over a period of *one second*. You cannot change N directly. However, you can use flag -benchtime to specify a benchmark run time and thus influence the number of iterations during a benchmark. For instance, the following runs the benchmark for a period of 5 seconds:

```
> go test -run=Bench -bench="Add|Sub|Scale" -benchtime 5s
PASS
BenchmarkVectorAdd-2      10000000               784 ns/op
```

```
BenchmarkVectorSub-2      10000000              810 ns/op
BenchmarkVectorScale-2    30000000              265 ns/op
ok      github.com/vladimirvivien/learning-go/ch12/vector        25.877s
```

Notice that even though there is a drastic jump in the number iterations (factor of five or more) for each benchmark, the average performance time for each benchmark function remains reasonably consistent. This information provides valuable insight into the performance of your code. It is a great way to observe the impact of code or load changes on performance, as discussed in the following section.

Comparative benchmarks

Another useful aspect of benchmarking code is to compare the performance of different algorithms that implement similar functionalities. Exercising the algorithms using performance benchmarks will indicate which of the implementations may be more compute- and memory-efficient.

For instance, two vectors are said to be equal if they have the same magnitude and same direction (or have an angle value of zero between them). We can implement this definition using the following source snippet:

```
const zero = 1.0e-7
...
func (v SimpleVector) Eq(other Vector) bool {
    ang := v.Angle(other)
    if math.IsNaN(ang) {
        return v.Mag() == other.Mag()
    }
    return v.Mag() == other.Mag() && ang <= zero
}
```

golang.fyi/ch12/vector/vec.go

When the preceding method is benchmarked, it yields to the following result. Each of its 3 million iterations takes an average of half a millisecond to run:

```
$> go test -run=Bench -bench=Equal1
PASS
BenchmarkVectorEqual1-2   3000000              454 ns/op
ok      github.com/vladimirvivien/learning-go/ch12/vector        1.849s
```

The benchmark result is not bad, especially when compared to the other benchmarked methods that we saw earlier. However, suppose we want to improve on the performance of the Eq method (maybe because it is a critical part of a program). We can use the −benchmem flag to get additional information about the benchmarked test:

```
$> go test -run=bench -bench=Equal1 -benchmem
PASS
BenchmarkVectorEqual1-2   3000000 474 ns/op   48 B/op   2 allocs/op
```

The −benchmem flag causes the test tool to reveal two additional columns, which provide memory allocation metrics, as shown in the previous output. We see that the Eq method allocates a total of 48 bytes, with two allocations calls per operation.

This does not tell us much until we have something else to compare it to. Fortunately, there is another equality algorithm that we can try. It is based on the fact that two vectors are also equal if they have the same number of elements and each element is equal. This definition can be implemented by traversing the vector and comparing its elements, as is done in the following code:

```
func (v SimpleVector) Eq2(other Vector) bool {
    v.assertLenMatch(other)
    otherVec := other.(SimpleVector)
    for i, val := range v {
        if val != otherVec[i] {
            return false
        }
    }
    return true
}
```

golang.fyi/ch12/vector/vec.go

Now let us benchmark the Eq and Eq2 equality methods to see which is more performant, as done in the following:

```
$> go test -run=bench -bench=Equal -benchmem
PASS
BenchmarkVectorEqual1-2   3000000   447 ns/op   48 B/op   2 allocs/op
BenchmarkVectorEqual2-2   5000000   265 ns/op   32 B/op   1 allocs/op
```

According to the benchmark report, method Eq2 is more performant of the two equality methods. It runs in about half the time of the original method, with considerably less memory allocated. Since both benchmarks run with similar input data, we can confidently say the second method is a better choice than the first.

Depending on Go version and machine size and architecture, these benchmark numbers will vary. However, the result will always show that the Eq2 method is more performant.

This discussion only scratches the surface of comparative benchmarks. For instance, the previous benchmark tests use the same size input. Sometimes it is useful to observe the change in performance as the input size changes. We could have compared the performance profile of the equality method as we change the size of the input, say, from 3, 10, 20, or 30 elements. If the algorithm is sensitive size, expanding the benchmark using such attributes will reveal any bottlenecks.

Summary

This chapter provided a broad introduction to the practice of writing tests in Go. It discussed several key topics, including the use of the `go test` tool to compile and execute automated tests. Readers learned how to write test functions to ensure their code is properly tested and covered. The chapter also discussed the topic of testing HTTP clients and servers. Finally, the chapter introduced the topic of benchmarking as a way to automate, analyze, and measure code performance using built-in Go tools.

Index

io.Reader interface
  about 236, 237
  readers, chaining 237, 239
io.Writer interface
  about 239, 241
IO
  with, readers and writers 236
iota
  using, in expressions 48

J

JSON API server
  about 287, 289
  API server client, in Go 290
  JavaScript API server client 291, 294
  testing, with cURL 289
JSON mapping
  controlling, with struct tags 262

L

label identifier 75
logical operators 52

M

map functions
  delete(map,key) 174
  len(map) 174
map
  about 170
  as parameter 174
  creating 171
  functions 174
  initialization 170, 171
  traversal 173
  using 172
methods 18
multi-file packages 133

N

named types 18
naming, packages
  about 134
  context, adding to path 135
  short names, using 135

unique namespace, using 134
net package
  about 267
  addressing 268
  client connections, accepting 271
  connection, dialing 268
  incoming connections, listening for 270
  net.Conn Type 268
  reference 267
net/http package
  reference 278
networked services
  writing 267
new() function 93
numeric types
  about 82
  complex number types 84
  floating point types 84
  numeric literals 84
  signed integer types 83
  unsigned integer types 83

O

objects, Go 18
operators
  about 50
  arithmetic operators 50
  assignment operators 51
  bitwise operators 51
  comparison operators 52
  decrement operators 50
  increment operators 50
  logical operators 52
  precedence 53
os package
  reference 244
os.OpenFile function
  about 245, 246

P

package identifier
  specifying 141
package visibility
  about 137, 138
  package member visibility 138